RHETORIC

Rhetoric has shaped our understanding of the nature of language and the purpose of literature for over two millennia. It is of crucial importance in understanding the development of literary history as well as elements of philosophy, politics and culture. The nature and practise of rhetoric was central to Classical, Renaissance and Enlightenment cultures and its relevance continues in our own postmodern world to inspire further debate.

Examining both the practice and theory of this controversial concept, Jennifer Richards explores:

- historical and contemporary definitions of the term 'rhetoric'
- uses of rhetoric in literature, by authors such as William Shakespeare, Mary Shelley, William Wordsworth, Jane Austen, W.B. Yeats and James Joyce
- classical traditions of rhetoric, as seen in the work of Plato, Aristotle and Cicero
- the rebirth of rhetoric in the Renaissance and the Enlightenment
- the current status and future of rhetoric in literary and critical theory as envisaged by critics such as Kenneth Burke, Paul de Man and Jacques Derrida.

This insightful volume offers an accessible account of this contentious yet unavoidable term, making this book invaluable reading for students of literature, philosophy and cultural studies.

Jennifer Richards is Professor in English at the University of Newcastle. She is the author of *Rhetoric and Courtliness in Early Modern Literature* and she has edited several collections of essays, including, with Alison Thorne, *Rhetoric, Women and Politics in Early Modern England* (Routledge, 2006).

THE NEW CRITICAL IDIOM

SERIES EDITOR JOHN DRAKAKIS, UNIVERSITY OF STIRLING

The New Critical Idiom is an invaluable series of introductory guides to today's critical terminology. Each book:

- provides a handy, explanatory guide to the use (and abuse) of the term
- offers an original and distinctive overview by a leading literary and cultural critic
- relates the term to the larger field of cultural representation

With a strong emphasis on clarity, lively debate and the widest possible breadth of examples, *The New Critical Idiom* is an indispensable approach to key topics in literary studies.

Also available in this series:

RHETORIC

Jennifer Richards

Routledge
Taylor & Francis Group

LONDON AND NEW YORK

First published 2008
by Routledge
2 Park Square, Milton Park, Abingdon, Oxon OX14 4RN

Simultaneously published in the USA and Canada
by Routledge
270 Madison Ave, New York, NY 10016

Routledge is an imprint of the Taylor & Francis Group, an informa business

© 2008 Jennifer Richards

Typeset in Garamond and Scala Sans by
Taylor & Francis Books
Printed and bound in Great Britain by
MPG Books Ltd, Bodmin

British Library Cataloguing in Publication Data
A catalogue record for this book is available from the British Library

Library of Congress Cataloging in Publication Data
A catalog record for this book has been requested

ISBN 978-0-415-31436-7 (hbk)
ISBN 978-0-415-31437-4 (pbk)

In memory of my mother

CONTENTS

SERIES EDITOR'S PREFACE

The New Critical Idiom is a series of introductory books which seeks to extend the lexicon of literary terms, in order to address the radical changes which have taken place in the study of literature during the last decades of the twentieth century. The aim is to provide clear, well-illustrated accounts of the full range of terminology currently in use, and to evolve histories of its changing usage.

The current state of the discipline of literary studies is one where there is considerable debate concerning basic questions of terminology. This involves, among other things, the boundaries which distinguish the literary from the non-literary; the position of literature within the larger sphere of culture; the relationship between literatures of different cultures; and questions concerning the relation of literary to other cultural forms within the context of interdisciplinary studies.

It is clear that the field of literary criticism and theory is a dynamic and heterogeneous one. The present need is for individual volumes on terms which combine clarity of exposition with an adventurousness of perspective and a breadth of application. Each volume will contain as part of its apparatus some indication of the direction in which the definition of particular terms is likely to move, as well as expanding the disciplinary boundaries within which some of these terms have been traditionally contained. This will involve some re-situation of terms within the larger field of cultural representation, and will introduce examples from the area of film and the modern media in addition to examples from a variety of literary texts.

Acknowledgements

This book could not have been written without the support of my Head of School, Linda Anderson, and it would not have been completed without the patience and encouragement of my editors John Drakakis, Liz Thompson and Polly Dodson. I have benefited from being able to share my ideas with Alison Thorne, and also with Dermot Cavanagh; his help during the writing of this book has been extraordinarily generous. He not only read all of the chapters more than once and never complained, but also showed willing to talk about rhetoric even when we were supposed to be on holiday.

Just after completing this book I took up a CRASSH fellowship at the University of Cambridge, and was reminded that nothing is ever quite finished. I would like to thank Rukmini Bhaya Nair, Willard Bohn, Becky Conekin, Garry Hagberg, Mary Jacobus, Jane Rendell and Laurence Simmons for the challenging and stimulating conversations in our weekly seminars which prompted me to take up my pen again. Last but not least is another group to whom I owe special thanks; these are the students of Emma Julieta Barreiro's English translation class at the National Autonomous University of Mexico. They read an early draft of Chapter 1 and gave me wonderfully frank and welcome advice, which I have tried very hard to follow! Their names are: Francisco Alarcón Cárdenas, Diana Almaguer Ortega, Sagrario Bravo Pintos, Lucina Cabrera de la Rosa, Patricia Domínguez Meneses, Jorge E. Hermosillo Gutiérrez, Emiliano Quintana Montaño, Virgina Zúñiga Martínez.

INTRODUCTION
WHAT IS RHETORIC?

I ask her whether she needs to change the macho culture of the Socialist Party, and indeed whether this is a realistic aim. 'It's too late,' she says with calm assurance. 'The changes you are talking about have already taken place. France is a very different country from what it was a generation ago, a decade ago, and the Socialist Party has been able to recognise those changes and reflect them. The fact that I am a woman is the least important aspect of that.'

The answer is a little too glib but none the less revealing. The same applies when she is asked about the rioting kids in the suburbs. 'Yes, I can understand them. It is true that I don't live in these suburbs – in fact I don't know any French politicians who do – but I have met these people. So, yes, I can have opinions on what happens.'

But didn't Mme Royal's hardline solution to the riots (military boot-camps for the rioters, she advocated at one point) simply borrow the *rhetoric* of Sarkozy and the parties of the far right? This is when the smile drops. 'Listen', she says in a surprisingly deep and gruff voice, 'I never said military camps, but that those rioters should do some military service as soldiers as a punishment for their actions.

This is not the same thing.' But don't soldiers live in military camps,
I persisted, and wasn't it an insult to ordinary soldiers? 'Let's move
the questions on', she snaps.

Andrew Hussey, 'Is France ready for a woman President?'
(*Observer Review*, 23 July 2006; emphasis added)

This is how one journalist attempts to discover and represent the
values of Marie-Ségolenè Royal, the first serious female contender
in the French presidential elections. Ségolenè was being feted
within the Socialist Party at the time of Andrew Hussey's article
because she speaks to 'the ordinary, hard-working people of
France' and to female voters of all social classes. More unusually,
she has also made a considerable impact upon Anglophone journalists and political commentators. Among the last group,
Hussey notes, Ségolenè is admired as much for her good taste
and fashion sense as her political acumen. However, as a self-
declared fan of the 'British way of life' and 'Blairisme', she is also
respected because she represents a different approach in French
politics. She is 'probably the only French politician of her generation', Hussey comments, 'who is willing and able to take on
the "social model" that most French people of the left see as an
integral part of their civilisation', and given her apparent closeness to 'the very English figures of Margaret Thatcher and
Supernanny', this suggests that 'if she ever does achieve power we
might indeed see a truly revolutionary force at work in France'.

And yet, as Hussey's warning word 'rhetoric' suggests in the
extract cited above, the image of Ségolenè may be different from
the reality. That is, she may be more conservative and traditional
than her language promises. Hussey is never quite sure what
Ségolenè stands for; he suspects her of borrowing the 'rhetoric' of
the 'right', equally, he distrusts the 'rhetoric that promotes her as
a breath of fresh air'. Throughout, he emphasizes the difficulty of
pinning her views down, of finding out what she really stands
for, so skilled is she at speaking tactfully, perhaps even tactically,
to her immediate audience. For example, he notes, she is 'not
quite what she seems on the question of the liberal economy'
and, in this way, he quietly distinguishes his own approach from
journalists who are seduced by Ségolenè's 'rhetoric'.

This is a small example but it helps to tell a bigger story about the resonance of the term 'rhetoric' in our own time. Most obviously, it reminds us that 'rhetoric' is not a word we want applied to our own speech or writing, not least because of its association with ostentatious or empty expression. The implication is clear: phrases that sound good but express little of a speaker's or writer's 'real' beliefs count as rhetoric. Yet, this is a recent development. The negative association I have just outlined is noted in the *Oxford English Dictionary* (2b), but the more favourable and longer-standing definition of this term is given precedence. This derives from Greek *rhētorikē*, 'the art of speaking', and it overlaps in modern English with 'oratory', a word of Latin origin that denotes skill in public speaking (*OED* 1a). Its classical origins help to define it as an 'art of using language so as to persuade or influence' and its 'body of rules' (*OED* 1a). It turns out, then, that rhetoric is not only a term we might apply to the speech or writing of someone we suspect of political 'spin'; it also connotes an 'art' in which one can be trained.

The idea that persuasive speech and writing can be theorized as an art, a body of rules, is represented in the handbooks that thrived in fifth- and fourth-century BC Athens and in first-century BC Rome. Many of these are overly technical – they multiply the number of rules beyond what is sensible or desirable – and this has drawn much criticism. Adam Smith (1723–90) dismisses them in his *Lectures on Rhetoric and Belles Lettres* as 'a very silly set of Books and not at all instructive' and he proposes instead a new rhetoric: a 'few observations' on effective speech and writing derived from common sense (Smith 1985: 26–27). Smith is teaching his students not how to persuade an audience, but rather how to express themselves appropriately: that is, how to express the 'sentiment' or 'affection' that is proper to their character (55). Nonetheless, though we may understand and indeed share this dislike of excessive prescription we should remember that in its inception the art was nothing more than an attempt to reflect on 'natural' eloquence. The handbooks set out to describe what persuades in *practice*.

Moreover, the art was developed under particular political conditions, in democratic Athens and republican Rome. In these states the importance of speaking well in the public forum or the law courts was essential to political life, and was deemed worth defending. Compare our dismissive conception of rhetoric as political spin with the defence of the art offered by the Roman orator Cicero in the opening pages of his youthful manual *De inventione* (*On invention*) (84 BC). For Cicero it is impossible to imagine a society without rhetoric. In the beginning, he argues, people were 'scattered in the fields and hidden in sylvan retreats'; they fought with one another over scarce resources until they were 'assembled and gathered' by a 'great and wise man' who, 'through reason and eloquence', transformed them 'from wild savages into a kind and gentle folk' (Cicero 1954: 1.2.2). This is a myth of the origins of society, and we might be wise to read it 'rhetorically'. After all, it offers a rousing opening to yet another manual in a competitive market. Moreover, it includes Cicero's commendation of the power of an orator, a 'great and wise man', to sway an audience at will. Even so, we may not want to dismiss this myth too quickly. For Cicero sees rhetoric as taming one audience in particular: men who would use force to satisfy their will. Without eloquence, he argues, the physically powerful would never have been *persuaded* 'to submit to justice without violence'. The man who held sway over others would never have suffered being 'put on a par with those among whom he would excel' (1.2.2).

The capacity of this remarkable skill to contest the abuse of power was famously demonstrated in Cicero's prosecution of the corrupt governor of Sicily in 70 BC, Gaius Verres; this has been expertly portrayed in Robert Harris' recent novel, *Imperium* (2006). Cicero proves his case against Verres with the help of documentary evidence and a series of witnesses, all of whom testify to the extent of his theft and extortion from the Sicilian people. However, he finally defeats Verres by using the testimony of a witness to imagine the final hours of one of his victims, a Roman citizen who was traduced wrongly without trial as a pirate and then tortured, maimed and finally crucified, all to hide the governor's corrupt dealings. This is how it is done:

'Would you repeat what he said, more loudly please, so that all can hear.'

'He said, "I am a Roman citizen."'
'So just that?' said Cicero. 'Let me be sure I understand you. A blow lands' – he put his wrists together, raised them above his head and jerked forwards, as if his back had just been lashed – 'and he says, through gritted teeth, "I am a Roman citizen." A blow lands' – and again he jerked forwards – '*I am a Roman citizen*'.

The conclusion to this speech works brilliantly: the Roman audience identify with this victim as one of their own. But they identify with him so profoundly because Cicero also makes them 'see' the injustice he suffered as if it happened before their very eyes. The point is made by Tiro, Cicero's slave and amanuensis and the narrator of *Imperium*: 'These flat words of mine cannot begin to convey the effect of Cicero's performance upon those who saw it. The hush around the court amplified his words. It was as if all of us now were witnesses to this monstrous miscarriage of justice. Some men and women ... began to scream, and there was a growing swell of outrage from the masses in the forum' (Harris 2006: 189).

Thanks to the early handbooks it is possible to arrive at a broad understanding of the art of rhetoric and the different persuasive strategies and 'proofs' that are appropriate to the aims of the rhetorician or orator: to persuade someone to an action, to acquit or condemn a defendant, and to praise or blame a public figure. Nonetheless, we should remember not only that there are differences among the classical theorists concerning the definition of rhetoric and its parts, but that there are also significant shifts in the art's conception and elaboration throughout its subsequent history.

In the Middle Ages the art of rhetoric was eclipsed by logic and grammar, its partners in the *trivium*, surviving primarily as part of the *ars dictaminis*, the art of letter-writing. Thereafter, the heyday of classical rhetoric is the Renaissance. Its rebirth in the fifteenth century was supported by the recovery in Italy of several Roman handbooks, the complete manuscripts of Quintilian's encyclopaedic *Institutio oratoria* in 1416 and of Cicero's *De oratore* and *Brutus* in 1421, the last a new discovery. These discoveries helped to raise rhetoric from its lowly place among the 'trivial' subjects; it moved to centre stage in school and university curricula. Rhetoric provided useful preparation for academic study, but it was also understood as an indispensable requirement for all forms of public activity. Education in this art was seen by classically trained humanists to shape the *vir civilis*, the civic-minded gentleman whose self-interest is, supposedly, subordinated to the service of the commonwealth, and whose rhetorical know-how enabled him to fulfil a public role, whether as courtier, magistrate or as servant to an aristocratic patron (Skinner 1996: 69).

However, despite the ambition of this recovery, we can also find the cause of later deterioration in the formal description of the art in the Renaissance. Sixteenth-century English handbooks reveal the narrowing of the art to 'style'. Many of these are concerned only with providing a taxonomy of linguistic devices, and it is this mechanical prescription that will be rejected in the eighteenth and nineteenth centuries, both by new rhetoricians such as the economist Adam Smith and poets, from Alexander Pope (1688–1744) to William Wordsworth (1770–1850). Humanist rhetorical training is also dismissed for political reasons: it is blamed for the Civil War that led to the execution of Charles I in 1649 and the eleven-year 'republic'. One of the fiercest attacks on traditional rhetoric was made by Bishop Thomas Sprat (1635–1713), an ardent Royalist and historian of the Royal Society, founded in the 'wonderful pacific year' of the Stuart restoration (1660). In this history, Sprat complains that rhetoric is only of interest to those 'who are bred up in *Commonwealths*, where the greatest affairs are manag'd by the *violence of popular assemblies*, and those govern'd by the most *plausible speakers*' (Sprat 1959: 19). Rhetoric is to be replaced by the rational, dispassionate methods of the natural philosopher, that is, the scientists of the Royal Society: observation, experimentation, demonstration and sober debate.

Sprat represents a turning point in the history of rhetoric. He helps us to understand our own popular dismissal of this art because he gives sharper expression to the two views of language which, according to Stanley Fish, have shaped the 'history of Western thought' (Fish 1989: 484):

on the one hand, language that faithfully reflects or reports on matters of fact uncolored by any personal or partisan agenda or desire;
and on the other hand, language that is infected by partisan agendas
and desires, and therefore colors and distorts the facts which it pur-
ports to reflect. It is the use of the second kind of language that
makes one a rhetorician, while adherence to the first kind makes one
a seeker after truth and an objective observer of the way things are.

(Fish 1989: 474)

This is a long-standing opposition. It emerges at the very
moment when a systematic understanding of the subject was
being consolidated in the fourth century BC. Famously, it is
articulated by Plato in his most anti-rhetorical of dialogues,
Gorgias (*c.* 387 BC), which contrasts the truth-seeking philosopher with the 'sophist', the teacher of mere rhetoric. However, it
is not until the consolidation of scientific method in the late
seventeenth century that the distinction between natural and
rhetorical language becomes entrenched, and the critics of
rhetoric are able to envisage its 'end' with any confidence.
Cicero's myth of the origins of society is revised: in Sprat's
account, the scientist replaces the orator as the founder of civil
society, and language and communication are refined. Quite
simply, in the late seventeenth century we became polite.

On this account, the history of rhetoric has a clear beginning
and end. Its demise is understood to coincide 'with that long and
arduous historical process that is often termed modernization'
(Bender and Wellbery 1990: 7). It is hard not to endorse this
persuasive and neatly organized narrative: antiquity and its
renaissances versus modernity. This is because the demise that
Sprat envisaged did in fact come to pass. For centuries rhetoric
was a compulsory subject of study for privileged boys and young
men. Since the nineteenth century, this art has been replaced by
other disciplines or sciences. Kenneth Burke lists some of these
interlopers in his preface to *Rhetoric of Motives* (1950): aesthetics,
anthropology, psychoanalysis, sociology (Burke 1969: xiii). Even
disciplines which have grown out of traditional rhetoric have turned
their backs on it, notably English studies. 'Rhetoricians were the
first professors to teach English literature and composition', Thomas

P. Miller argues, 'but when literary studies became professiona-
lized in the nineteenth century, scholarship on rhetoric began to
be marginalized as the discipline came to concentrate on philo-
logical studies and a few literary genres' (Miller 1997: 3).
Rhetoric still survives in many English departments in the USA,
but usually only as practical training in 'Rhetoric and Composition', a course of study that prepares students for academic life.
As one of its advocates explains, teachers in this field range 'from
Aristotle to business writing', and cover 'teaching entering students how to write and read academic discourse, training gradu-
ate students to work in the classroom, and collaborating on
recruitment and outreach with high schools and community lit-
eracy programs' (Miller 1997: 6). Because teachers of Rhetoric
and Composition purportedly serve other disciplines, helping
students of 'literature' or 'science' with their academic writing,
their status within the academy is often regarded as menial: teachers of Rhetoric and Composition are the *lumpenprofessoriat* of
English departments (Rhodes 2004: 54). They are usually 'part-
timers' or 'transient faculty', often with doctorates in Literature,
who engage in the kind of practical work that 'the true literary
scholar does not do' (Neel 1995: 62, 75).

This difficult relationship has also not been helped by the so-
called linguistic turn in the humanities in the mid-twentieth
century; this is predicated on a new 'art' or science of language,
linguistics. Thanks to the work of the Swiss linguist Ferdinand
de Saussure (1857–1913) in the first decade of the twentieth century, our view of how language works has changed radically. Language is no longer deemed a resource that can be deployed at will
by the skilful orator; rather, it is conceived as a self-determining
and self-contained system: meaning is constituted by systematic
patterns of similarity and difference between signs.

Excitement at the possibilities this new science presented for
cultural criticism led Roland Barthes to declare in the mid-
1960s that rhetoric was, if not dead, then certainly on its last
legs, and that this was a very good thing. His remarkable essay,
'The Old Rhetoric: an aide-mémoire' ('L'Ancienne Rhétorique,
aide-mémoire'), a transcription of a seminar taught at the Ecole
pratique des hautes etudes in 1964 and 1965, shows us how far

rhetoric has declined. 'The Old Rhetoric' is a counter handbook. It offers one of the most engaging accounts of the art of rhetoric and its varied history that I have come across in researching for this book. Yet Barthes is not interested in reviving the discipline. On the contrary, he tells its history so thoroughly in order to ensure that we do not forget what was so seductive and oppressive about it. He wants to make sure that those who succeed the rhetoricians as theorists of language do not reproduce their mistakes. Barthes marks the passing of rhetoric from a living discipline to an object of critical or 'ideological' scrutiny (Barthes 1988: 47). One might say that our dismissive use of the term 'rhetoric' encompasses this insight; it resonates with a popular understanding of the art of rhetoric's oppressive history.

So why dedicate a book to the study of an art that is dead or dying? The simple answer to this question is that, whatever I might have said so far, Barthes was a little premature in announcing the demise of rhetoric. Indeed, the declaration of its passing is itself a rhetorical gesture: for example, Sprat's veneration of the plain style is a rhetorical choice rather than a declaration that the discipline has reached a conclusion. The same can be said of Barthes. What better way to announce innovation than to declare the death of the oppressive system that preceded it? Yet rhetoric survives as both a practice and an idea, if not quite as an ideal. From the eighteenth century scientists may have declared rhetoric dead, but more recently it is called upon to remind us that there is no objective, truthful language that can lift us above the uncertain realm of persuasion. In 'discipline after discipline', writes Stanley Fish:

> there is evidence of what has been called the interpretive turn, the realization ... that the givens of any field of activity – including the facts it commands, the procedures it trusts in, and the values it expresses and extends – are socially and politically constructed.
>
> (485)

In the late twentieth century a series of studies appeared which independently debunked the idea of an objective, disinterested language of science: Donald McCloskey's *The Rhetoric of Economics*

(1985), which exposes as illusory the social scientist's defence of his or her method as 'impersonal', and Thomas Kuhn's *The Structure of Scientific Revolutions* (1962), which is 'rhetorical through and through' because it reveals how tacit assumptions determine the 'facts' that scientific methods supposedly prove (Fish 1989: 210–11).

We might add to Fish's list Alan Gross' *The Rhetoric of Science* (1990), which challenges explicitly the claim that the sciences lie outside the uncertain field of persuasion. Gross is not arguing 'that science is oratory'. On the contrary, he is arguing that 'like oratory, science is a rhetorical enterprise centred on persuasion' (Gross 1990: 6). Scientific writers are traditionally expected to be clear, lucid and objective; they are encouraged to argue from the facts in hand and to abstain from emotional pleas and ethical inducements. In particular, they are expected to avoid the use of figurative language, since this betrays the semantic congruity between word and thing. And yet where is the semantic congruity between word and thing, we may well wonder, in such well-worn metaphors as 'magnetic field', or 'sound wave'? Scientific writing can be subjected to rhetorical analysis, Gross insists. Reports, for example, can be analysed according to the three genres of rhetoric: judicial, deliberative and epideictic. If a report 'reconstructs past science in a way most likely to support its claims', then it can be viewed as an example of 'judicial' rhetoric; if it 'intends to direct future research' then it is 'deliberative'; if it celebrates 'appropriate methods' then it is 'epideictic' (10). Emotional appeals play a role in peer review, while anger and indignation are 'part of the machinery of persuasion' when they are called upon to refute or support a claim (14). Finally, conviction in scientific writing rests not only on 'uninterpreted brute facts' but also on their description and arrangement (11).

Rhetoric is ubiquitous, Gross suggests, it is just that we no longer recognize this. The way in which he alerts us to this is by applying the classical system to the speech and writing of academics who claim to be above persuasion. We might repeat this gesture for political journalists whose dismissive view of rhetoric as 'spin' makes them inattentive to the persuasive strategies that they also use casually every day. Thus, even as he is busy debunking the 'rhetoric' of Ségolenè and her supporters, Hussey is in turn constructing a different argument which relies on the same rhetorical proof, notably the discovery of female exemplars with whom Ségolenè can be suggestively compared. On his account, Ségolenè is closer to posh 'Margo from *The Good Life*' than Audrey Hepburn, as one of her smitten commentators had suggested. This type of analysis effectively demonstrates the fallacy of the two views of language: the distinction that is traditionally drawn between 'natural' and 'rhetorical' expression. But we might go further still in debunking this commonplace distinction, by exposing just how profoundly rhetoric permeates all language: in effect, by establishing that language is essentially and inescapably rhetorical.

This was the argument of a young German philosopher in the late nineteenth century, Friedrich Nietzsche (1844–1900), who was employed to teach rhetoric at the University of Basle in 1872–73. In his 'Lecture Notes on Rhetoric', probably written in 1874, Nietzsche set out to contest the idea of rhetoric as a resource which the skilled orator can draw upon. How can we understand rhetoric as an art, he asked, when we cannot control its linguistic effects? Nietzsche's insight is that the figures of speech classified in traditional rhetorical manuals do not represent a special case of linguistic variation and ornamentation; rather, these constitute all language. So-called literal words, he argues, are figures too: for example, the word 'snake' (in Latin *serpens*) means an image of a creature crawling. We are so accustomed to using this term without thinking about it that we have forgotten its origins as a metaphor (Nietzsche 1983: 107–8). This is a far-reaching insight for it underscores how misguided is the Enlightenment attempt to define a new science of communication which favours literalness, and so bypasses the vagaries of rhetoric.

Nietzsche's interest in rhetoric found new students in the late twentieth century. Roland Barthes may have declared the rhetorical system dead in the 1960s; just a few years later, however, Paul de Man (1919–83) was to develop Nietzsche's thesis in a different way to contest this linguistic turn. De Man is not arguing that all language is figurative, but that all speech acts are susceptible to both a grammatical and a rhetorical reading. For this reason we cannot dismiss rhetoric quite as readily as Barthes was prepared to do, for this only conceals difficulties of interpretation and communication. Perfectly grammatical sentences, de Man demonstrates, can be read figuratively; meanwhile, a poet's commanding use of a range of figures may be undermined when the same lines are read grammatically. Rather like Nietzsche, though, de Man concludes that it is impossible to *apply* the tropes and figures 'artfully' in our speech and writing with absolute confidence; they are always in some way outside our control.

This book traces this complex history of the art, from the debate about how it is constituted in antiquity and beyond to its profound rejection as a rational system in the work of Nietzsche and de Man. Of the many different theorists of rhetoric, de Man offers by far the most radical re-engagement with the classical art; this is because he rejects completely the promise of linguistic control that the idea of rhetoric as an *art* implies. De Man gives us a different way of conceiving the trajectory of the history of rhetoric: modernity signals not the end of rhetoric but rather an increased awareness of how 'rhetoricality' saturates every aspect of our linguistic experience.

Does this mean that there is no going back? The story told about classical rhetoric is always structured as a narrative of decline, and there are good reasons for this. It is difficult to defend the revival of an ancient system which, although associated with early 'democratic' states, still allowed a coercive system of inequities and exclusions to be maintained. The democracy of ancient Athens during which rhetoric first flourished is very different from its modern conception. Athens may have 'pioneered the practice of a self-ruling citizenry' in which each citizen was given the 'chance and duty to participate in the decisions and practices that framed their lives', but citizenship was not extended to women, foreigners or slaves (Honohan 2002: 16, 29).

Nonetheless, there are problems also in endorsing a narrative which defines the overthrow of an oppressive rhetorical culture and its 'system' as a moment of enlightenment. Many of de Man's insights into the nature of rhetoric are already noted by this art's 'traditional' theorists, though they carry a different resonance. Rhetoric is generally defined as an art of persuasion; this is certainly the starting point of the revisions proposed by Nietzsche, Barthes and de Man, who reject it as a rational system. However, ancient orators already understood that rhetoric exceeds its definition as a system, hence the reluctance of some theorists to offer rules for every eventuality. Moreover, there is acknowledgement that its methods involve not just the acquisition of a skill but active critical reflection. This is a possibility raised, at least, in one distinctive Roman handbook which fits uncomfortably in the standard history of rhetoric, Cicero's *On the ideal orator* (*De oratore*) (55 BC). In this text, Cicero refuses to recognize that rhetoric is an 'art', and he rejects the technical approach to its teaching represented by the Roman handbook tradition. We need to pay attention to this because Cicero has something important to say about the scope of rhetoric as a philosophical method. *On the ideal orator* is a dialogue, and this form constitutes the process of its argument. In this dialogue, speakers modify or change position rather than offer straightforward technical advice; they do so to illustrate the key argument of this text, that argument on different sides is the shared method of the orator and the philosopher, *including* Plato who, Cicero claims, understood the contingency of 'truth'.

I want to pause over this unanticipated alternative approach to rhetoric in antiquity. According to this view, rhetoric is more than a taxonomy of linguistic devices and persuasive strategies; it is also a process of argument, a way of thinking which understands that all positions are ultimately arguable. This understanding of rhetoric is valuable, I want to emphasize, not just because it helps us to persuade someone to do our bidding or to take our side, but because it lies at the heart of philosophical speculation. In this rhetorical tradition what is valued is the capacity to change one's mind, to go back and unravel positions or viewpoints that seem natural and unremarkable.

I draw attention to this alternative approach not simply in order to correct the narrow conception of rhetoric on which the rejection of the system so often rests in modernity, but also to enable our exploration of the kind of *literary* writing which demonstrates the flourishing of this process of argument. When we think of rhetoric as an art of persuasion we usually imagine its form of expression as the public oration or political speech; but there is a literary dimension to rhetorical practice too. In particular, the classroom practice of declamation, of argument *pro* and *contra* on any issue, informs the development of vernacular literature in the sixteenth century. The most famous beneficiary of this kind of rhetorical training, as we will see later in this book, is William Shakespeare. However, we might also describe as 'rhetorical' those writings which are not informed by formal training in rhetoric, but which engage their readers in a process of deliberation on different sides. I want to explore this dimension by comparing two texts, written some two hundred years apart, both of which challenge our assumptions about the gendering of 'persuadability': Philip Sidney's *Arcadia* and Jane Austen's *Persuasion*.

Philip Sidney's immensely popular prose romance, written in the 1570s, explores the adventures of two young princes in Arcadia, a nation whose ruler, Basilius, has secreted himself and his family in a rural retreat after receiving an oracle that predicts his overthrow. Basilius' relinquishing of his court is the catalyst for the romance's complicated plots and nearly tragic ending: namely, our two princes, Pyrocles and Musidorus, fall in love with Basilius' daughters and set about trying to gain access to them. *Arcadia* is a romance which explores political questions of masculine good government; but it is also preoccupied with the dangers of and necessity for rhetoric. It is Sidney's two-sided approach to this topic, which derives from his training in rhetoric, that interests me.

Initially, Sidney seems to be warning his readers of the dangers of rhetoric. Book 1 represents a debate between the love-stricken prince Pyrocles and his sensible friend Musidorus. The former defends his decision to disguise himself as an Amazon in order to gain access to the youngest daughter of Basilius. He is visibly effeminized by the experience of falling in love, but there is also a strong insinuation that his 'unmanliness' shows in other ways; namely, his ability to debate rationally is adversely affected. He defends his disguise in a confused way, and makes contradictory claims in support of love, presenting himself as motivated, on the one hand, by spiritual ambition, and on the other hand, by sexual desire. Musidorus is alarmed: 'it utterly subverts the course of nature in making reason give place to sense, and man to woman' and he reminds his friend of the fate of Hercules, the classical strong man who was transformed by love into a 'distaff spinner' (Sidney 1985: 18). And yet it is the transvestite Pyrocles who wins the debate with his newly emotive oratory, principally by asserting, quite simply, that he *is* a slave to his passion and then, 'gushing out abundance of tears and crossing his arms over his woeful heart', he sinks 'to the ground'. Pyrocles is putting into practice the kind of advice given in the Roman handbooks on how to conclude a speech effectively. This is all too much for Musidorus: he falls down as well and 'kissing the weeping eyes of his friend' he now seeks to make amends for his 'over vehement' speech (22).

The dangers of this sympathetic response become immediately apparent because Musidorus now falls in love with the elder daughter of Basilius, Pamela, and he attempts to elope with her. The nadir of the romance is reached when Musidorus is over-powered by the sight of Pamela sleeping, and contemplates her rape, an assault that is prevented by the arrival of 'a dozen clownish villains' (177). Beyond this, the complications of these love interests lead indirectly to the accidental 'death' of Basilius, and the final book of the *Arcadia* depicts the trial of Musidorus and Pyrocles, who are accused of undermining the Arcadian state and of Basilius' murder. Eventually, it emerges that Basilius has only drunk a sleeping potion and his unexpected awakening after the condemnation and sentencing of the princes forestalls a tragic ending. However, before we are offered this *deus ex machina*, we watch the court-room drama unfold; it is here that we are given the opportunity to change our minds, and to rethink the place of emotion in judgement-making.

If we expect a straightforward moralization of the dangers of passion at this point in the fiction then we will be disappointed. The complicating factor of the trial is that the presiding judge is Euarchus, the father of Pyrocles. Euarchus is the epitome of the impartial judge; despite his closeness to the two accused, he refuses to be swayed by their emotional appeals, or by the evidence of their otherwise good character. He will not be moved, and in this respect he may seem to provide a longed-for antidote to the love-stricken princes. And yet, rather than improving his judgement, the reader watches him making crucial mistakes. Musidorus and Pyrocles have transgressed, but the harsh death penalty meted out to them by Euarchus, strictly according to Arcadian law, is an uncomfortable conclusion, and it distresses the onlookers. Having ridiculed emotional responses throughout *Arcadia*, Sidney now turns the tables on us. In this final episode he poses to the reader difficult questions about whether it is right to regard 'virtue' and 'vice' as absolutes, and about where we should lay blame when things go wrong in a state. Sidney represents the act of *being* persuaded as feminine and effeminizing throughout most of *Arcadia*, until its last book, when these gender assumptions are challenged, and the value of an emotive response reconsidered.

My second example is by a woman writing more than two centuries later, and who was most certainly not trained in oratory: Jane Austen's *Persuasion* (1818). This novel presents as a problem the 'persuadability' of its heroine, Anne Elliot, the overlooked and under-valued daughter of the vain and snobbish Sir Walter Elliot. Anne has to pay the price for having broken off an engagement to the undistinguished but loving Frederick Wentworth in her youth; when he returns to her life seven years later as Captain Wentworth, a man of considerable fortune, she discovers that her love for him has not diminished, but that it is not returned. The reason given for her original decision is that she was persuaded, perhaps too easily, by her aunt, Lady Russell, who deemed him unworthy. 'She was persuaded', the narrator explains, 'to believe the engagement a wrong thing – indiscreet, improper, hardly capable of success and not deserving it' (Austen 1970: 56). This is understood by Anne herself, whose recollection of this decision is much more critical:

> She had used him ill; deserted and disappointed him; and worse, she
> had shewn a feebleness of character in doing so, which his own
> decided, confident temper could not endure. She had given him up

to oblige others. It had been the effect of over-persuasion. It had been weakness and timidity.

(86)

Anne must now bear the brunt of his resentment and disapproval when he apparently falls for her neighbour Louisa Musgrove, valuing in her the very qualities of forthrightness and determination that she supposedly lacks:

yours is the character of decision and firmness. ... It is the worst evil of too yielding and indecisive a character, that no influence over it can be depended on. – You are never sure of a good impression being durable. Every body may sway it; let those who would be happy be firm.

(110)

Yet, in its gentle course, this novel will change our view of the meek Anne as her tractability is revealed as the real strength of her character. Louisa comes to be seen as rash and obstinate: her wilfulness leads to a serious accident and Wentworth is indecisive and uncertain in his attempt to rescue her. His conviction that Anne is weak, and the high value he places on decisiveness, makes him unyielding towards her. It also perpetuates the silencing and misrepresentation that defines her experience of family life. Wentworth is fascinated by Louisa because he is similarly wilful and refuses to engage in dialogue with Anne. By the end of the novel, though, he has learned 'to distinguish between the steadiness of principle and the obstinacy of self-will, between the daring of heedlessness and the resolution of a collected mind' (244), and Anne is given the opportunity to answer his criticism and, this time, is listened to: 'I was right in submitting to [Lady Russell]', she concludes, 'if I had done otherwise, I should have suffered more in continuing the engagement than I did even in giving it up, because I should have suffered in my conscience ... if I mistake not, a strong sense of duty is no bad part of a woman's portion' (248).

We might suppose that the novel concludes rather conservatively, by endorsing female duty and the relinquishment of personal desire. However, it is not Anne's proper sense of duty to her dysfunctional family that constitutes its 'moral'; rather, it is the unpersuadable, unyielding mind that judges too quickly which is put on trial. The importance of being persuaded is summed up in the final chapter when Lady Russell, who originally convinced Anne that she should reject Wentworth, admits that she 'had been unfairly influenced by appearances'. She recognizes that 'because Captain Wentworth's manners had not suited her own ideas, she had been too quick in suspecting them to indicate a character of dangerous impetuosity' (251). What is valued at the end of this novel is the capacity to change one's mind, to admit that one was wrong.

My opening question 'what is rhetoric?' has proven a little harder to answer than expected. Principally, this is because different traditions provide radically different answers to this question: rhetoric is an art, but it is not; rhetoric is dead, but it thrives. Certainly, the dictionary definitions to which I first turned to explain the term scarcely do these complexities justice. Mostly in this introduction I have considered the disputed definition of rhetoric as an art; in the first chapter we will explore the origins of this definition in more detail. But throughout this book I am also interested in the difficulty of reducing persuasiveness to a system. This resistance to systematic definition and elaboration has its own important legacy, and its end point, I will suggest in the final chapter of this book, is the troublingly unsystematic Kenneth Burke. Burke extends the emphasis on persuasion in traditional rhetoric in two ways: first, he seeks to understand how we act on ourselves and others in both an inadvertent as well as an overt manner. Second, he adapts the exercise of argument on different sides to effect a series of dizzying reversals which aim to develop a way of interacting and cooperating that is 'strong enough to keep "states of domination" at bay' (Wess 1996: 204). It is with these two possibilities that this book will conclude as a way of identifying the enduring possibilities that remain within the rhetorical tradition.

1

THE CLASSICAL ART

BEGINNINGS

Rhetoric is not only concerned with debate, but has always seemed to provoke it. In this chapter, I want to consider how the key terms of the disputes originated principally because the disagreements elicited by this way of thinking about language have repercussions that continue into the present. We can summarize this debate quite simply at the outset as a question: is rhetoric a means to knowledge or simply an aptitude or a skill that helps us to persuade, regardless of the truth of the matter? As we shall see the responses this produces have some profound consequences.

In the West, the rhetorical tradition is believed to have originated as a self-conscious practice in Sicily in the fifth century BC. No texts survive from this period, but a story or myth does: after the overthrow of the tyrant Thrasybulus, the citizens initiated lawsuits to reclaim confiscated land and they began to systematize the use of persuasive speech to help them to win their cases. The earliest surviving handbook, though, is Athenian rather than Sicilian and it dates from the fourth century BC. This is Aristotle's *Rhetoric* (c. 332 BC), a text which has shaped all subsequent understanding of the subject. This work is regarded as seminal because it establishes that rhetoric is an art. As George Kennedy argues, it 'organizes its subject into essential parts, provides insight into the bases of speech acts, creates categories and terminology for discussing discourse, and illustrates and applies its teaching so that they can be used in society' (Aristotle 1991: ix).

This is an important contribution to the defence and definition of an 'art' that had already provoked doubts over its entitlement to be regarded as one. Aristotle's antagonist is his predecessor Plato (428–347 BC), especially in two of his most important dialogues: *Gorgias* and *Phaedrus*. In these dialogues Plato presents the philosopher Socrates' excoriation of rhetoric as a mere knack and a branch of flattery that is concerned with suasion rather than the truth. Rhetoric aims to please and gratify its makers as well as influence its recipients, but the satisfactions it offers are closer to those provided by a good meal rather than philosophical enquiry (Plato 1964a: 462c–d).

Socrates' attack has had a significant legacy and even theorists of rhetoric can be seen to demonstrate his point. Some five hundred years later Quintilian (*c.* 35 BC–AD 95), Professor of Latin Rhetoric under the emperor Vespasian and author of this art's most comprehensive handbook, *On the training of the orator* (*Institutio oratoria*), defines oratory as 'the science of speaking well' (Quintilian 2001: 8.Pr.6). Socrates might well have agreed with this and, equally, with Quintilian's insistence that the 'art' of the orator 'comprises various means of creating belief' (5.8.1). This depends on a range of learned techniques, many of which aim to arouse an audience's emotions. An orator, he tells us, should seek to 'entice' an audience 'with delights, drag them along by the strength of [his] pleading, and sometimes disturb them with emotional appeals' (5.14.29).

What is so different about Aristotle's *Rhetoric*, and the reason why it is central to defences of rhetoric, is its argument that this art does indeed lead to knowledge, albeit of a practical kind: the kind that helps us to resolve disputes, to reach agreements and to ascertain what is probably true. In relation to this last point Aristotle is commended for providing this art with a logical basis; he explores the method of reasoning specific to its practitioners.

Aristotle proposes that we consider rhetoric as an art that has a philosophical as well as a pragmatic purpose and defines it as 'the faculty of observing in any given case the available means of persuasion' (Aristotle 1984: 1355b, 26–27). This means that it helps us to make decisions when the matters under consideration are uncertain. Rhetoric is integral, in Aristotle's view, to both the discovery and presentation of knowledge, and this brings it closer to philosophical endeavour.

This chapter takes account of the technical defence and elaboration of rhetoric. My aim is to provide an introduction to the classical system, some of its key terms and its so-called standard history. I begin by exploring Plato's formative attacks on this 'art' in *Gorgias* and *Phaedrus* because these works provide a crucial context for understanding Aristotle's defining contribution as well as the scope and limitations of the later Roman technical tradition; we need to understand a little about both of these dialogues in order to grasp the significance of this key moment of origin in the rhetorical tradition as it has come to shape the defensive stance of its standard history. However, a perhaps unexpected reason for attending to these is that it will enable us also to understand how for one Roman theorist, Marcus Tullius Cicero, Plato rather represented a positive beginning: his attack on rhetoric can also be seen as a rhetorical gesture which brings to light the shared method of the orator and the *sceptical* philosopher, argument on different sides. This is the beginning of a different defence of rhetoric, not as a useful skill, but as a 'critical' method, as a way of thinking.

PLATO'S ATTACK

Plato was a follower of Socrates, who was executed by the civic authorities in Athens in 399 BC for impiety. Socrates appears as the leading disputant in almost all of Plato's dialogues, which explore a wide range of subjects, including the proper education of male citizens in the ideal republic and the right and wrong kinds of homoerotic love. However, rhetoric is a recurring preoccupation, and it is against this 'knack' that Socrates' own philosophical style of enquiry is contrasted by Plato in his dialogue

Gorgias. Socrates is critical of the method of the sophists, their tendency to argue different sides of an issue. We can see this method in one of the few surviving speeches of the sophist Gorgias (483–376 BC), the figure who comes under scrutiny in Plato's dialogue of that name. Gorgias came from the city of Leontini in Sicily and settled in Athens in 427 BC where he taught rhetoric to young men with the means to pay for this education. He did not write rhetorical handbooks, nor was he a teacher of rhetoric per se. Rather, he taught the practical skills of civic participation; his teaching of rhetoric as an aspect of this is best described as 'unsystematic'. His idea of rhetoric is really embodied in his practice, in performed speeches such as the *Encomium of Helen* (Kennedy 1994: 19). This sets out to exonerate the legendary Helen of Troy from the dishonour of abandoning her husband and country, and it does so by offering a range of different possibilities to explain her behaviour, while refusing to affirm any one of them.

> For either it was   by the will of Fate
>   and   the wishes of the Gods
>   and   the votes of Necessity
> that she did what she did,
>   or   by force reduced
>   or   by words seduced
>   < or   by love possessed. >
>
>   (Dillon and Gergel 2003: 78)

The sophists have had something of a 'renaissance' in the last two decades, especially among teachers of Rhetoric and Composition, who discover in their pedagogic and philosophical practice a potential model for their own teaching of rhetoric. Thus, Jasper Neel provocatively describes his own work as 'sophistry', and Stephen Mailloux advises that 'we are presently within a third sophistic' (Mailloux 1995: 1–2). For sophists like Gorgias, rhetoric is not a means to communicate persuasively 'truths' discovered through philosophical enquiry. Rather, it is a means to knowledge and understanding in the absence of a priori truth. The sophists are known as 'philosophical relativists'; that is, they are recognized as being 'skeptical about the possibility of knowledge of universal truth' (Kennedy 1994: 7). Protagoras had famously written a treatise which began by endorsing a subjective relativism: 'Man is the measure of all things'. In contrast, Gorgias' surviving speech *On Nature* evinces a radical scepticism: nothing exists, or if it exists it cannot be known, or if it can be known then it cannot be communicated.

It is this relativism, this openness to different possibilities, that has proven attractive to contemporary teachers of Rhetoric and Composition because it offers a new direction for both the writing of the history of rhetoric and the pedagogy of rhetoric teaching itself. Thus, Susan Jarratt reclaims specific stylistic devices and argumentative strategies for contemporary historians of rhetoric: *antithesis*, the pairing of opposite words; *parataxis*, the loose and non-hierarchical association of clauses; *antilogy*, the opposing of one argument with another or discovering contradictions in an argument; and, finally, *anagogy*, the exploration of different positions, demonstrated in the quotation from the *Encomium to Helen* above. These techniques, she argues, encourage openness to 'a multiplicity of possible causal relations', and they challenge the idea of a continuous, progressive history that dominates standard accounts of rhetoric; they allow for coterminous histories (Jarratt 1991: 10–12, 21, 103).

Nonetheless, despite such interest, the sophists remain the negative starting point of standard histories of rhetoric. The value of the position taken by Gorgias, George Kennedy argues, is that it 'opens up a place for rhetoric in debate and a need to argue both sides of an issue as persuasively as possible'. However, 'it also opens up a place for skill in "making the weaker the stronger cause"' (Kennedy 1994: 8). It is this problem that Socrates is highlighting in *Gorgias*. For Socrates, the sophists are concerned with suasion rather than the truth. They argue any side of the question so long as it pleases and gratifies the audience (Plato 1964a: 462c–d).

Let us take a closer look at this dialogue. *Gorgias*, probably written around 387 BC on Plato's return from a trip to Sicily, is deemed the foundational example of anti-rhetorical thinking. It is also the first text in which the Greek term denoting public speaking, *rhētorikē*, appears (Kennedy 1994: 3). This dialogue is organized in three parts: Socrates converses with the sophist Gorgias and then, when this breaks down, his followers Polus and Callicles step in. Gorgias understands that the province of rhetoric is 'persuasion', and he sets out to defend its utility in moral terms. For example, a rhetorician might persuade a patient to take essential medicine when the real expert, the physician, has failed to convince him (Plato 1964a: 456b). This does not make rhetoric 'moral' exactly, but it does mean that it is useful: it can help to make people 'better'. This defence of rhetoric, however, is undermined by Socrates. The problem with Gorgias' defence is that he has already commended the power of the orator elsewhere. For example, when he suggested that someone who possesses rhetorical expertise will be able to persuade the real experts to serve his interests: 'you will make the doctor ... your slave,' he argued, 'and your businessman will prove to be making money, not for himself, but for another, for you' (452e). Gorgias' moral defence of rhetoric will be dropped later in the dialogue: Polus argues that rhetoric is 'good' because it empowers those who wield it, while Callicles advises that it helps us to avoid suffering at the hands of others. This last claim is undoubtedly a pointed allusion to the judicial condemnation of the real Socrates in 399 BC. Both speakers, however, succeed only in condemning themselves from their own mouths.

Socrates famously argues in *Gorgias* that rhetoric is a 'knack' because it produces pleasure, not knowledge. It serves only to gratify the whims of the people rather than leading them to a deeper understanding of what constitutes good citizenship (462a). The problem, according to Socrates, is that the rhetorician lacks rational understanding of the moral issues he defends or contests. For example, though Polus may be 'well trained in rhetoric' he does not know what counts as Good (471d). He thinks that having power is a good thing because it makes one happy, even if this ultimately involves harming others; on his view it is better to do wrong than to suffer.

Socrates takes the moral high ground, insisting that a person is 'better' if he acts justly, 'worse' if he acts unjustly (470c), and he undermines Polus' position by attacking his process of argument.

From the very beginning of the dialogue Polus is characterized as a speechifier, as someone who is more interested in making longwinded orations than in conducting a conversation (448d). When countering Socrates, for instance, Polus engages in 'rhetorical refutation'; this is the practice, deployed so successfully in the law courts, of calling upon witnesses to support a position. One such 'witness' cited by Polus to disprove Socrates' argument is Archelaus, the slave whose willingness to murder secured him the throne of Persia (470d–471d). Is he not a happy man, Polus asks? Socrates rejects this method of refutation and its conclusion because it is easy for a witness to provide false testimony. False witnesses include, for Socrates, all those members of an audience who think that Polus' conventional view makes sense. Just because Polus is giving voice to popular opinion does not make him right.

To counter this Socrates employs a different style of refutation, setting out to reveal that everyone agrees with him. By prompting his antagonist to answer directly and concisely the questions he poses, Socrates forces Polus to retrace his steps. In so doing, he also practically demonstrates the difference between the rhetorical style of the sophists and the conversational method of the philosopher. So, for example, thanks to Socrates' questioning, Polus is invited to distinguish between what is admirable and contemptible, the very categories he mistakenly collapsed in his longwinded speech. This will lead him to acknowledge what he initially failed to see: first that doing wrong is more contemptible than suffering wrong, and then, that because it exceeds suffering wrong in harmfulness it is also 'worse' (475c–d). Once this point is conceded Socrates can then challenge Polus' citation of Archelaus as a false witness in a different way, staking out his surprising and rather contentious claim that he is an unhappy man who does not use rhetoric to denounce himself, his family and his friends (480b–c).

Verbose orating and the use of example as proof are two rhetorical techniques criticized by Socrates in his dialogue with Polus. A third is the practice of arguing on different sides of an issue, though, curiously, Socrates is accused of this same trick by the third speaker, Callicles. Exasperated by the ease with which

Socrates has unsettled Polus, as well as by his outlandish claims for the proper function of rhetoric, Callicles accuses him of being deliberately contrary: 'if you are serious and what you say is true, then surely the life of us mortals must be turned upside down and apparently we are everywhere doing the opposite of what we should' (481b–c). Yet, argues Socrates in self-defence, he is saying the same thing over and over again, whereas Callicles is ready to 'constantly shift to and fro' his views according to the whims of the Athenian Assembly (481d). Socrates is not at all concerned about the fact that his views run contrary to popular opinion so long as he is not 'out of tune with' himself (482c). He speaks like 'a true mob orator', declares Callicles (482c), though it is Socrates who will eventually silence his opponent, exposing as wrong-headed his belief that unrestrained passion is the route to happiness, as well as his failure to 'say the same things about the same subjects' (491b).

Central to Socrates' engagement with Callicles is his comparison of the rhetorical and philosophical ways of life. Callicles' way of life involves the manly activities of 'speaking in the Assembly and practicing rhetoric', but, Socrates argues, this does not mean that it is better than the contemplative path chosen by the philosopher (500c). In contrast to the philosopher, the sophist does not try to improve the mind of his listeners; his objective is merely their gratification. Sophists do not seek to order and organize their subject; consequently, they do not succeed in ordering the minds of their listeners. The aristocratic Callicles argues that a happy man is one who can indulge his desires freely and he defends rhetoric as a means to this end. In contrast, Socrates insists that the philosopher's careful management of both his mind and body constitutes the true source of happiness. Moreover, he adds, it is widely recognized that 'the heavens and the earth, gods and men, are bound together by fellowship and friendship, and order and temperance and justice'. It is the refusal to recognize this truth that leads sophists like Callicles to over-reach themselves (508a).

In the end, Socrates concedes that the best course is to avoid both doing and suffering wrong. The difficult issue is how we can manage that. Socrates' attempt to address this prompts him to reiterate his claim that the proper function of rhetoric is self-denunciation. Criticizing the amorality of Archelaus is one thing, but how do we address the mistakes of a great leader like Pericles who failed to improve the Athenians not because he didn't try, but because in giving them what they thought they wanted he unintentionally harmed them? Gratifying the people is not the same as improving them. What is needed is the method of refutation in which philosophers like Socrates excel, and which encourages critical self-reflection. Only then will we be faced with the difficult questions that we need to ask of ourselves if we are to lead moral and happy lives. The dialogue ends with Socrates relating a myth about the Isles of the Blessed, in which, on his view, the only lucky people to gain admittance after death will be self-disciplined philosophers like himself.

Gorgias is not Plato's only discussion of rhetoric. Curiously, some fifteen years later he wrote another dialogue, *Phaedrus*, in which he explores the basis of a philosophical rhetoric. *Phaedrus* is a dialogue of two halves, each of which reflects critically on one of the two contemporary forms of rhetorical instruction: on the one hand, the memorization of a performed speech, on the other, the rhetorical handbooks. All Greek citizens were expected to represent themselves in law courts. The sophists provided a broad liberal education for the elite, offering training in judicial oratory 'incidentally'. Those who could not afford such an education might employ a speech-writer to help them, and if this proved too expensive, they could always consult the rhetorical handbooks which offered an orientation in judicial oratory, outlining the parts of a speech and the main features of each (Kennedy 1963: 52–58).

Phaedrus opens with a young man, Phaedrus, recounting a speech about homoerotic love which he has just heard 'the ablest writer of our day' deliver (Plato 1964b: 228a). This writer is Lysias. Socrates, who is in love with Phaedrus, seeks to disabuse him of his good opinion of Lysias, and he does so by offering two 'better' orations of his own. The first supports his antagonist's claim that it is preferable to receive the affections of a man who is not in love with you on the grounds that such a lover is more rational. The second explains why the mad, impassioned lover, presumably like Socrates himself, is to be preferred. He will argue, paradoxically, that the impassioned lover is in fact the more rational of the two because he is motivated, not by lust, but by a desire to know the 'idea' of the Good which he sees represented in his beloved. This second speech supposedly represents Socrates' own views though he will later disclaim this. Why is Socrates the better speaker according to Plato? Socrates' first oration is technically the more proficient. It includes all the parts of a speech laid out in the handbooks: it has a prologue, a narration, a proof of the argument and an epilogue. Yet, despite its formal excellence, Socrates is not happy with its content. He believes that both he and Lysias have offended the god of Love. It is for this reason that he decides to offer a second speech defending the opposite argument. This second speech is not a formal oration. Rather, it uses a myth about a charioteer trying to control two horses to explore and demonstrate the nature of the soul. Socrates distinguishes between two kinds of soul: on the one hand, the soul of a forgetful man like Lysias who does not remember his divine, immortal origins, on the other hand, the soul of a philosopher who uses properly the material reminders of this world, such as the beauty of a young man, to recall this innate knowledge. On this account, Socrates' eloquence is divine. He claims not to know the source of his new eloquence. In other words, he is not a skilled rhetorician. Rather, it is strongly suggested that he is inspired by love for Phaedrus, whose beauty recalls to him the idea of the Good (244a–257b). This is why Socrates is deemed the better speaker: he understands the human soul and the idea of the Good and, better still, he is in love. This is the kind of love that leads one to nurture the beloved, not to exploit them.

The distinction between good and bad rhetoric, or rather between eloquence and rhetoric, is clarified in the second half of the dialogue. Plato analyses the form of Lysias' speech, revealing its lack of coherence according to the criteria set out in the rhetorical handbooks; he also criticizes these manuals for their empty formalism. Socrates recalls some of the key contributors to the technical tradition and the various terms they have coined to describe the parts of a public oration, only to dismiss this type of knowledge as superficial (269b). At the end of *Phaedrus* he goes yet further, attacking the technical innovation of writing itself on the grounds that it atrophies memory (274c–275a). According to myth, Socrates explains, it was the deity Theuth who 'invented' writing, along with arithmetic, geometry, astronomy and dice games. This invention, however, was rejected by the king of Egypt, Thamous or Amon, on the grounds that it 'will implant forgetfulness in [people's] souls; they will cease to exercise memory because they rely on that which is written, calling things to remembrance no longer from within themselves, but by means of external marks' (275a). For Socrates, it is only the reasoning process, represented in living speech or dialogue (*logos*), that makes us truly 'remember' what and who we are. Significantly, it is also in this part of the dialogue that Plato offers a positive statement of what constitutes a true rhetoric. The 'true rhetorician, the real master of persuasion' (269c–d), Socrates argues, depends on a profound understanding of the nature of the human soul and its parts; this is acquired by the application of the art of reasoning or dialectic (271a–b). That is, the right orator needs to know how many types of soul there are and he must also closely observe how each one is affected by different events, and he must watch in turn to see how his persuasiveness affects their conduct. Only then can he be said to be wise, and only then can he be said to be eloquent:

> Since the function of oratory is in fact to influence men's souls, the intending orator must know what types of soul there are. Now these are of a determinate number, and their variety results in a variety of individuals. To the types of soul thus discriminated there corresponds a determinate number of types of discourse. Hence a certain type of hearer will be easy to persuade by a certain type of speech to take such and such an action for such and such reason, while another type will be hard to persuade. All this the orator must fully understand, and next he must watch it actually occurring, exemplified in men's conduct, and must cultivate a keenness of perception in following it.
>
> (271 c–e)

Only with this rhetoric will he be able to lead the soul of his beloved towards the Good, the virtue of temperance. Only then, too, will he become the temperate lover who seeks to empower and enlighten his beloved rather than to exploit him.

A case can be made for viewing positively Plato's contribution to the debate about rhetoric. We might begin to make this case by asking whether the positive engagement with rhetoric in *Phaedrus* represents a change in position for Plato. Socrates tells us repeatedly in *Gorgias* that he always says the same thing about the same issue. Perhaps this is right: in both dialogues the moral philosopher Socrates values self-restraint and equates this with the well-ordered mind. In this respect, there is no change in Socrates' philosophical position. Nonetheless, we might also give some credence to Callicles' representation of Socrates as a slippery speaker, one who argues on different sides of an issue, rather like a sophist. It is not just that Plato places contrasting characters in fictional debates, and so engineers a debate that Socrates will always win; he also seems to *invite* ongoing disagreement. This is noted by the literary critic James L. Kastely. Socrates' dismissal of rhetoric in *Gorgias* as a 'knack', he suggests, should not be seen as 'his final word on rhetoric, but rather his opening of rhetoric for discussion'. If we are attentive to the dialogue form of Plato's writings then it is indeed hard to take Socrates' pronouncements at face value. It is difficult not to be dissatisfied with many of his arguments: his claim, for instance, that the true rhetorician should denounce himself. Similarly provocative is Socrates' isolation at the end of *Gorgias*, the fact that 'no one will talk to him'. Socrates' insistence that the proper use of rhetoric depends on self-denunciation only works if the reader is willing to denounce him too, and his final isolation invites us to do just this since it highlights his failure to persuade (Kastely 1997: 36, 32). The same provocations are offered to the reader of *Phaedrus*, which ends unexpectedly with Socrates' brief commendation of the young Isocrates, one of Athens' most famous sophists, and a prediction that he will make contemporaries like Lysias look like 'very small fry' in years to come, especially if 'a sublimer impulse [should] lead him to do greater things' (Plato 1964b: 279a). Meanwhile, Socrates' assertions on what counts as a true rhetoric are perhaps not meant to be extracted from the text and reiterated in our own speech or writing as 'gospel'; to do this would mean that Plato had failed to make us *think*. Plato's choice of the dialogue form works well rhetorically because it invites further deliberation.

At the end of this chapter we will explore one example of just such an engagement with Plato's two dialogues, Cicero's *On the ideal orator* (*De oratore*) (55 BC). However, the reading of them just outlined does not usually carry much weight in standard histories which seek to defend rhetoric as a practical art. Both of Plato's dialogues are regarded as resolutely anti-rhetorical. In standard histories Callicles' hostility to Socrates in *Gorgias* prompts a denunciation of Plato's hypocrisy, not a re-engagement with the form of the dialogue. Plato 'never allows Socrates' opponents to go back over his arguments critically', protests Brian Vickers, 'but forces them to accept Socrates' terms and Socrates' tempo' (1988: 94). This is just as Callicles complains. Meanwhile, the outlining of a philosophical rhetoric in *Phaedrus* is not taken seriously. Socrates' insistence that the true rhetor-ician should study the different types of soul and understand how each one is affected by different events is considered impossible to put into practice. The apparent softening of Socrates' approach since *Gorgias* is regarded as misleading. The common starting point of the standard histories remains Plato's denunciation of rhetoric in *Gorgias*. Historians dismantle his opposition, usually by emphasizing his anti-democratic views, and then defend the usefulness of rhetoric to democratic debate (Barilli 1989; Vickers 1988). The proper scheme standard histories outline is not to be found with the sophists. Indeed, Plato's disparagement of their style as over-wrought and manipulative has mediated their modern critical evaluation. Thus, Kennedy observes that some of the sophists' surviving speeches display 'an empty verbosity and self-indulgence' (Kennedy 1980: 39), while Renato Barilli notes 'a total lack of caution' in Gorgias' works: 'the argumentation is all on the side and in favour of the emotional and irrational power of words' (Barilli 1989: 5). Rather, the articulation of the true scheme is attributed to one of Plato's pupils, Aristotle. His *Rhetoric* recognizes the shortcomings of the technical and sophistic tradi-tions; it eschews the emphasis in the handbooks on the parts of a speech, and it details this art's logical method of argument.

ARISTOTLE'S *RHETORIC*

The likely origin of *Rhetoric* is lecture notes; it was probably written at different times but never fully revised (Kennedy 1994: 55). Perhaps because of this *Rhetoric* is a difficult text, densely written and often contradictory. Nonetheless, it marks the beginning of the rhetorical canon because it is seen to address directly Plato's attack on the sophists in *Gorgias* and the technical tradition in *Phaedrus*. Mainly, Aristotle (384–322 BC) defends rhetoric as a necessary, albeit a secondary art. It is an essential art, for example, for the persuasion of uneducated or uneducable audiences. In contrast to Plato, who berated the popular appeal of the sophists in *Gorgias*, Aristotle argues instead that it is in fact necessary 'to use, as our modes of persuasion and argument, notions possessed by everybody'. Furthermore, he also argues that a rhetorician must be able to argue 'on opposite sides of a question':

> not in order that we may in practice employ it in both ways (for we must not make people believe what is wrong), but in order that we may see clearly what the facts are, and that, if another man argues unfairly, we on our part may be able to confute him.
>
> (Aristotle 1984: 1355a, 27–34)

Arguing on opposite sides is important, after all and despite Socrates' apparent hostility, because it enables us to discover the stronger case and to persuade a popular audience of its rightness.

When it comes to theorizing the 'art' itself, *Rhetoric* begins where *Phaedrus* left off, with an attack on the technical hand-books. These books are too preoccupied with the techniques for arousing the emotions and, as Plato had complained, with the formal organization of a speech (1354a). Aristotle avoids this second problem by focusing attention on the stages of composition, also known as the 'activities of the orator': invention, or the discovery of the available means of persuasion; disposition, or the arrangement of this material; and, finally, style. He does not ignore the parts of a speech which, like Plato, he lists as four, but these are dealt with in the last book, under style.

Throughout *Rhetoric* Aristotle privileges one of these activities over the others: 'invention', the discovery 'in any given case [of] the available means of persuasion' (Aristotle 1984: 1355b, 26–27). Quite simply, Aristotle understands that the 'means of persuasion' must be invented before they can be arranged in a speech (Wisse 1989: 84). As Roland Barthes elegantly puts it, *Rhetoric* 'foregrounds the structuration of discourse (active operation) and relegates to the background its structure (discourse as product)' (Barthes 1988: 48). Under 'invention', Aristotle identifies three means of persuasion or proof: *logos*, or rational argument; *ethos*, the speaker's character, particularly his 'trustworthiness'; and *pathos*, the emotions aroused in an audience. In the pre-Aristotelian handbooks criticized by Socrates in *Phaedrus*, *ethos* and *pathos* are restricted to the opening and concluding parts of a speech. This is because it is deemed advisable to try to conciliate the judges at the beginning of a speech by giving them the impression that one is of good character since this will make them more willing to be persuaded; meanwhile, the emotions of the judges should be roused at the end of a speech so as to stir them to action (Kennedy 1963: 91, 94). Aristotle not only makes *ethos* and *pathos* 'means of persuasion' or 'proofs' in their own right, and thus central to the whole speech rather than just a part of it, but he also understands that *ethos* can be rational. This is because a listener will consciously evaluate a speaker's reliability (Wisse 1989: 29–36).

Aristotle's main contribution to the defence of rhetoric, however, was to detail its particular methods of logical proof (*logos*). He identifies two kinds: the 'example' and the 'enthymeme'. The example approximates 'induction' in logic: it involves demonstrating that something is so from 'a number of similar cases' (1356b, 14). For instance, 'that Dionysius, in asking as he does for a bodyguard, is scheming to make himself a despot' can be demonstrated with the earlier example of Peisistratus, who 'kept asking for a bodyguard in order to carry out such a scheme, and did make himself a despot as soon as he got it; and so did Theagenes at Megara'. All of these, Aristotle concludes, are 'instances of the one general principle, that a man who asks for a bodyguard is scheming to make himself a despot' (1357b, 30–35).

Aristotle's interest does not really lie with the example, but it is still worth pausing over this form of proof for a moment longer. The use of example has proven important to the *querelle des femmes*, from the medieval French aristocrat Christine de Pizan to Camille Paglia. Mostly, feminist defences in this genre offer examples of worthy or notable women, seeking to establish as a general principle that women possess intellectual and moral equality with men, as well as pointing to how female contributions to the arts and sciences are written out of history. This is consonant with Aristotle's brief advice on the 'example'. But often the example can be used to provoke further reflection, or to expose inconsistencies in expected lines of argument. One particularly provocative use of this 'proof' to defend the rights of women is offered in *A Letter to the Women of England, on the Injustice of Mental Subordination* (1799) by the colourful Mary Robinson (1758–1800), actor, poet and polemical writer. Robinson is often conventional in her use of this proof, reaching back into antiquity for 'examples' of notable women, including Quintilian's three eloquent Roman matrons (Robinson 2003: 55). But some of her examples are rather more flamboyant and disconcerting, notably so the 'true story' she tells to 'prove that the mind of WOMAN, when she feels a correct sense of honour ... can rise to the most intrepid defence of it' (49–52). This example reads like a story from an Italian novella: 'A foreign lady of great distinction' meets her lover on the eve of their marriage; when he invites her to grant him his conjugal rights a day early, she is astonished but conceals this and resolves to be revenged; she deceives her lover into meeting her secretly later that night, and then shoots him. Our heroine is found guilty of murder, but she is not condemned to die because her promise to 'marry him that night', or rather, to have sex with him, is deemed by judge and jury 'so powerful an argument of her love for the deceased' that they determine 'no other motive could have produced so dreadful an event' (51). With this example Robinson goes way beyond proving a woman's 'correct sense of honour'; she also challenges our assumptions about what a correct sense of honour might actually mean.

For Aristotle, though, it is the enthymeme rather than the example that is the most powerful of rhetorical proofs, mainly because it earns the rhetorician the most applause. The enthymeme means literally 'something "held in the mind"' (Kennedy 1994: 59). Enthymemes are often recognizable in English by their form: usually, two sentences joined by a conjunction or by a conjunctive adverb, such as 'therefore' or 'consequently'. For example: our peace is under threat therefore we must go to war. An enthymeme demonstrates that if certain propositions are true then 'a further and quite distinct proposition must also be true in consequence' (Aristotle 1984, 1356b, 15–16). In the example just cited, the conclusion that we must go to war can be deduced from the premise that 'our peace is under threat'. Unlike the premises of a syllogism, which are certain, the premises of an enthymeme are 'derived from probabilities' familiar to an audience. As a result, a key premise is often implied rather than stated in full (1357a). In our example, the missing premise might be stated as 'war safeguards peace'. Identifying a missing premise is important because only then can we test the strength or weakness of an argument. In this case, the premise that 'war safeguards peace' is of course highly contentious; the refutation of this enthymeme should address this.

How might this work in practice with a more complex example? Let's consider Prime Minister Tony Blair's use of this argument in his 'Address to the Nation', delivered two nights after he gave the order for British troops to be sent to Iraq:

> For 12 years, the world tried to disarm Saddam, after his wars in which hundreds of thousands died. UN weapons inspectors say vast amounts of chemical and biological poisons, such as anthrax, VX nerve agent, and mustard gas remain unaccounted for in Iraq. So our choice is clear: back down and leave Saddam hugely strengthened; or proceed to disarm him by force.
>
> (Blair 2003)

Critics of the war in Iraq focused on the claim that Saddam Hussein had not been successfully disarmed. The subsequent failure to discover weapons of mass destruction in Iraq undermined the integrity of the government's position; it appeared, retrospectively, as if they or, indeed, parliament and the country, had been misled.

However, we can also see how coercively Blair's argument works in this speech if we focus on the missing premise of this enthymeme: that war safeguards peace. This silent assumption propels us towards the narrow options with which we are being presented: tackle Saddam or back down at your peril. The choice that is emphasized, tackle Saddam now, is supported by an example that Blair repeatedly and discreetly invokes throughout the speech. He appeals to collective memory of the failure of the policy of appeasement which was pursued so futilely by the British government in the 1930s: 'it is true, as we British know – that the best way to deal with future threats peacefully, is to deal with present threats with resolve' (Blair 2003).

How does a rhetorician 'invent' the examples and enthymemes that will support his or her position? Or rather, where can we find the means of persuasion that will support our standpoint? For Aristotle arguments can be found with the help of the 'abstract patterns of inference' (Leff 1983: 220), or 'topics' listed in *Rhetoric*. The topics are one of the more challenging aspects of classical rhetoric, not least because of the difference in their conception between Aristotle and the Roman theoreticians, but also because they are alien to contemporary habits of organizing a speech or essay. Probably, the term 'topic' referred to 'a "place" in a handbook or text that could be imitated and adapted to a new context by a speaker' (Kennedy 1994: 61). Aristotle distinguishes between 'common topics', abstract lines of reasoning which are 'common' to a range of questions, moral, scientific and political, and the 'special topics', which are particular to the genres of rhetoric. The common topics are not ready-made arguments or essentialist assumptions; they do not constitute the materials of argument. Rather, they offer a series of possible 'forms' which explore relationships: for example, similarity, difference, degree, cause and effect, contradiction.

One of the five common topics listed in *Rhetoric* derives from the abstract relation of more or less (1397b). This topic assumes that when we compare two or more things we discover differences that are by degree rather than absolute: for instance, we might use this topic when deciding which is the lesser of two evils. An example of this topic in use is Martin Luther King's argument that the stumbling block to black liberation is the 'white moderate' wedded to social 'order' rather than 'justice', not the card-carrying racist: 'Shallow understanding from people of good will is more frustrating than absolute misunderstanding from people of ill will. Lukewarm acceptance is much more bewildering than outright rejection' (King in Corbett 1990: 348–49).

The 'special topics', on the other hand, represent generally held beliefs and values appropriate to each of the three genres of rhetoric. Aristotle argues that rhetoric functions in three crucial genres. First, forensic or judicial rhetoric is concerned with past events; it is used primarily in law-courts to accuse or defend. Second, deliberative rhetoric is concerned with future events; its action is exhortation or dissuasion. Third, demonstrative rhetoric, also known as display or epideictic, is concerned with the present: its context is usually commemorative occasions and its function is praise or blame. Inevitably, owing to these different functions, each genre has its own lines of reasoning. The most extensive treatment of the special topics, though, concerns deliberative rhetoric, the objective of which is 'happiness' (*eudaimonia*). Accordingly, Aristotle lists the constituent parts, which include virtue, gentle birth, virtuous friends, wealth, beauty, good reputation and lots of offspring (1360b). Deliberative rhetoric is about expediency, that is, it is concerned with the means to happiness rather than with what happiness actually is; the special topics which inform debate about this represent what can be described as the Good, with what brings happiness. Aristotle lists uncontroversially good things, including 'happiness' and its parts as well as 'justice', 'courage' and so on, but also types of argument that can be called upon when a 'good' is controversial, for instance:

> That is good of which the contrary is bad. That is good the contrary of which is to the advantage of our enemies. ... That which most people seek after, and which is obviously an object of contention, is also a good. ... Again, that is good which has been distinguished by the favour of a discerning or virtuous man or woman etc.
>
> (1362b–1363a)

Sometimes the rhetorician is presented with two options, both of which are expedient. In this case, 'he' will need to decide which is more expedient, and in order to do so can draw upon a different set of topics concerned with 'the greater good'. For example:

> of two things that which stands less in need of other things is the greater good, since it is more self-sufficing. ... Again, that which is an origin of other things is a greater good than that which is not. ... what is rare is a greater good than what is plentiful. ... More generally: the hard thing is better than the easy, because it is rarer; and in another way the easy thing is better than the hard, for it is as we wish it to be. ... Again, one thing is more honourable or better than another if it is more honourable or better to desire it etc.
>
> (1364a–b)

Reading lists of topics is not much fun unless, of course, one is looking for something to say. When preparing a public speech, however, these lists were evidently 'aids to composition, well tried methods of stimulating thought, and safeguards against the haphazard selection of ideas' (Dixon 1971: 27). But I would also argue that these lists can be a well tried method of stimulating thought for the literary writer too, who may use them to expose the self-interested exploitation of familiar arguments by untrustworthy characters; this is the case in the opening books of John Milton's *Paradise Lost* (1674), in which the fallen angels deliberate on their next course of action.

In particular, we can use this system to assess the claims of their leader, Satan, that Hell offers a republican alternative to a Heaven governed by a tyrannical God. Most readers find it hard to resist Milton's fallen angels. In the early books of *Paradise Lost* they are epic heroes who have fallen in the field of battle, rebels against an oppressive and nepotistic God who has anointed his 'Son' the Messiah. Informing this reading is discomfort with the closed dialogue represented between God and the Son in book 3. It is difficult to distinguish between these two characters, who appear wrapped up in mutual admiration:

O Son, in whom my soul hath chief delight,
Son of my bosom, Son who art alone
My Word, my Wisdom, and effectual might,
All hast thou spoken as my thoughts are, all
As my eternal purpose hath decreed.

(Milton 1998: 3. 169–72)

This comes after we have experienced the debate in the Council of Hell in book 2, which represents a diverse range of characters, the fallen angels, Moloch, Belial, Mammon and Beelzebub, all of whom express quite distinctive viewpoints. Not surprisingly, later readers have suspected that Milton's sympathies lie, unconsciously, with Satan and his crew. Yet, as I want to suggest, the energy of this contest of clashing viewpoints takes on a different cast in a reading alert to its rhetorical design.

The fallen angels have been invited by Satan to debate whether they should continue their battle against Heaven with open war or with 'covert guile' (2.41). Of the several disputants only Moloch actually responds to this question explicitly, declaring that his 'sentence is for open war' (2.51). Belial immediately shifts ground, advising that they do nothing. Mammon introduces a new polemic, the advantages of peace over war. The victor of the debate, though, is the last speaker, Satan's second-in-command, Beelzebub, who returns to the original question, advising that they wage war covertly, directing their revenge against God's newest creation, the 'puny inhabitants' of a new paradise, Adam and Eve (1.367). These speeches are concerned with future action, that is, with the question of what is the happier course of action, and more specifically, with whether a second attack on God is expedient. Thus, they are examples of deliberative oratory, though not uncomplicatedly so. Collectively, the disputants consider what will distress their enemy most, and explore the scope and limits of their power to wage war again, but mainly they seek to establish a direction of action based on the 'greater good'. In their falsely reasoned debates, however, this comes down to 'the lesser evil'. The destruction that God may unleash on the rebellious angels if they attempt a second war, Moloch despairingly reasons, cannot be worse than the situation they find themselves in. Why, then, would they hesitate:

> to incense
> His utmost ire? Which to the highth enraged,
> Will either quite consume us, and reduce
> To nothing this essential, happier far
> Than miserable to have eternal being.
>
> (2.95–99)

Belial recognizes that a second failed rebellion may in fact leave them in a worse condition; their punishment may lead to more pain and further constraint, not oblivion. Therefore, it is better, he reasons, to accept their 'fate' and do nothing rather than invoke God's anger again (2.196–99). Mammon paradoxically invites the unrepentant angels to 'seek / Our own good from ourselves' (1.252–53), arguing that they can 'Thrive under evil' (1.261). Beelzebub's final contribution is the best in the sense that he advises 'the easier enterprise' (1.345); his cowardly, spiteful proposal is the most likely to succeed.

In an epic poem that is all 'about knowing and choosing', or rather, about the exercise of free will, and where the exploration of this complex issue is grounded partly in 'Milton's own choice and rhetorical use of a panoply of literary forms' (Lewalski 1985: 1), then the rhetorical decisions of Satan and his bad company are revealing. The rhetorical genre they have chosen, John M. Steadman explains, 'emphasizes their obduracy in crime'. Had they chosen instead the genre of forensic oratory then they would have been guided to reflect critically on the justness of their past actions (Steadman 1968: 244). It is notable, for instance, that none of the disputants counsels repentance.

The diatribe against the tyranny of God by the grand rhetorician Satan in book 1 persuaded William Blake that Milton was 'of the Devil's party without knowing it' (Blake 1980: 107). However, the speeches in book 2 not only show that the fallen angels remain obdurate in crime, but also indicate why: even among themselves they have no opportunity to exercise free will. The debate has a foregone conclusion. Beelzebub's successful

argument merely repeats what Satan had already advised at the
end of book 1 (Milton 1998: 2. 645–62).

THE ROMAN ART

Aristotle is by far the most important theoretician of rhetoric to
many historians. In contrast, the Roman contributions seem
derivative and overly technical. On this there is general agreement. Aristotle is respected because he provides the art with a
logical basis, and in so doing, defends it from Plato's influential
attack in *Gorgias*, whereas the technical organization of the
Roman handbooks tends to recall why Plato found the art so
treacherous in the first place. Two of the handbooks drawn upon
in this section will help us to understand why. The anonymous
Rhetoric for Herennius (*Rhetorica ad Herennius*) (*c.* 100 BC) is a
practical guide for working lawyers; it provides precise
instruction on what should be said in court, at what point in a
speech and how. Meanwhile, Quintilian's encyclopaedic twelve
volume *On the training of the orator* (*Institutio oratoria*), written
in the first century AD, offers a complete education in rhetoric for
school boys.

   In addition to being the most venerated theorist in the standard history of rhetoric, Aristotle is also an important starting
point in critical histories that have provided the basis for a different engagement with this tradition. In his 'Lectures Notes on
Rhetoric', Friedrich Nietzsche (1844–1900) finds the rhetoric of
the Roman orator and republican Cicero 'crude and distasteful
compared to that of Aristotle' (Nietzsche 1983: 103). In the late
twentieth century, Roland Barthes reaches a similar conclusion.
All rhetoric, he argues, is fundamentally 'Aristotelian'; 'all the
didactic elements which feed the classical manuals come from
Aristotle' (Barthes 1988: 20). It is important to note this consensus because it reminds us that rhetoric is conventionally
defined as an 'art'; mainly, recent debate has been concerned with
improving it or replacing it with a more scientific study of language, linguistics. The technical focus of the Roman handbooks
undoubtedly contributes to this view of rhetoric, though there is
one important exception. Cicero's dialogue *On the ideal orator* (*De*

oratore) (55 BC) contests the very idea that rhetoric can be deemed an art, and indeed, refuses to detail its rules straightforwardly. This text will be considered at the end of this chapter; all we need note for the time being is that this Roman handbook is not well regarded either, only this time the reason given is that it is not systematic enough.

Barthes is undoubtedly right to suggest that 'all the didactic elements which feed the classical manuals come from Aristotle.' The Roman theorists inherit his division of the genres, and they also understand that each genre has its own set of 'commonplaces'. In addition, they derive from Aristotle the three activities of the orator – invention, disposition and style – though they add two further activities: memory (*memoria*), or the memorizing of a speech; and its delivery (*pronuntiatio*). However, there are many differences too. In general, the concern of the Roman handbooks is with the practicality of delivering a judicial oration, and this affects both how they are organized and the advice they offer. If, as Barthes argues, Aristotle's *Rhetoric* 'foregrounds the structuration of discourse (active operation) and relegates to the background its structure (discourse as product)' (Barthes 1988: 48), then we might say that the Roman handbooks relegate to the foreground their concern with 'structure', with 'discourse as product'. That is to say, they are organized around the parts of a judicial oration, and in this respect they recall pre-Aristotelian rhetoric (Wisse 1989: 78).

The number of these 'parts' varies from book to book. *Rhetoric for Herennius* lists six parts, while Quintilian increases this to seven. According to the latter, the orator needs to structure his discourse in the following way: first with a prologue or exordium, in which the orator tries to win the goodwill of an audience by representing his character in the best light; then a narration of what is supposed to have happened; the division of the points that will be treated; the proof of the argument; the refutation of an opponent's arguments; the digression, which is an occasion to entertain the audience or beautify a speech; and the epilogue or peroration, used to sum up the speaker's position and to arouse strong emotion. However, it is not the naming of these parts that calls for our attention, but rather how one of the key activities of the orator is distributed in relation to these, 'invention'.

If we remember, Aristotle describes 'invention' as encompassing three different kinds of proof – *ethos*, *pathos* and *logos* – all three can be invoked at any stage in an oration. Of these, though, the discovery of examples and enthymemes, discussed under *logos*, is by far the most important activity, not least because it earns the rhetorician the most applause. These are derived from Aristotle's topics, which are organized according to the three genres. In the Roman manuals, *logos* is restricted to the parts of speech identified above as the proof and refutation, while the topics are *'loci communes'* or 'common-places'. That is, they are ready-made arguments organized according to types of legal defence (Cicero 1954: 2.48ff.). I find helpful Barthes' imagining of them as the filling out and fixing of what were Aristotle's original 'empty forms' of reasoning. The Roman commonplaces become 'a storehouse of stereotypes, of consecrated themes, of full "pieces" which are almost obligatorily employed in the treatment of any subject' (Barthes 1988: 67). The anonymous *Rhetoric for Herennius* offers fulsome classification of the commonplaces that can be called upon to support different types of defence in court. This is known as status theory. Orators must work out the position they are taking through a process of elimination. Did X kill Y? If he or she did, was it a matter of self-defence? Or, are there mitigating circumstances, such as service to the state? Once the basic defence is determined the orator should then run through the stock arguments or commonplaces appropriate to this (Cicero 2001: 32–33).

This stockpile of arguments emphasizes the fact that the Roman manuals are hands-on guides in the art of persuasion. They 'stem from a desire to create an academic discipline', a list of arguments 'which could be memorized' and 'which applied to classroom exercises' (Kennedy 1972: 116). Arguments can be discovered and applied as the need arises. Nonetheless, there is a downside to this technical approach. 'As a way of analysis', writes Jakob Wisse, 'this system is quite adequate, and it probably helped boys beginning to learn rhetoric to see the central issue of a case. But the exhaustiveness aimed at for such checklists of topoi, of all possible arguments in all possible cases, also has some disadvantages' (Wisse 1989: 94). Indeed, there has long been an understanding that this attachment to a rule-bound approach to speaking persuasively can have a constraining effect on intellectual enquiry.

This sounds dull and formulaic no doubt, and the Roman theoreticians would probably agree. Though Quintilian gives considerable attention to rational proofs, mainly in book 5, he also shifts Aristotle's emphasis, identifying the orator's art with emotive appeal. At the start of book 5 he complains of those famous 'authorities', such as Aristotle, 'who have held that the sole duty of the orator was to instruct'. Earlier theorists 'believed that the emotions were to be excluded' on the grounds that it was 'wrong for the judge to be diverted from the truth by pity, favour, anger, or the like' (5.Pr.1). Quintilian could not disagree more. Unless we 'can entice' an audience 'with delights, drag them along by the strength of our pleading, and sometimes disturb them by emotional appeals' then 'we cannot make even a just and true cause prevail' (5.14.29). Later, in book 6, he argues that this ability is the skill of the orator:

> [T]here are, and always have been, a fair number of speakers capable of discovering with some skill what it is that their Proofs require. I do not despise them, but I think that the limit of their usefulness is to ensure that the judge is not ignorant of anything. If I may speak my mind, they are very proper people to instruct real orators in the facts of the case. But the man who can carry the judge with him, and put him in whatever frame of mind he wishes, whose words move men to tears or anger, has always been a rare creature. Yet this is what dominates the courts, this is the eloquence that reigns supreme. Arguments, for the most part, spring out of the Cause, and the better side always has more of them, so that a man who wins on Arguments knows only that his advocate has not failed him. But where force has to be brought to bear on the judges' feelings and their minds distracted from the truth, there the orator's true work begins. . . . Of course, Proofs may lead the judges to *think* our Cause the better one, but it is our emotional appeals that make them also *want* it to be so; and what they want, they also believe.
>
> (6.2.3–6)

Ethos and *pathos* are the proofs associated with the emotions. Only in the Roman handbooks, they are not really 'proofs' at all, but rather a series of techniques that enable the orator to affect judgement. Moreover, they are relegated to the opening and closing parts of an oration, the prologue or exordium and epilogue or peroration, respectively (Wisse 1989: 78, 85). Of the two, *ethos* is associated with milder emotions, and for this reason it is suited to the exordium, the part of a judicial oration in which the orator aims to 'prepare the hearer to be more favourably inclined towards' his cause (Quintilian 2001: 4.1.5). This often depends, in the first place, on the perception of the orator as a good man because, Quintilian explains, he is likely then to be seen as a 'trustworthy' rather than 'partisan' witness (4.1.7). Making a good impression might involve emphasizing one's lack of preparation, or fear of being outflanked by an opponent since '[t]here is a natural prejudice in favour of people who have difficulties, and a scrupulous judge is already ready to listen to an advocate who does not present a threat to his integrity'. At the very least he should conceal his artfulness for the simple reason that we are more persuadable when we believe that a speaker is not a skilled orator (4.1.9–10).

Techniques for arousing *pathos*, strong emotions such as anger, hate or pity so as to sway the judgement of the audience at the end of an oration, include the simple gesture of 'bringing the accused into court dirty and unkempt, and their children and parents with them' as well as the display of 'blood-bespattered clothing, the unbandaging of the wounds, the stripped bodies with the marks of the scourge' and so on, the aim being to 'confront people's minds directly with the facts', bringing a crime to the eyes of an audience, so to speak (6.1.30–31). The definitive example of this technique in action is Antony's display of the blood-stained cloak of Julius Caesar during his funeral oration, which 'drove the Roman people to fury', and plunged the republic into civil war: 'It was known that he had been killed; his body lay on the bier; but it was the clothing, wet with blood, that made the image of the crime so vivid that Caesar seemed not to have been murdered, but to be being murdered there and then' (6.1.31).

Quintilian's list of techniques for producing *pathos* also includes, more worryingly, the affectation of sincerity. To achieve this, Quintilian advises, we must 'assimilate ourselves to the emotions of those who really suffer', so that 'our speech spring[s] from the very attitude that we want to produce in the judge' (6.2.27). How can an orator achieve this? This depends above all on a vivid imagination. The orator with a vivid imagination will 'show the greatest power in the expression of emotions' (6.2.29). For this enables him to convey to his audience *enargeia*, a 'quality which makes us seem not so much to be talking about something as exhibiting it' (6.2.32). This is the same technique that Shakespeare displays to devastating effect when Iago gives the 'ocular proof' Othello demands of Desdemona's adultery by making him 'see', or really, vividly imagine, the sexual betrayal that did not happen (Shakespeare 2005: 3.3.365):

IAGO	There are a kind of men
	So loose of soul that in their sleeps
	Will mutter their affairs. One of this kind is Cassio.
	In sleep I heard him say 'Sweet Desdemona,
	Let us be wary, let us hide our loves',
	And then, sir, would he grip and wring my hand,
	Cry 'O, sweet creature!', then kiss me hard,
	As if he plucked up kisses by the roots,
	That grew upon my lips, lay his leg o'er my thigh,
	And sigh, and kiss, and then cry 'Cursèd fate,
	That gave this to the Moor!'
OTHELLO	O, monstrous, monstrous!

(3.3.420–30)

Iago artfully persuades Othello that Cassio's supposed sleep-talking is 'a foregone conclusion' of Desdemona's guilt (3.3.433). He successfully appeals to his unfounded fears rather than his reason. Did Plato not have good cause to dismiss rhetoric as a dangerous 'knack' which gratifies, enflames and misleads rather than educates an audience?

Another important difference between Aristotle's *Rhetoric* and the Roman handbooks concerns the treatment of style or *elocutio*.

It is not so much that the general advice changes: in both traditions great importance is attached to correct use of language, clarity, intelligibility and propriety or 'decorum'. And in both, three styles are distinguished: the grand, the middle and the low. The grand style is emotive and ornate; it is suited especially to a peroration, in which the orator should try to arouse the emotions of his audience. The middle style, in contrast, offers a midway between the ornate grand style and the idiomatic low style. However, there is divergence over the treatment of the stylistic devices, the tropes and figures which are used, mainly, to ornament speech.

Aristotle's treatment of these is very brief, and his attention is taken by one trope, metaphor, which 'gives style clearness, charm, and distinction as nothing else can' (1405a, 8–9). Discussion of this, moreover, is concerned with its 'proper' use. For instance, Aristotle advises that there must be 'harmony' between the two things being compared in a metaphor. Inappropriate metaphors produce a 'frigid' style, for example, when 'Gorgias talks of "events that are green and full of sap", and says "foul was the deed you sowed and evil the harvest you reaped"' (1406b, 9–10). Compare this with the very full account offered in the Roman manuals. The author of *Rhetoric for Herennius* lists some two hundred tropes and figures in book 4 of his treatise, while Quintilian dedicates two volumes to their elaboration: book 8 is concerned with tropes and book 9 with figures of speech.

Quintilian's remains the most comprehensive treatment, and the divisions that he outlines can be usefully recounted here. The term 'figure', he notes, often serves as a catch-all term for linguistic effects which involve either a substitution of one word for another which affects meaning ('trope'), or a change in syntactic structure for emphasis or ornament ('figure' or 'scheme'). The term 'trope', Quintilian explains, signifies 'language transferred from its natural and principal meaning to another for the sake of embellishment' (9.1.4). This category includes familiar 'tropes' like metonymy, when one word is substituted for another (8.6.23), synecdoche, when the term for a part of a thing is substituted for the whole, or vice versa (8.6.19), and also metaphor (*translatio*). This last is also the first trope discussed by Quintilian, on the grounds that it is 'the commonest and far the most beautiful', and also because it 'adds to the resources of language by exchanges or borrowings to supply its deficiencies' so that 'nothing goes without a name' (8.6.4–5). A metaphor, he explains, involves the transference of a verb or noun from a place where it properly belongs to another where 'the "transferred" term is better than the "proper" one', or, indeed, where there is 'no "proper" word': for example, when farmers describe a vinebud as a 'gemma' or gem 'or speak of the crops as "thirsty" or the harvest as "in trouble"' (8.6.4–6). In this respect, it represents the very idea of the trope itself, but it can also be thought of as a 'shortened form of Simile'. For example, he 'acted "like a lion"' is a simile whereas 'he is a lion' is a metaphor (8.6.8–9). This trope can be used artfully to adorn a speech, to move an audience's feelings or to place something vividly 'before our eyes' (8.6.19).

In contrast, 'figures' involve a structural alteration of a sentence or a grouping of words rather than a change in meaning (8.6.67). This is a more complex category because it includes both grammatical figures and rhetorical figures. Grammatical figures can be understood as 'innovations in speech' which would most likely be regarded as errors if they were not deliberately applied. Their benefit is that they alleviate 'the tedium of everyday stereotyped language' (9.3.2–4). An example of a grammatical figure is parenthesis or *interpositio*, when we insert a remark in the middle of a sentence, modifying the original assertion or complicating it (9.3.23). In the example that follows, taken from *The Defence of Poetry* (c. 1579), Philip Sidney is advising the poet to follow the example of the 'courtier' who uses linguistic devices 'naturally' because he is copying their 'practice', but perhaps also, since this term serves both as a noun and a verb, just to practise them. This is not a difficult argument to grasp when stated like this, but Sidney's formulation makes us pause to really think about the paradox it implies, that one can do something artfully, without knowing what one is doing: 'the courtier, following that which by practice he findeth fittest to nature, therein (though he know it not) doth according to art, though not by art' (Sidney 1989: 247). The parenthesis draws attention to this curious possibility because it complicates the original assertion; this is reinforced by two rhetorical figures of speech which are used in the same sentence: *epistrophe*, the reiteration of a word at the end of a clause or sentence ('art'), and *antithesis*, the opposition of contrary words or sentences ('according to art, though not by art').

In contrast, as these last two examples suggest, rhetorical figures describe changes in 'word arrangement' (9.3.2); they are more 'potent' than grammatical figures because they do 'not wholly depend on the linguistic form', but give 'charm and also force to the thought itself' (9.3.28). There are many ways in which word arrangement can be modified, and Quintilian explores these in detail. Figures that involve 'addition' include the doubling of words or terms either for amplification, for example '"I have killed, I have killed, not Spurius Maelius," where the first "I have killed" states the fact and the second emphasises it', or for *pathos* ('Ah! Corydon, Corydon!') (9.3.28). Another figure of addition is *gradatio* or climax, which literally means a staircase or a series of steps, and it represents the consecutive use of parallel words or sentences to convey gradation: 'Who controls Berlin, controls Germany; who controls Germany controls Europe; who controls Europe controls the world' (Burke 1969: 57–58). Other figures depend on sound for their effect, and in this group Quintilian includes *paranomasia* or *adnominatio*, for example when we repeat a word, but 'with a deeper meaning': 'Since our enemy is a human being, he is human' (9.3.67).

Under 'rhetorical figures' we find those devices which 'seek elegance of speech by means of similar, equal, and balancing words' (9.3.74). This category includes two figures that were very common in Elizabethan writing, *antithesis* and *isocolon*, the latter being the term for clauses or phrases of equal length. In my next example, taken from *The Spanish Tragedy* (*c.* 1589–93), these two figures are used along with *epistrophe*: the formal patterning of these lines draws attention to the opposition between 'love' and 'fear' which is the subject of the exchange:

> BALTHAZAR   'Tis I that love.
> BEL-IMPERIA   Whom?
> BALTHAZAR   Bel-imperia.
> BEL-IMPERIA   But I that fear.

```
BALTHAZAR    Whom?
BEL-IMPERIA  Bel-imperia.
```

(Kyd 1986: 3.10.96–97)

No doubt such formal patterning seems highly artificial to us now. People just do not talk like this! Nonetheless, these devices allow Kyd to convey dramatically the precariousness of Bel-imperia's situation in a male-dominated world, and her awareness of this. Prior to this scene, Bel-imperia's brother, Lorenzo, has murdered her lover Horatio, and then abducted and imprisoned her to further the love interests of the son of the Viceroy of Portugal, Balthazar, from which he also expects to benefit. This scene represents Balthazar's first tentative and unimaginative attempt to court Bel-imperia. Let us read the lines again in the context of the three-way exchange between Balthazar, Bel-imperia and Lorenzo:

```
LORENZO      He whispereth in her ear.
             But Bel-imperia, see the gentle prince,
             Look on thy love, behold young Balthazar,
             Whose passions by thy presence are increas'd,
             And in whose melancholy thou mayst see
             Thy hate, his love; thy flight, his following thee.
BEL-IMPERIA  Brother, you are become an orator,
             I know not, I, by what experience,
             Too politic for me, past all compare,
             Since last I saw you; but content yourself,
             The prince is meditating higher things.
BALTHAZAR    'Tis of thy beauty, then, that conquers kings:
             Of those thy tresses, Ariadne's twines,
             Wherewith my liberty thou hast surpris'd;
             Of thine ivory front, my sorrow's map,
             Wherein I see no haven to rest my hope.
BEL-IMPERIA  To love, and fear, and both at once, my lord,
             In my conceit, are things of more import
             Than women's wits are to be busied with.
BALTHAZAR    'Tis I that love.
BEL-IMPERIA  Whom?
```

BALTHAZAR	Bel-imperia.
BEL-IMPERIA	But I that fear.
BALTHAZAR	Whom?
BEL-IMPERIA	Bel-imperia.
LORENZO	Fear yourself?
BEL-IMPERIA	Ay, brother.
LORENZO	How?
BEL-IMPERIA	As those
	That what they love are loath and fear to lose.

(3.10.78–99)

Balthazar uses the tired tropes of the Petrarchan lover to court Bel-imperia, describing his subjection to her by mixing two metaphors: he is imprisoned by her beauty; he is the lost traveller who does not know where he will land. Balthazar's metaphors are particularly ill chosen: Bel-imperia is a prisoner in a very unsafe place, caught as she is by the treachery of the person closest to her, her brother. The *antithesis* between love and fear that she plays upon here emphasizes this. Her initial response to Balthazar might be loosely paraphrased thus: how can I think about love when I am frightened? Balthazar misunderstands her; he thinks she is asking for clarification, and so explains that he means that he is in love. The inappropriateness of this declaration is drawn out again as Bel-imperia further plays on the *antithesis* between love and fear, though this time she articulates her fear as their staccato dialogue is played out in reverse: 'But I that fear'. And when pressed by her brother further, she offers this explanation: she fears herself. What does this mean? In fact, Bel-imperia's meaning is left tantalisingly uncertain. Does she anticipate her role as a revenger? In which case, she is afraid of what she might do. Or is she insinuating that she fears to lose what she loves, her own life?

A figure of speech is concerned with 'the presentation of a thought'; in contrast a figure of thought 'resides in the conception' of a thought (Quintilian 2001: 9.1.16). This is a difficult distinction to grasp, but Quintilian tries to clarify this with a dramatic example taken from Cicero's Second Speech against Verres, in which Cicero turned away from the judge to address the absent Dolabella, Verres' partner in crime: 'Now, now, Dolabella, neither for you nor for your children'. The first part of this sentence involves the figure of speech *conduplicatio* ('Now, now') for emphasis; but the turning away from the judge is an example of the figure of thought *apostrophe* (9.1.16). This last is a 'remarkably effective' way of appealing to the emotions of an audience (9.2.38).

Finally, both tropes and figures of speech can sometimes function as figures of thought. When we say the opposite of what we mean we are using the trope 'irony'. However, 'irony' (*dissimulatio*) also serves as a figure of thought if 'pretence involves the whole meaning, and is transparent rather than openly avowed'. As Quintilian clarifies, when irony is used as a trope, 'the contrast is between words and words', and when it is used as a figure the contrast is rather 'between the meaning and the words'. In addition, the figure of irony can cover whole passages, even a 'whole life', as the example of Socrates suggests: he 'was called an *eiron*', Quintilian notes, 'because he played the part of an ignoramus who marvelled at the supposed wisdom of others' (9.2.45–46).

Delivery, one of the two activities additionally covered in the Roman manuals, is concerned with the means of effective presentation, especially, the use of gesture and tone. The treatment of 'memory' underlines the more mechanical approach of the later tradition. Roman orators relied on a good memory to recall the points of a case in the correct order, the arguments made by an antagonist in court so they can respond to them fully, and also their own speeches so that they could appear 'extempore'. To support this they deployed a range of techniques. Memory is a distinct art, the origins of which are recalled by Cicero in an anecdote in *On the ideal orator* (*De oratore*). According to this story, Simonides of Ceos (*c.* 556–468 BC) is the sole survivor of a disaster when guests at a banquet are killed by a collapsing roof. Simonides remembers where each guest sat, and he is thus able to identify the crushed bodies for burial. Reflecting on his natural skill he makes the discovery 'that order is what most brings light to our memory' (Cicero 2001: 2.353–54).

Rhetoric for Herennius provides the most detailed early account of memory training. The orator who wants to train his memory must create a 'background' for storing images, usually an architectural location such as a house; this enables the orderly retrieval of the images which are used to mark the objects or words to be remembered. These images should be vivid and remarkable to aid memory. For example, the author of this manual explains how a prosecutor might keep in mind the details of a convoluted case involving a number of witnesses and accessories in which a defendant is accused of killing a man with poison in order to obtain an inheritance. He might do so by imagining the victim in bed with the defendant at the bedside 'holding in his right hand a cup, and in his left tablets, and on his fourth finger a ram's testicles' ([Cicero] 1954: 3.xx.33). This last image is especially opaque, but to a Roman orator it vividly represents the presence of the witnesses (Latin, *testes*). *Rhetoric for Herennius* offered an orderly account of mnemonic techniques and it provided the basis for the art's later development (Yates 1984: 1–26).

CICERO: REJECTING THEORY

The idea that rhetoric is an art of persuasion derives from the Greek and Roman traditions we have just surveyed. Yet, though this elaboration of rhetoric as a system is quite complex and varies in important details from Aristotle to the Roman theoreticians and beyond, it is also rather limiting. It fixes our sense of rhetoric as a technical subject, one in which the professional orator or rhetorician is 'expert'; in relation to this, it perpetuates a misplaced distinction between spontaneous and trained expression, and sincere and 'rhetorical' speech and writing.

I am not saying that rhetoric should not be viewed as a technical art. Obviously, speech or writing that is deliberately patterned and decorated with the kind of linguistic devices listed in handbooks can be discerned as 'rhetorical'. Quintilian is quite insistent that it is only expressions which are 'feigned and artificially produced' that can be 'regarded as Figures' (9.2.27):

> We pretend that we are angry, happy, frightened, surprised, grieved, indignant, desirous of something, or the like. ... Some people call this Exclamation, and count it among Figures of Speech. When these

> expressions are sincere, they do not come under our present topic;
> but if they are feigned and artificially produced they are undoubtedly
> to be regarded as Figures.
>
> (Quintilian 2001: 9.2.26–29)

Quite simply, a spontaneous exclamation is not rhetorical, but an affected one is. According to Quintilian's definition, *The Spanish Tragedy* is 'rhetorical'. In the passage we looked at above, Kyd is using a range of figures to convey the mental state of his character, Bel-imperia. There is an element of deliberation and care in the representation of this character's sense of her situation. However, Quintilian's strict definition of what can be called a figure presents us with a problem. How, for example, should we describe the speech of those women litigants, contemporaries of Kyd's, who had no rhetorical training and yet represented their plight and interests movingly, when given the opportunity? Is this not 'rhetorical' or 'persuasive' too? I am thinking of the fifteen-year-old orphan, Joan Smith, the story of whose abduction and enforced marriage to a cousin, Henry Eaton, recalls the difficulties faced by Kyd's Bel-imperia. This was recounted in an Elizabethan court in 1575 thus:

> she ys verye younge and of very simple sence and capacities fatherles
> and motherles. ... she sayeth also that she had never anie acquain-
> tance before with the sayde Henrie Eaton neyther did shee ever love
> him or ever had anie occasion by giftes or tokens or other familiar
> continuance or talke so to do onelye throughe the feare and treach-
> erie aforesaide neyther had shee ever or hathe anie likinge of hym
> but hathe and dothe utterlie dissente from hym and all his compa-
> nions craftye and moste ungodlye devises and practises in this
> behalfe.
>
> (Cited in Laura Gowing 1996: 253–54)

This tale is far more straightforward than the dramatic scene in *The Spanish Tragedy*, but it is also carefully and movingly structured, pitting the teller's simplicity and vulnerability sharply against the immoral behaviour of Eaton and his 'craftye' and 'ungodlye' companions.

I would suggest that despite Quintilian's clarity on the matter of what counts as a 'figure', or his emphasis on the artfulness of rhetoric, it is not always easy to distinguish between the knowing and unprompted use of linguistic devices, between practised and spontaneous expression. We might pose the problem thus: at what point in an act of expression does an element of calculation become apparent? This problem can be highlighted with the figure of frank speech, *parrhesia* or *licentia*. Quintilian discusses this effect alongside 'exclamation' to explain what he means by a 'figure'. We may not think of frank speech as rhetorical, he notes, 'for what is less "figured" than true freedom?' Nonetheless, 'flattery is often concealed under this cover': for example, if the orator uses praise to alleviate the concerns of an audience. Such frankness, which is evidently staged, should be considered as a rhetorical effect. Yet, it is still possible for the orator to use *licentia* knowingly *and* sincerely. David Colclough notes that Cicero suggests this possibility. His rhetorical treatise *Orator* defends the importance of emotional appeals to oratory, and *licentia* is one figure he discusses in relation to this. For example, he advises the orator to 'take the liberty to speak somewhat boldly', acknowledging that this includes flying 'into a passion' or protesting 'violently' (Cicero 1939 [*Orator*]: 40.138). We know from Cicero's other writings that he thought that inflaming emotion is 'something which needs to be artfully effected by the orator, but also experienced by him in order to be properly persuasive' (Colclough 2005: 29–30). One way in which such sincerity can be achieved is through the vivid imagining or *enargeia* we considered above, which enables the orator to 'seem not so much to be talking about something as exhibiting it' (Quintilian 2001: 6.2.32). Frankness, it turns out, can indeed be both artful and sincere.

The difficulty of making a distinction between sincere and rhetorical expression is encountered again in the argument Cicero offers in *On the ideal orator*, that a rhetorician is most persuasive when any impression of rhetorical 'knowingness' is concealed. Unknowingness is evidently a contrived effect here, but it can also, of course, be knowingly unpremeditated: after all, practise can make techniques or devices, initially known only abstractly, habitual, so that they are used at the right time without studied consideration in just the same way that a fluent speaker might deploy them unconsciously when she speaks to a topic with commitment and passion. It is hard to say what is artful and what natural here.

Let us consider an ordinary example of such 'unknowingness'. The fact that I have never received formal training in the art of rhetoric means that I can honestly represent myself to you as a 'plain speaker'. Indeed, in this book I am writing about a subject, rhetoric, that I have never been taught. I am not using any special techniques to persuade you of the importance of rhetoric or my trustworthiness as an authority on this subject. Rather, I can only offer my opinion, telling you what I think about the practice of speaking and writing persuasively.

Most of what I have just declared is actually true, but it is also an example of an old persuasive trick noted in the rhetoric books. Here is the character Antonius in Cicero's *On the ideal orator* making the same claim, and in so doing, establishing his *ethos*, or trustworthiness, as a plain speaker: 'I shall teach you, students, what I have not learned myself, namely, what I think about every facet of speaking' (Cicero 2001: 2.29). In this rhetorical manual such a device is made explicit because it is described belatedly as a figure of thought, *dissimulatio* or 'irony' (2.269). Its naming enables the reader to identify, retrospectively, a device which they have experienced the character Antonius using, apparently quite effortlessly and to great effect. I will elaborate this differently. Within the fiction that Cicero has constructed, we can assume that the skilful Antonius knows of this device, and so one could say that this is an example of a speaker 'hiding' his artfulness, and indeed this is suggested by a second character, Crassus, who accuses him of doing just this. However, because Cicero has chosen to write a dialogue rather than a technical manual, he also brings to our attention the fact that you do not need to know the name of this device to use it effectively, or to understand its use: *dissimulatio* is used 'naturally', and often quite unselfconsciously, to facilitate social exchange every day. It is also used quite naturally and to great effect, I should add, by the arch-antagonist of rhetoric, Socrates.

In *On the ideal orator* Cicero has gone to great lengths to emphasize the simple point that 'eloquence' depends on speaking 'naturally' rather than 'artfully', not least by choosing to depart from the conventional format of the rhetorical manual. In its opening paragraphs Cicero dismisses his first manual, *On invention* (*De inventione*), as that 'sketchy and unsophisticated work that found its way out of my notebooks when I was a boy' (1.5). *On the ideal orator* is written in contrast as a dialogue, and its subject and form openly recall Plato's *Phaedrus* (1.28). It is given a location, the Tuscan villa of Lucius Crassus who had retired there, we are told, in order 'to reinvigorate himself' during a period of political tumult (1.24), and a set of characters. Crassus and Antonius are the main speakers, though other friends and colleagues are also present. They intervene at different stages of the dialogue in order to contest points raised by either speaker and to encourage further elucidation and discussion. *On the ideal orator* covers the same ground as contemporary handbooks. It offers plenty of technical advice, although Cicero follows Aristotle rather than his contemporaries who focus too narrowly on the parts of a speech. However, because of its dialogue form, this treatise never treats the 'art' systematically. We might question the wisdom of this decision because it makes this handbook a challenging read. Instead of describing rhetorical devices according to the genres, as Aristotle does, or the parts of a speech, as his contemporaries do, Cicero begins to debate. Moreover, he does so in a way which appears unexpectedly to endorse Socrates' complaint that rhetoric is a mere knack.

This is an unexpected turn, but it is characteristic of this difficult dialogue, which cannot seem to make up its mind what rhetoric 'is', or indeed, what we should consider as the source of eloquence. In fact, *On the ideal orator* is full of such unexpected turns, making it hard to identify its argument. For example, Cicero tells us very early on that he believes that 'eloquence is founded upon the intellectual accomplishments of the most learned', whereas his brother Quintus believes instead that eloquence depends 'on natural ability and practice' (1.5). These contrasting views are represented in the dialogue by Crassus and Antonius respectively. Yet, rather than being able to choose confidently between Cicero and Quintus, or between the dialogue's two speakers, we find that these positions are readily confused. Crassus is identified as Cicero's mouthpiece, yet it is not clear he wins the debate. Indeed, it is hard at times to tell that the two interlocutors are opponents not only because they are self-contradicting, but also because they agree on so many key issues. For example, in book 1 Antonius contests Crassus' more ambitious claims for the orator by arguing that his sphere of activity should 'be restricted to the ordinary practice of public life in communities' (1.260). Crassus complains that Antonius has made the orator a kind of 'laborer', but he also expresses his suspicion that Antonius is not saying what he actually thinks but is rather 'showing us that amazing penchant [he has] for refutation' (1.263). In fact, Crassus will be proved right. In book 2 Antonius compromises his original position when he celebrates the scope of eloquence, and then confesses that he had previously argued against Crassus only in order to 'entice these pupils away from' him (2.40).

The dialogue is full of such contrary arguments, but there is one point on which Crassus and Antonius do agree: that oratory is not an 'art'. In book 1 of *On the ideal orator* Crassus argues that oratory can be considered an art only in the loose sense that the procedures that are followed in public orations 'have been observed and recorded'. It is not a discipline, he suggests, because 'every aspect of our judicial and political thinking is variable and adapted to an ordinary and popular way of thinking' (1.108–9). Meanwhile, Antonius repeats this argument in book 2, and advances a new claim, that because the orator does not possess knowledge, then the method proper to him is argument on different sides of an issue, just as he and Crassus are demonstrating in this dialogue:

> It seems to me that oratory, when considered as an ability, is a splendid thing, but that it is no more than average when viewed as an art. After all, an art deals with such things as are known, while the whole activity of the orator is based not on knowledge but on opinions. We speak before audiences that are ignorant, and we also say things about which we are ignorant ourselves. Accordingly, on the

same issue they have now one view and judgment, then another, while we ourselves often plead opposite cases. I mean the latter not only in the sense that Crassus sometimes argues against me or I argue against him – and in that case, either of us must necessarily be saying something that it not true – but also in the sense that, on the same issue, each of us supports now one opinion, then another – whereas not more than one can be true.

(2.30)

This is just as Plato had complained in *Gorgias*.

On the ideal orator is, apparently, a badly organized handbook which foolishly accommodates Plato's attack on rhetoric. However, Plato is being drawn upon as an ally as well as an antagonist in *On the ideal orator*, and the difficulties of its process of argument help to complicate the original opposition between rhetoric and philosophy: the gradual, incremental process of argument represented in this dialogue makes us question what we think we know about oratory, and its status as an art or discipline.

Like Plato, Cicero is interested in understanding the source of eloquence and, like Plato, he recognizes the need to compose a different kind of 'rhetoric' or manual to explore this. For Cicero, eloquence is both a rhetorical skill, a capacity 'to amplify and give distinction' to any topic in a 'marvellous and magnificent way' (1.94), and also the source for 'wisdom': the same process of reasoning which is represented by Crassus and Antonius is shown to underpin understanding as well as eloquence. 'I contend that this method of thought and expression, this power of speaking,' Crassus insists in book 3, 'is what the Greeks of old called wisdom' (3.56). One cannot be eloquent without wisdom, or wise without eloquence. This was always understood in antiquity, prior to Socrates, because the same people 'taught both right actions and good speech' and 'gave instructions for living and for speaking'. It was only when students were shut out of matters of state that this symbiosis was threatened, that philosophy, poetry, music and so on emerged as distinct disciplines (3.57–58), and the attack on rhetoric was tolerated. Indeed, Crassus recalls, while some individuals still taught the skills of living and speaking, notably the sophist Gorgias, others emerged who 'shirked politics and its responsibilities on principle; they criticized and scorned the practice of speaking. The most important among them was Socrates' (3.59). Yet, in a twist in the argument, Crassus acknowledges that despite his criticisms, Socrates also relies on these same methods (3.67–68). He is akin to the very sophists he attacks.

The difficult argument of *On the ideal orator* might be clarified as follows. The orator will not become eloquent by studying manuals alone. Instead, as Crassus explains, the orator needs to exercise his natural talent in a number of ways: the reformulation in the vernacular of 'the speeches of the great orators from Greece' (1.155); the memorizing of one's own writings and their testing in 'the front line of the forum' (1.157); and the study of law, poetry and histories. This is what Cicero means when he insists that 'eloquence is founded upon the intellectual accomplishments of the most learned'. The training programme described by Crassus supports these accomplishments, and much more. It becomes clear that Antonius disagrees with Crassus only superficially. For both speakers are also recommending, and indeed demonstrating, the orator's practice of arguing on different sides of an issue. The orator must read as widely as possible, Crassus argues, but he must not only read poetry, histories and so on but also, 'for the sake of practice, praise, expound, correct, criticize, and refute them'. Indeed, Crassus emphasizes, the orator 'must argue every question on both sides, and on every topic [he] must elicit as well as express every plausible argument' (1.158). He must do so, not only to gain understanding, but in order to adapt this knowledge to persuade popular audiences. But this is only part of Cicero's argument. This method, which brings together Crassus and Antonius, is also shared with philosophers, at least with those who can be regarded as the successors of Socrates, the so-called Academic Sceptics.

This is a counter-intuitive position, hence, I think, the difficulty of Cicero's dialogue. He is trying to undercut what seems to be an agreed opposition between rhetoric and philosophy. In fact, *On the ideal orator* suggests that this opposition is 'rhetorically' constructed; there is agreement between Crassus and Antonius, and, as it turns out, between them and Plato's Socrates.

Antonius is arguing towards this position even as he seems to be arguing against it. For example, in book 1 he agrees with Crassus that a facility in speaking is supported by 'a knowledge extending over the principles and nature of all objects and arts', but he also notes that this 'is a difficult thing to accomplish'. In any case, he adds, this kind of philosophical study may very easily lead the orator 'away from the popular way of speaking that we normally use in the forum' (1.80–81). The opposition between rhetoric and philosophy is reasserted in the example he offers of the Stoic philosopher Mnesarchus, who he claims to have heard debating 'the duty and properties of the orator' in Athens. Antonius recounts how Mnesarchus defended the same argument as Crassus, that 'no-one was an orator unless he was wise'. However, his logical style of argument 'was quite thorny and meager, and completely out of touch with the way we think' (1.83–84). Meanwhile, even as Antonius is disagreeing with Crassus, and insisting on the difference between the philosopher and the orator, a seed is sown that will allow for their eventual rapprochement. Mnesarchus was not an eloquent defender of rhetoric, but the philosopher who attacked rhetoric for being merely a technical art was. This philosopher was the Academic Sceptic Charmardas, a member of the Academy founded by Plato in the fourth century BC. Charmardas argued that wisdom belongs to the philosophers, not the rhetoricians, whose 'trivial handbooks' are 'crammed with talk of prooemia and epilogues, and other nonsense of that sort'. Meanwhile, 'not a syllable was to be found' in them about the constitution and managing of communities or the tempering of the passions (1.85–86). This is just as Socrates argues in *Phaedrus*, and Crassus and Antonius are insisting on in this dialogue. The reason that Charmardas is the more persuasive of the two, Antonius explains, is that he 'spoke with much greater fullness on the same topic, though not in order to reveal his own opinion – for this was the inherited custom of the Academy, always to oppose all comers in debate' (1.84). This also is the method used by Crassus and, more obviously, by Antonius.

Plato is the starting point of the standard histories of rhetoric, though he appears in the guise of its arch-antagonist. These histories are invariably defensive; they begin by dismantling Plato's opposition, usually by emphasizing his anti-democratic views, and then proceed to defend the importance of rhetoric to democratic debate, appealing to Aristotle's theorization of it as a pragmatic art. Aristotle's *Rhetoric* is preferred to the technical Roman manuals of the first centuries BC and AD because it provides rhetoric with a logical basis, but it is to the Roman tradition that we are most likely to turn for our understanding of rhetoric as a system.

Unsurprisingly, it is hard to find a place for Cicero's unusual and challenging dialogue in this account of the art. The random twists and turns of its argument have left many historians of rhetoric struggling to find its focus. Brian Vickers finds *On the ideal orator* 'cumbersome' and 'inefficient in exposition' (1988: 34), while George Kennedy, who has more sympathy for Cicero, notes that while this dialogue has 'charm', its form 'covers up some imprecision'. *On the ideal orator* 'is entirely too much like a real conversation in which people forget what they have said or change their views for the sake of argument or politeness' (Kennedy 1972: 226). Yet, such criticism stems from a commitment to defending rhetoric as a body of rules which serves a practical end, whereas Cicero's purpose is quite different. He reminds us that we need also to rethink the rhetorical tradition even as we theorize it as a system, and he does so, moreover, by recasting Plato in the role of the 'ideal' orator: the speaker who is 'eloquent' because he is both wise and a moving speaker.

But let us be sure we understand the claim he is making. In Cicero's view, Plato is not simply using the methods of the orator to disseminate his wisdom, as Aristotle advises; rather, he uses these methods because he understands that he cannot possess certain knowledge. This is the source of his wise eloquence. In response to one interlocutor's rehearsal of the philosophical dismissal of rhetoric as merely an art of plausible speaking in public, Crassus argues that it was Plato and the Academic Sceptics who 'invented this line of argument'; but then he recalls that he also read '*Gorgias* with some care, together with Charmardas', and recognized with admiration the 'way in which, while making fun of orators, [Plato] appeared to be a supreme orator himself' (1.47). This is reiterated in book 3: Socrates was 'the first to establish the practice ... of not revealing his own view, but of always arguing against any view that anyone else would assert', and he did so, Crassus insists, because he believed 'that there is no certainty that can be grasped either by the senses or by the mind' (3.67). This is the beginning of a different defence of rhetoric as a 'critical' method, which prompts us always to think again and to recognize that no conclusion is ever absolute.

2

RHETORIC RENEWED

This chapter explores the revival of rhetoric in early modernity, both the Renaissance and the Enlightenment. The first section explores the fate of the 'art' of rhetoric as it is represented in the handbook tradition. It considers, first, the narrowing and adaptation of the Roman art in Renaissance manuals and, second, the increasing resistance to the theorization of 'good' speech and writing in the eighteenth century which led to the valorization of 'common sense' as the only standard the writer should follow. However, in the Renaissance rhetoric was not only an art; it was also a training programme, for boys at least, one which involved the practice of arguing on different sides. In the second section, I consider how this classroom practice is understood by literary critics to inform the structuring of Shakespeare's drama; I also consider whether this is a practice that can be seen to extend beyond the Renaissance public theatre, to literary writings which explore an argument, or take part in a debate. Rhetorical training is a masculine privilege, yet, this does not mean that its techniques and effects are practised only by those who attended grammar school and university. Mary Shelley's *Frankenstein* (1818, 1831) is not the product of an intense rhetorical training in the way that Shakespeare's plays are, but her reading of John Milton's *Paradise Lost*, which is drawn upon in this novel, undoubtedly informs its structure, as well as its preoccupation with assessing the eloquence of contrasted characters: Dr Frankenstein and his monstrous Creature. In the final section of this chapter we return to the problem of rhetoric conceived too narrowly as an art to explore how its rejection in post-Romantic writing shapes an important stage in literary history, mainly the privileging of the poetic imagination unshackled from rhetorical rules. And yet the advice that accompanies this, as I will argue, also makes 'rhetorical' good sense.

RENAISSANCE TO ENLIGHTENMENT

The heyday of rhetoric belongs to democratic Athens and republican Rome, when there was an opportunity to debate publicly and a great deal invested in succeeding. Roman theoreticians understood the history of this art as intimately connected with the fate of these states. The great Roman historian Tacitus (AD *c.* 56–117) believed that rhetoric declined after the collapse of the republic and with the rise of imperial forms of government. He outlined this process in his *A dialogue on oratory* (*Dialogus*). The interlocutors in this dialogue agree that the rhetoric of a hundred years before, embodied most spectacularly in the words and actions of Cicero, the great republican orator, has now been warped to expedient and selfish purposes: it is 'gain-getting', 'greedy for human blood', and characterized by 'wantonness of language, by shallow-pated conceits, and by irregular arrangement' (Tacitus 1914: 12, 26). Different reasons are offered for this decline: poor education, narrow reading and lack of discipline at home, but there is also concern about the over-theorization of rhetoric at school. The problem is that 'practise' has been replaced by 'theory', by the technical elaboration of the art. The speakers remind themselves that whatever Cicero 'accomplished as an orator, he owed not to the workshops of the rhetorician, but to the spacious precincts of the Academy' (32). Oratory is nourished by the experience of advancing an argument in public, of refuting others and being, in turn, refuted (34). Rhetoric flourishes

best in 'times of trouble and unrest' (37), when there is something to argue about and the opportunity to do so. By the same
token, when a speaker does not have a 'spacious field in which to
expatiate without let or hindrance' his eloquence 'lose[s] all its
strength and pith' (39). The last phrase captures the quality of
imperial rhetoric according to Tacitus.

Given this pessimism about the survival of eloquence under
empire, we might wonder about the fate of rhetoric in Europe in
later centuries, in political states which lacked any vestige of a
public sphere, or in which emotional displays in public life were
just deemed 'impolite'. Rhetoric is always represented as being
'in decline'. Tacitus is just one of many historians who recall
with nostalgia a more virtuous, mythical age. So appealing is
this vision that it is easy to overlook the imperial aspirations of
republican Rome. And yet his lament is in some sense prophetic:
after the fall of the Roman Empire the process he describes
became more drastic. In the Middle Ages rhetoric was eclipsed
by logic and grammar, its partners in the *trivium*, surviving only
as part of the highly technical *ars dictaminis*, the epistolary art.
For these reasons it has been common to describe the rhetorical
culture of the Middle Ages in terms of fragmentation, dis-
memberment and disintegration (Vickers 1988: 214–53; Monfasani 1976: 241–48). Yet, the discipline was to enjoy another
moment of apotheosis during the Renaissance and Tacitus might
have savoured the reason for this. Such a moment of dramatic
'rebirth' and renewal in fourteenth-century Italy was made possible, in part, because the political conditions were right: the
newly recovered art of rhetoric underpins the disputative culture
of the emergent city states such as Florence, whose defenders self-
consciously recalled the republican culture of Cicero's Rome
(Baron 1938). This was also supported by the recovery of several
Roman handbooks, the complete manuscripts of Quintilian's
encyclopaedic *Institutio oratoria* in 1416 and of Cicero's *De oratore*
and *Brutus* in 1421.

However, the optimism of the Italian city states in the fifteenth century was overtaken by the collapse of the Florentine
republic in 1512 and the occupation of Northern Italy by Spanish troops. Correspondingly, the rhetorical confidence of the early

humanists, their attempt to recover the vital culture of republican Rome, was replaced by a more entrenched scepticism concerning the capacity of rhetoric to persuade citizens to act virtuously, for the good of the commonwealth. It was also replaced by a narrower conception of the 'art' of rhetoric, which is represented in the handbooks produced in the second half of the sixteenth century. These also tell a story of fragmentation. The English handbooks, for example, are really style manuals; they focus on one activity of the orator, *elocutio* or style, listing and illustrating the tropes and figures. Meanwhile, invention and disposition, the discovery and arrangement of content, become the activities of the logician.

Let's consider in a little more detail how the seeming expansion of rhetoric's influence conceals a story of fragmentation. We can pursue this by examining the development of the handbook tradition over the course of the Renaissance and into the Enlightenment, the subject of this section. I will begin with Henry Peacham's English style manual, *The garden of eloquence* (1577). This opens confidently enough. In his preface, Peacham recalls the terms of Cicero's defence of oratory in *On the ideal orator (De oratore)*. 'Wisedome doe reqyure the light of Eloquence, and Eloquence the fertility of wysedome', he argues, explaining that he has written this manual to help to realize this union (Peacham 1577: A2v). However, these two treatises could not be more different. As we saw in the last chapter, the dialogue *On the ideal orator* establishes that 'eloquence' depends on the exercise of argument on both sides, a method shared by orator and philosopher alike. In contrast, Peacham argues that the source of eloquence is the 'flowers' of rhetoric, the tropes and figures. *The garden of eloquence* is just a taxonomy of these. It quickly becomes clear, moreover, that Peacham's art of rhetoric might serve less noble interests than 'wisdom'. Or, to put this another way, we might understand his broad term 'wisdom' in a narrower sense, as a pragmatic ability in the service of self-interest. Thus, Peacham boasts of the power that the skilful use of figures gives to the orator, allowing him to 'leade his hearers which way he list, and draw them to what affection he will' (Peacham 1577: A3r). This is strengthened in the second edition of 1593, in which the orator is celebrated as the 'emperour of mens minds and affections, and next to the omnipotent God in the power of perswasion' (Peacham 1593: AB3v).

The narrower scope of rhetoric is also discernible in the slight changes that Peacham makes to the description of some figures of speech, perhaps notably to *licentia*. The author of *Rhetoric for Herennius* tells us that this figure of frankness is used when 'we yet exercise our right to speak out' in the company of those 'to whom we owe reverence or fear ... because we seem to be justified in reprehending them, or persons dear to them, for some fault'. It also includes gestures of 'palliation' that aim to assuage any annoyance caused: for example, phrases such as 'I here appeal to your virtue', 'I call on your wisdom', 'I bespeak your old habit' ([Cicero] 1954: 4.49–50). We can see this figure in use in act 4 scene 2 of William Shakespeare's *The Tragedy of Julius Caesar* (*c.* 1599), when the republican Brutus unflinchingly confronts Cassius, his co-conspirator in the assassination of the dictator Julius Caesar, about rumours that he has been taking bribes. Cassius' response is immediate and angry: 'When Caesar lived, he durst not have moved me'. 'For your life you durst not', is Brutus' clarifying rejoinder (4.2.111–17). However, Brutus also attempts to assuage Cassius' anger, not by flattery but by bringing him back to his better self: 'Was that done like Cassius?' (4.2.132). Moreover, this attempt also includes Brutus' self-indictment as he reflects on the action of confronting Cassius, and so restores the equality of their friendship again: 'I was ill-tempered too' (4.2.170). If we compare this with the advice that Peacham gives on avoiding offence we can see how much this republican frankness recreated by Shakespeare has dwindled: the directness of a speaker is to be alleviated 'by *craving* parden afore hand, and by shewing the necessitie of free speech in that behalfe, or by some other like formes of *humble submission* and modest insinuation' (Peacham 1593: sig. R1r; cited in Colclough 2005: 56; emphases mine).

Not all handbooks are limited to *elocutio*. The first comprehensive rhetorical manual in English was Thomas Wilson's *Arte of Rhetorique* (1553). This rehearses the Roman system, detailing the parts of a speech and the activities of the orator, and it also lists some eighty tropes and figures. Moreover, Wilson also adapts Cicero's defence of the civilizing power of eloquence for a contemporary, protestant readership. He explains in his opening chapter how after the Fall 'Menne lyved Brutyshlye' until orators 'appoynted of God called theim together by utteraunce of speache, and perswaded with them what was good'. Without this gift of eloquence, he argues, humankind would never have been brought 'to lyve together in felowshyppe of life, to mayntayne Cities, to deale trulye, and willyngelye to obeye one another' (Wilson 1982: 18–19). Yet, we may well wonder whose interest such eloquence is intended to serve. For the civil society that Wilson imagines is created and preserved by rhetoric is one in which everyone knows their place:

> what manne I praye you being better able to maintayne him selfe by valeant courage, then by living in base subjection: would not rather loke to rule like a lord, then to lyve like an underlynge: if by reason he were not perswaded that it behoveth everye man to lyve in his owne vocation, and not to seke anye higher rowme, then whereunto he was at first appoynted?
>
> (19)

Without eloquence, that is, who 'woulde digge and delve from morne till evening' (19)? Many of the examples that Wilson uses to illustrate the figures listed in this manual reinforce this emphasis on social order. His example of the figure 'regression' (*regressio*), 'when we repeate a worde eftsones, that has been spoken, and rehearsed before', is illustrated thus: 'Thou art ordeined to rule other, and not other to rule thee' (406). While *dissolutum* or 'Wordes loose', that is, words 'uttred without any addicion of conjunctions, such as knitte woordes and sentences together', is explained with this example: 'Obeye the Kynge, feare his lawes, kepe thy vocacion, doo right, seke rest, like well a little, use all menne, as thou wouldest thei should use thee' (407).

In response to my question 'whose interest does this art serve?' we can surmise a university-educated humanist like Wilson himself, one of the 'singuler' men, whose eloquence makes him 'halfe a God' (20). *The Arte of Rhetorique* is written with such social climbers in mind, but also with a view to recommending their skills to aristocratic patrons. In the aristocratic dedication of this book, Wilson defends rhetoric with the example of the power of Cinneas, the orator who, 'through the eloquence of his tongue, wanne moe Cityes unto him, then ever him selfe shoulde els have bene able by force to subdue'. '[W]hat greater delite do we know,' Wilson concludes, 'then to se a whole multitude with the onely talke of a man ravished and drawen whiche waye him liketh best to have them?' (5–6).

Not surprisingly, recent critical interest is suspicious of the 'rhetoric' of the handbooks. The defences of this art in prefaces, along with the examples used to illustrate its 'flowers', reveal that the preoccupation with the regulation of language in this period is uncomfortably associated with social and political control. Thus, Patricia Parker detects in the proliferation of grammatical and rhetorical manuals in the sixteenth century an eagerness to control both language and social and political behaviour. Illustrations of figures in the English manuals, she notes, frequently 'turn into illustrations of the social order the figure would rhetorically reflect' (Parker 1987: 99). We have seen this with Wilson's treatment of *regressio* and *dissolutum*, but it is not hard to find other examples: thus, George Puttenham translates *'gradatio'* or 'climax' as the 'Marching figure' (Puttenham 1936: 208). The use of this figure, Parker notes, can insinuate a proper relation to political authority, as in this example taken from John Hoskins' rhetorical handbook, *Directions for Speech and Style* (1599): 'You could not injoy your goodnes without government, nor government without a magistrate, nor a magistrate without obedience' (Parker 1987: 99, 250–51, n. 4; Hoskins 1935: 12). However, another worrying aspect of this, as Parker has also argued, is the way in which this linguistic regulation also serves to naturalize gendered social hierarchies. It is to this crucial issue that I now turn.

Since its inception, rhetoric has been the preserve of a masculine elite. Only male citizens were given training in it because only this group had the opportunity to debate publicly. We see the effect of this in the Roman manuals, which tend to explore the loss of this opportunity or its ineffective application in explicitly gendered terms. For Quintilian, for example, good oratory is manly; it entails wielding arguments as weapons in a quest for domination in the public arena. In contrast, bad oratory, which seeks to please rather than to win, is deemed effeminate. In *On the training of the orator* Quintilian complains of the passing of an exercise that the Romans had used 'as it were to fence with foils as practice for the battles of the courts', declamation, or argument on different sides. Because declamation is no longer an intrinsic part of rhetorical training, he complains, pleading has become overly preoccupied with pleasing an audience, with the result that modern orators have 'lost their muscle'. In a memorable passage, he suggests that teachers of oratory are 'guilty of the same offence as slave-dealers who castrate boys in order to increase their attractions' (Quintilian 2001: 5.12.17). The orator should rather follow the example of the gladiator Doryphorus and other 'warlike and athletic youths', who are 'equally well fitted for war and for the wrestling ring' (5.12.21).

These values are inherited by Renaissance theorists, who reflect negatively on the possibilities for female persuasive speech. Rhetorical education is again, with a few notable exceptions, the preserve of a male elite. The humanist educator Juan Luis Vives (1523) explains why: rhetorical training has no utility for women, he argues, because to engage in public debate is to compromise one's sexual modesty (Watson 1912: 54–55). One hundred years later William Gouge (1622) is still recommending that the words used by a woman in the company of her husband should be 'few, reverend and meeke' on the grounds that silence 'implieth a reverend subjection' (Gouge 1976: 281–82). Meanwhile, others suggest that women would just not be any good at it. Richard Brathwait argues that the natural garrulity of women, their tendency 'to *flow* in words, but *droppe* in matter' makes them incapable of properly selecting persuasive arguments from lists of commonplaces (Brathwait 1640: 70; Heard 2006).

These attitudes are shaped by and reproduced in the style manuals. In these, unruly language and deceitful figures are frequently gendered as feminine (Parker 1996). Thus, Puttenham likens the trope *occupatio* or *paralepsis*, the making light of a matter, to 'the maner of women, who as the common saying is, will say nay and take it' (Puttenham 1936: 232). Meanwhile, rhetorical forcefulness is often described in terms of an array of similes and metaphors which liken it, in equal measure, to rape and sexual pleasure. Theoreticians often talk about rhetoric as binding, seizing and ravishing the listener, and of overpowering their will (Rebhorn 1995: 159–60). Or they dwell on the seductive pleasure of rhetorical display. For example, the rhythm of rhetorical prose is described by John Rainolds in *Oratio* as 'suffus[ing] most pleasingly the senses of the auditors with the sweetness of its modes' (trans. Rebhorn), while George Puttenham 'defines rhythm even more suggestively as "a certaine flowing utterance by slipper [i.e. easily pronounced] words and sillables, such as the toung easily utters, and the eare with pleasure receiveth"' (Rebhorn 1995: 159, 155; citing John Rainolds 1940: 48; Puttenham 1936: 91).

Suspicion of the art of rhetoric is not new, as we have already seen, though the concerns raised vary enormously. The work of Patricia Parker in the 1980s drew attention to the preoccupation of the *art* of rhetoric with the ordering of language *and* social relations; she sees this as a precursor to the growing concern in the seventeenth century with the development of the plain and orderly virile style of Enlightenment science (Parker 1996). Nonetheless, from the late seventeenth century attacks on rhetoric are inspired by the anxiety that the Renaissance art is not orderly *enough*. Thomas Sprat was an ardent Royalist and historian of the Royal Society, founded in the 'wonderful pacific year', as he sees it, of the Stuart restoration (1660). In his *Historie of the Royal Society* (1667) he holds the humanist revival of rhetoric in the Renaissance directly responsible for the Civil War, the brief period covering two decades in which England was constituted as a republic. 'They who are bred up in *Commonwealths*, where the greatest affairs are manag'd by the *violence of popular assemblies*, and those govern'd by the most *plausible speakers*', Sprat argues, 'busie themselves chiefly about *Eloquence*' (Sprat 1959: 19). Orators were the founders of civil society, according to the classical theorists of rhetoric and their Renaissance imitators. In the canonical version of this myth offered by Cicero, which Thomas Wilson repeats, men originally lived as savages, roaming the wilderness like animals, pitted one against the other until they were persuaded by 'eloquence and reason' to form societies (Cicero 1954: 1.2.2). Sprat maintains this myth but replaces its protagonist with the scientist or natural philosopher. The members of the Royal Society, he argues, have reformed their methods of argument; they have sought to 'free' intellectual enquiry 'from the Artifice, and Humors, and Passions of Sects' in order 'to render it an Instrument, whereby Mankind may obtain a Dominion over *Things*, not only over one another's *Judgements*' (62). Moreover, they have done so by separating 'knowledge of *Nature*, from the colours of *Rhetorike*, and the devices of *Fancy*'. In addition, the scientists have preserved 'a singular sobriety of debating, slowness of consenting, and moderation of dissenting' which is altogether free from faction. They have returned to a 'primitive purity' of expression, enacting in their conversations 'a close, naked, natural way of speaking; positive expressions; clear senses; a native easiness: bringing all things as near the Mathematicall plainness, as they can' (113).

A second influential contributor to this orderly reformation of rhetoric is Thomas Hobbes (1588–1679). From the early seventeenth century he had been arguing that a speaker's persuasiveness should depend, not on the rhetorical construction of trustworthiness or *ethos*, but on the integrity of evidence. He rejected habits of rhetorical thinking and composition: the assumption that historical examples yield 'general truths', the dependence on generally accepted beliefs as argumentative proof, the use of emotion to sway decisions, and, most worryingly, the way in which the delivery of a speaker, or their use of the figure of redescription, *paradiastole* can change 'the meanings of utterances so pervasively that there "is scarce any word that is not made Equivocall"' (Skinner 1996: 261, 263, 269, 278). Hobbes was particularly hostile to this kind of linguistic slipperiness on the grounds that it engenders moral ambiguity; it creates a 'world in which there will be no possibility of reaching any rational agreement about the application of evaluative terms, and no prospect in consequence of avoiding a state of unending confusion and mutual hostility' (282). It is imperative that the two-sidedness facilitated by such figures is replaced by a more secure process of investigation and communication. In his view, the orator had to be supplanted by the political 'scientist', for whom the clear definition of terms is the starting point of a reasoning process that leads to demonstrative truths.

What happens to rhetoric in the context of these attacks? Perhaps the first thing to note is that this art does not decline completely. In his later writings Hobbes recognizes that the moving power of eloquence is important for the dissemination of scientific reasoning (Skinner 1996: 347). But rhetoric is changed by such attacks inevitably, and by the political and cultural changes that produced them. In the eighteenth century, Adam Potkay notes, 'eloquence' was associated with the 'sublime' or grand style of classical deliberative oratory, though it served mainly 'as a metonymy for an imagined *scene* of ancient oratory in which the speaker moves the just passions of a civic assembly and implants a sense of community with his words' (Potkay 1994: 2). In his essay 'Of Eloquence' (1742), the Scottish Enlightenment philosopher David Hume (1711–76) makes a plea for the revival of ancient eloquence in British politics, although he fails to suggest how this might be reintroduced. However, by the time this essay was revised and published for the last time in 1770, Hume had changed his mind, and expressed his disapproval of eloquence on the grounds that it is 'impolite' (Potkay 1994: 4).

There is a perception that eloquence has inevitably declined, but there are also attempts to shape a new rhetoric, a simplified art that meets with the needs of a polite and commercial society. To underscore the changes in the conception of the art of rhetoric in the eighteenth century I want to compare George Puttenham's treatment of the figure *periphrasis* in *The Arte of English Poesie* (1589) with its description and illustration in Alexander Pope's *PERI BATHOUS or, The Art of Sinking in Poetry* (1727), the co-authored production of the Scriblerus club, which also included Jonathan Swift, John Gay and John Arbuthnot. Puttenham describes *periphrasis* as a linguistic going 'about the bush', when one chooses many words to represent 'that thing which we desire to have knowen' without saying what it is, and he gives as an example some lines that he claims to have written about Elizabeth I:

> Whom Princes serve, and Realmes obay,
> And greatest of Bryton kings begot:
> She came abroade even yesterday,
> When such as saw her, knew her not.
>
> (Puttenham 1936: 193)

This is a gallant example of this figure, the immodest Puttenham advises, because it is 'used discretely' (193), but it is easy to get this wrong, for instance if the subject 'which should have bene covertly disclosed by ambage, was by and by blabbed out', as in this example:

> The tenth of March when Aries received,
> Dan Phoebus raies into his horned hed.

This is a poor example because the reference to March gives away the subject of the lines, which is the season Spring (194). A better rendering of these lines and a better example of *periphrasis*, he offers, would be:

> The month and daie when Aries receivd,
> Dan Phoebus raies into his horned head.
>
> (194)

Compare this practical analysis with Pope's description of *periphrasis* as 'an aid to Prolixity' and his choice of example:

> A waving Sea of Heads was round me spread,
> And still fresh Streams the gazing Deluge fed.
>
> (Pope 1987: 184)

The point of this figure, Pope notes, is 'to give the Reader the Pleasure of guessing what it is that the Author can possibly mean; and a Surprize when he finds it'. If we ponder these lines for long enough, then we will 'come at last to find it means a *great Crowd*' (184).

It is not entirely clear that Pope would have approved of Puttenham's 'good' examples. Nor is it likely that he would have approved of the detail of his art. *The Arte of English Poesie* runs to three volumes. In contrast, the aim of *The Art of Sinking in Poetry* is satire. It is a mock handbook, a bathetic riposte to the revival of a style manual from the first century AD, *The Art of the Sublime*, and its eager imitation. *The Art of Sinking in Poetry* is not offering practical guidance on how to use the rhetorical figures; rather it ironically defends the national importance of mediocre poetry, and proposes to supply its art. Everything that Pope recommends should be taken in the opposite sense, and this extends to the idea of an 'art' itself. 'I will venture to lay down, as the first Maxim or Cornerstone of this our Art', Pope declares, 'That whoever would excel therein must studiously avoid, detest and turn his Head from all the Ideas, Ways and Workings of that pestilent Foe to Wit and Destroyer of Fine Figures, which is known by the name of *Commonsense*' (176). The idea that bad poetry needs an art can be turned around to mean instead that only 'art' produces bad poetry. We can deduce, then, that common sense produces good writing. The examples that Pope uses to illustrate this art are all derived from contemporaries. In one way or another, they illustrate the lack of what classical rhetoricians would call 'decorum' or fittingness, and what Pope and his contemporaries might understand as 'taste'. Here is another example from the *Art of Sinking*, this time of 'amplification', the figure which, for Wilson, 'consisteth mooste in Augmentynge and diminishynge of anye matter', (Wilson 1982: 249), and for Pope, the hunting out of further 'circumstances . . . that are far-fetch'd, or unexpected, or hardly compatible':

> When *Job* says in short, *He wash'd his Feet in Butter*, (a Circumstance some Poets would have soften'd or past over) hear how it is spread out by the Great Genius:
>
> > With Teats distended with their milky store,
> > Such numerous lowing Herds, before my Door,
> > Their painful Burden to unload did meet,
> > That we with Butter might have wash'd our feet.
>
> (183–84)

The Art of Sinking in Poetry implies that good writing is in some sense unteachable. Pope is not the first to argue this. We encountered a similar argument in Cicero's *On the ideal orator*, the speakers of which insist that eloquence cannot be learned from technical manuals. It might be supposed that the conversation among the Scriblerians, which resulted in this *Art*, recalls the practice of arguing on different sides recommended by Cicero's speakers as an antidote to pedantic rule-following. Only, *The Art of Sinking in Poetry* does not formulate this as an approach exactly; rather, it invites the reader to develop a sense of 'good' poetry from a critical engagement with its bad literary examples. Pope is assuming, of course, a reader who shares his good taste. Puttenham is similarly concerned with the 'proper' or fitting use of figures, but his focus in the *Arte of English Poesie* remains on their description. We could say that Puttenham is teaching us how to use the figures, and Pope illustrating the errors of their over-teaching. In this respect, Pope represents a different approach to 'rhetoric'. He marks the beginning of a shift from the practical study of the devices of persuasive speaking and writing to 'criticism': that is, to the activity of *reading* which is concerned with taste and literary judgement (Rhodes 2004).

This transition was to be acknowledged and institutionalized, not in London among groups like the Scriblerians, but north of the border, in mid-century, post-union Scotland. The history of this transition has been traced most recently by Neil Rhodes. His story begins with Robert Watson, who used the terms 'rhetoric' and 'criticism' interchangeably in his university lectures at St Andrews in 1758, though it was not until the publication of Henry Home, Lord Kames' *Elements of Criticism* in 1762 that 'criticism' properly replaced 'rhetoric', and a practice of tasteful reading was born. Or rather, as Rhodes explains, it was Kames who clarified that 'it is the business of criticism to develop taste not by laying down a rigid aesthetic code, but by addressing the feelings: "criticism tends to improve the heart not less than the understanding"' (Rhodes 2004: 199, 221; citing Kames 1763, 2nd edn: 1.9–16).

This is quite a transformation. We began this section with Henry Peacham's boast that the orator who studies the tropes and figures will be able to 'leade his hearers which way he list, and draw them to what affection he will' (Peacham 1577: A3r), and we now find that the orator has become a polite reader who has somehow internalized unspoken standards of good taste. To understand how we can move from the orator to the reader, from rhetoric to criticism, I want to consider the treatment of 'style' by a contributor who stands between Pope and Kames: this is Adam Smith, whose *Lectures on Rhetoric and Belles Lettres* were delivered at the University of Edinburgh in 1748–51 on the instigation of Kames, and then at the University of Glasgow in 1751–63. The title of these lectures indicates this moment of transition: Smith is teaching rhetoric *and* 'belles-lettres', that is, rhetoric and a combination of 'literary criticism and what we might now call creative writing', and which aimed to form the polite values that would fit the student 'for easy intercourse in society' (Rhodes 2004: 197). Smith does understand the rhetorical system, and discusses it in some detail, even if only to dismiss it. Typical of this approach is his contempt for earlier handbooks with their 'divisions and sub-divisions' of the tropes and figures. These, he complains, are 'generally a very silly set of Books and not at all instructive'. However, since he understands that 'it would be reckoned strange in a system of Rhetorick intirely to pass' them by, he will 'offer a few observations on them though not on the same plan as the ordinary writers proceed' (Smith 1985: 26–27). I want to emphasize the importance of this difference. The *Lecture Notes* are Smith's 'notes' as transcribed by two students, so we might not expect them to offer a very systematic account of the new rhetoric. And yet, Smith is also obviously keen to draw his students' attention to his departure from 'silly' manuals; he offers only a 'few observations'. This makes it hard to grasp immediately what is innovative about his reconception of rhetoric because it is not explicitly theorized. Nonetheless, we can discern both what he values as good writing and how he teaches this by comparing his advice on style with Aristotle's.

In Book 3 of *Rhetoric*, Aristotle gives the following advice on 'appropriate' or fitting style, which Smith both adopts and adapts:

Your language will be *appropriate* if it expresses emotion and character, and if it corresponds to its subject. 'Correspondence to subject' means that we must neither speak casually about weighty matters, nor solemnly about trivial ones; nor must we add ornamental epithets to commonplace nouns, or the effect will be comic. ... To express emotion, you will employ the language of anger in speaking of outrage; the language of disgust and discreet reluctance to utter a word when speaking of impiety or foulness; the language of exultation for a tale of glory, and that of humiliation for a tale of pity; and so on in all other cases.

This aptness of language is one thing that makes people believe in the truth of your story.

(Aristotle 1984: 1408a, 10–20)

This emphasis on clear and appropriate expression is easily discernible in Smith's lectures, from the first surviving lecture (Lecture 2), which outlines the importance of 'Perspicuity of stile' (3). To achieve this, Smith advises, speakers should use 'expressions' that are free from ambiguity: that is, they should avoid using synonyms and choose native words wherever possible; these should be placed in a 'natural' order, so that their meaning is quite unambiguous. Lecture 4 considers the strengths and flaws of the English language of which speakers need to be aware and Lecture 5, 'the arrangement of a sentence' (21). Moreover, Smith echoes Aristotle's advice on the appropriateness of metaphors: the writer or speaker must not mix metaphors, and should ensure that there is propriety between the things being compared. No metaphor can have 'beauty', Smith explains 'unless it be so adapted that it gives the due strength of expression to the object to be described and at the same time does this in a more striking and interesting manner' (29). Thus, John Milton always kept his metaphors 'within just bounds': for example, when he compares 'the grating of hell gates to the thunder'. Had he 'compared the noise of the gates of a city to thunder' instead, then 'the metaphor would not have been so just, and still less if to the door of a private house' (30). The point is that such a comparison would have been ridiculous; it would have been out of proportion.

All of this is sensible advice, and we may wonder how exactly Smith is departing from *classical* rhetoric. In many respects, he is returning a corrupted rhetoric to its origins. However, there is one very important difference, and this is nicely summarized by Stephen J. McKenna: 'For Aristotle, if you are clear, you will be appropriate; for Smith, if you are appropriate, you will be clear' (McKenna 2006: 81). The 'perfection of stile', Smith argues, 'consists in Expressing in the most concise, proper and precise manner the thought of the author, and that in the manner which best conveys the sentiment, passion, or affection with which it affects or he pretends it does affect him and which he designs to communicate to his reader' (55). For Smith, propriety is not simply derived from using the right kind of rhetorical device at the right moment; it is also achieved by writing 'in character', by conveying sympathetically one's 'sentiment' or 'affection' or those of the characters one creates. For this there is really only one rule, and that is to follow the dictates of common sense which govern polite social interchange as well as 'Criticism':

> This you'll say is no more than common sense, and indeed it is no more. But if you'll attend to it all the Rules of Criticism and morality when traced to their foundation, turn out to be some Principles of Common Sence which every one assents too; all the business of those arts is to apply these Rules to the different subjects and shew what their conclusion is when they are so applyed. Tis for this purpose we have made these observations on the authors above mentioned. We have shewn how fare they have acted agreably to that Rule, which is equally applicable to conversation and behaviour as writing. For what is that makes a man agreable company, is it not, when his sentiments appear to be naturally expressed, when the passion or affection is properly conveyed and when their thoughts are so agreable and naturall that we find ourselves inclined to give assent to them.
>
> (55)

Of the several writers that Smith commends in his lectures each one seems 'to have acted agreably to that Rule'. That is, each one 'speaks in his own stile and such an one as is agreable to his generall character', so that there is no single style that Smith can recommend (55–56). Thus, Jonathan Swift is by nature a plain man, and tends to speak bluntly rather than observing the 'common civilities' (36); this is reflected in his prose style and choice of subject matter. Not only is his language 'always correct and Proper', without the use of any 'ornaments' (48), but his naturally 'morose temper' has led him to write about particular subjects, mainly to ridicule 'the gayer follies' (49). Arguably, this is another way in which he expresses his sense of propriety, for the follies he satirizes are examples of excess, of unfitting or disproportionate conduct. This is in sharp contrast to his contemporary, the third earl of Shaftesbury. Rather than following the dictates of common sense, Shaftesbury has 'formed to himself an idea of beauty of Stile abstracted from his own character' (56); this happens to be, mistakenly, the 'pompous, grand and ornate Stile' (59). Smith is establishing a new 'rhetoric' for an improved age.

Smith is better known as an economist than as a rhetorical theorist, though there is a link between the two. It is 'our propensity to truck, barter, and exchange one thing for another', Smith argues early in *The Wealth of Nations*, suggesting that this is a 'necessary consequence of the faculties of reason and speech' (Smith 1998: 21). Trade is, for Smith, yet another form of communication. More importantly, though, he understands that different economies need different rhetorics. Quite simply, the rabble rousing of popular oratory has no place among a people whose passions have been refined by commerce and luxury. This is one of the aims of his lectures, to redefine an 'art' of language that enables easier expression, easier communication, and to recognize that language is itself refined as a society becomes more polite. Smith understands this as inevitable and progressive, and this gives him the confidence to break away from an old rhetoric. Whereas Renaissance humanists are tied by their veneration for ancient languages and cultures, Smith dismisses the Latin and Greek languages as 'primitive'. It is only with the 'intermixture of different nations', when one person was 'at a loss to express himself in the other language', that the complex grammars of these ancient languages were simplified (13). Thus, the declension of nouns in Latin is replaced gradually with prepositions in the romance languages. By the same token, the 'silly books' of the rhetoricians, with their subdivisions of the tropes and figures, are replaced by critical understanding. Indeed, figurative language is most likely to be found, not in the company of refined gentlemen, but in Billingsgate, 'in the lowest and most vulgar conversation' (34). For too long we have viewed ornate speech and writing as beautiful, yet the 'most beautifull passages', Smith argues, 'are generally the most simple', and he invites his auditors to discover the truth of this for themselves by comparing two stanzas from Pope's *Essay on Man*:

> Lo, the Poor Indian whose untutored mind
> Sees God in clouds and hears him in the Wind etc.
>
> Behold above around and underneath
> All nature full and bursting into birth etc.
>
> (Pope 1966: 244, 248)

Of the first stanza Smith suggests that the 'words watery waste had been better exchanged for Ocean but that Rhime required them'. Of the second, he notes approvingly that 'there is not any one figurative expression, and the few there are in the other are no advantage to it' (33–34).

The culmination *and* complication of this distinction between figurative and literal, primitive and civilized language can be found in the work of the French Enlightenment thinker, Jean-Jacques Rousseau (1712–78). In his 'Essay on the Origin of Languages' (*Essai sur l'origine des langues*), unpublished during his lifetime, Rousseau uses this distinction as a way of conceiving the progress of human history. 'Man did not begin by reasoning', argues Rousseau, 'but by feeling', and it was the passions, love, anger, hatred, fear and pity, which produced the 'first voices'. The first societies used language to express the passions, not reason, and it is only with the development of civil society 'as needs increase, as [men's] dealings get more entangled', that language 'changes in character' and 'becomes more precise and less passionate'; language then 'substitutes ideas for sentiments, and no longer speaks to the heart but to reason' (Rousseau 2001: 256). This is a *myth* of enlightenment conceived, paradoxically, as the overcoming of myth and error; it is also a story of the development of rational communication. Rousseau imagines that when a primitive man encountered a fellow man for the first time his fear at this sighting gave him the idea that this fellow was a 'giant'. The word 'giant' is coined to describe the first men; later, men will learn from this mistake, and realize that this giant is just a man like themselves, not a god or hero. Understanding involves seeing something for what it is, not when it is disguised by the illusory ideas and poetic figures inspired by the passions. The word 'giant' is a substitution for the 'passion' which the first sighting of a fellow human represents to the primitive man. In time, men came to recognize this word as 'metaphorical'. The word is then used by someone only when he or she is 'moved by the same passions as had produced it' (Rousseau 2001: 252–54).

We have come a long way from Cicero's sense of the potential of human societies for improvement through 'eloquence' to a conception in the Enlightenment of civilization as the overcoming of its irrational force. Nonetheless, there is a paradox at the heart of Enlightenment engagements with the tropes and figures, and this is highlighted by Rousseau who conceives of 'enlightenment' as representing loss as well as progress. What is lost is a capacity to be moved *and* to act politically. The development of language in a civil society, Rousseau writes, owes much to the art of writing; this art allows for the analysis of a language and it also supports commerce by enabling 'travellers' to learn other tongues. However, it also fixes and 'adulterates' language because 'it substitutes precision for expressiveness'. 'In writing one is forced to use every word in conformity with common usage', Rousseau complains, 'but a speaker alters the meanings by his tone of voice, determining them as he wishes; since he is less constrained to be clear, he stresses forcefulness more' (260). As a language becomes more refined it loses its 'genius'; it grows 'frigid and monotonous', wanting the emotive force of ancient eloquence (260, 265).

This argument is finally developed in the pessimistic chapter of this essay, 'The Relation of Languages to Governments', in which Rousseau laments the fixing of modern civil societies: 'nothing can be changed in them any more except by arms and cash, and since there is nothing left to say to the people but, *give* money, it is said with posters on street corners or with soldiers in private homes; for there is no need to assemble anyone; on the contrary, subjects must be kept scattered; this is the first maxim of modern politics' (298–99). In the ancient world eloquence was necessary because 'persuasion occupied the place of public force' (298). In modernity, however, only violence and money have the power to change anything. If an orator tried to harangue the people of Paris in the Place de Vendôme, they would hear only that he was shouting, not what he was saying.

LITERATURE AND RHETORIC

At the beginning of this chapter I noted that rhetoric is understood to decline in the course of its history; mainly, this is because the formal art is narrowed to one activity or stage of composition, style. Another way of describing this decline is to say that rhetoric becomes literary (Kahn 1985: 38–39). In the eighteenth century, as we have seen, rhetoric is reformulated as 'criticism': to many this is the precursor of what we now consider to be 'English studies' (Rhodes 2004), to others it constitutes the 'betrayal' of rhetoric (Jarratt 1991). However, well before this, rhetoric is taught as an art of *composition*, and in this respect, it is deemed responsible for the development of vernacular literature. Historians of rhetoric usually think of this as a diminishment of the possibilities of rhetoric. Writers and literary scholars might equally view this association rather negatively too. It is not obvious how literature is served by a rhetorical training. We might well wonder what the Roman art, originally expanded to help lawyers prosecute or defend successfully in court, has to offer the poet, novelist or playwright. Though many of the examples I have used to illustrate the tropes and figures have been drawn from literary writings, other examples suggest how ungainly the enthusiastic application of these can be. Pope's *Art of Sinking in Poetry* exposes how rhetoric produces bad poetry, though this perception was already a source of comedy in Shakespeare's *Love's Labours Lost* (*c.* 1594/5). His pedantic schoolmaster Holofernes, for instance, has too much *copia*, as this tired example of *periphrasis* or circumlocution suggests:

The deer was, as you know – *sanguis* – in blood, ripe as the pome-
water who now hangeth like a jewel in the ear of *caelo*, the sky, the
welkin, the heaven, and anon falleth like a crab on the face of *terra*,
the soil, the land, the earth.

(Shakespeare 2005: 4.2.3–7)

Holofernes, as Colin Burrow remarks, exposes the possible 'night-
marish' consequences of rhetorical training that focuses too intently
on spotting and naming tropes and figures: 'an ability to para-
phrase, circumlocute, and ornament in a manner that serves no
instrumental purpose at all' (Burrow 2004: 16).

When we know a little more about the programme of rhetorical training in the Tudor classroom the benefits of rhetoric for
the literary writer become harder still to envisage. Training in
rhetoric in sixteenth-century England was a painstaking process,
one closely associated with the learning of Latin. School boys
were first given elementary sentences, usually moral phrases, to
enable them to grasp the rules of Latin syntax. After using these
to master 'accidence', they would then read dialogues, later Latin
letters and plays, excerpting from these texts phrases which they
could adapt grammatically in their conversations and writings,
but which they could also imitate for 'rhetorical' effect (Mack
2005: 6–7). Students were encouraged to spot stylistic devices,
and to collect these as well as any 'commonplaces' which they
discovered as they read, not Aristotle's 'lines of reasoning' but
rather moral sentences (*sententiae*): proverbs, maxims or pithy
sayings, ready-made phrases. These were excerpted and stored in
'commonplace books' under headings ('places') so as to facilitate
their easy retrieval for future use. This aimed to develop *copia*, a
rich store of linguistic devices and knowledge which the student
could apply as and when the need arose.

This sounds a dry and tedious process, hardly conducive to
imaginative self-expression. We can see the danger of the
mechanical process of selecting, storing and reproducing sayings in an 'anti-play' by Eugène Ionesco, a practitioner of
Theatre of the Absurd in 1950s Paris. The bizarre process of
composition that he describes as inspiring the writing of *The
Bald Prima Donna* (*La Cantatrice Chauve*) recalls this process;

and it illustrates wonderfully the absurdity of stockpiling commonplaces. In his counter-notes to this, titled 'The Tragedy of Language', he explains that the genesis of *The Bald Prima Donna* is his attempt to learn English from an 'English–French Conversation Manual for Beginners'. From this manual he 'conscientiously copied out phrases', planning to learn these off by heart, only to discover, in the process, that he 'was learning not English but some very surprising truths': for example, 'that there are seven days in the week', which he 'happened to know before', or that 'the floor is below us' (Ionesco 1964: 181). Initially he decided to teach these 'essential truths' to his peers through drama, and he made the play 'by stringing together phrases taken from [his] English manual' (183). Its characters, the Smiths and the Martins, are also the stars of his English–French Conversation Manual; in play and manual alike they 'utter the same maxims, and perform the same actions or the same "inactions"' (183). But what began as imitation turned into something more complex as the 'simple sentences' which he had 'so painstakingly copied into [his] schoolboy's exercise book ... changed places all by themselves' and 'became garbled and corrupted' (184). The result is a dialogue that makes no sense, with interlocutors mouthing often mangled or nonsensical maxims and unable to find common ground; such anti-dialogue eventually produces anger and frustration. It also offers us a glimpse of humanist rhetorical training taken to its mechanical extreme:

MRS MARTIN	I can buy a pocketknife for my brother, but you could not buy Ireland for your grandfather.
MR SMITH	One walks on one's feet, but one keeps warm with the aid of coal and electricity.
MR MARTIN	Sell a pig today, eat an egg tomorrow.
MRS SMITH	In life you've got to look out of the window.
MRS MARTIN	You may sit down on a chair, when the chair hasn't any.
MR SMITH	One can always be in two places at once.
MR MARTIN	The floor is below us and the ceiling is above us.
MRS SMITH	When I say 'yes', it's only a manner of speaking.

MRS MARTIN   We all have our cross to bear.

MR SMITH   Describe a circle, stroke its back and it turns viciou

(Ionesco 1958: 32,

And yet despite this revealing parody of linguistic training, the method it satirizes did produce, in the Renaissance at least, some astonishing writing that constantly broke free of apparent constraints. It is easy to forget that the selection and stockpiling of figures and commonplaces is only one part of the process. Once collected, the devices and commonplaces supported the classroom exercise of declamation, the practice of arguing on different sides of a problem. If we concentrate on the significance of this process we can extend radically our understanding of the period's rhetorical culture beyond the emphasis in its handbooks which focus narrowly on *elocutio*.

Shakespeare's work is perhaps the most stunning example of the resources and opportunities that rhetorical argument could offer to the Renaissance writer. His use of moral sentences is well recognized; it is often seen as enabling exploration of ethical problems from many different sides. As Peter Mack notes, *The Tragedy of King Lear* (c. 1605–6) is typical in this respect because it tests a character's use of moral comment or judgement against the action of the play as well as against the counter-responses of other characters. For example, when the destitute and disguised Edgar uses the commonplace of fortune's wheel to demonstrate that events must improve, he is challenged by the insight of Gloucester, his blind father:

> O gods! Who is't can say 'I am at the worst'?
> I am worse than e'er I was.
>
> (Shakespeare 2005: 4.1.25–26; Mack 2005: 18)

We are given two perspectives. Edgar argues that it is premature to judge that one is truly enduring the harshest blows of fortune; Gloucester, in contrast, counters by arguing that his bad fortune will never be ameliorated. Yet, it is typical of the play's impulse to speak 'to and fro' in conflicting argument that Edgar must later rebuke his father's despair as an abandonment of the will to

. 'What, in ill thoughts again? Men must endure / Their ɔing hence even as their coming hither. / Ripeness is all. *Come ɔn.*' (5.2.9–11; emphasis added). 'And that's true, too,' Gloucester acknowledges this time (5.2.12). After all, earlier in the play Gloucester is far from being a reliable judge of experience. In the second scene, he is persuaded as to Edgar's treachery and indulges in some sententious reflections on this as a symptom of broader temporal and cosmic decline. Such betrayals are of a piece with the 'late eclipses in the sun and moon' (1.2.101). This moralized conception of cosmology is subjected to devastating critique by Gloucester's truly treacherous son, the illegitimate Edmund. He portrays his father's ruminations as an example of 'the excellent foppery of the world' (1.2.116), a gross instance of presumption concerning the providential significance of essentially petty human actions. Moral commentary is placed in some estranging contexts throughout *King Lear* and this forces us to evaluate its limits. Indeed, some deeply unpleasant and malicious speakers can talk an alarming degree of sense. It is not misplaced then to sympathize with the strictures Regan addresses to her father concerning the need for 'discretion' in Lear's old age. Why does he need such a redundant and, she claims, troublesome retinue of followers? Yet, it is this commonsensical observation concerning Lear's indulgence of his household that provokes his great speech on the true nature of 'need' and this lays bare the impoverishment of her pragmatic calculus of necessity:

> O, reason not the need! Our basest beggars
> Are in the poorest thing superfluous.
> Allow not nature more than nature needs,
> Man's life is cheap as beast's.

> (2.2.438–41)

For some students at least, this emphasis on collecting sentences and then debating them evidently did prove fruitful, aiding dramatic composition. We might argue from this that rhetoric, rather than being diminished by its association with literature, in fact extends the 'sphere of literature' since the process of writing and also of reading or spectating constitutes an act of deliberation between alternative perspectives (Kahn 1985: 38–39). This is an aspect of literary writing before and after the Renaissance, but the revival of declamation in the classroom in the sixteenth century informs the structural ambivalence of many texts in this period in particular. Because issues are routinely presented from different perspectives, readers and audiences engage in a process of reflection with regard to even the most familiar problems and ideas.

The interpretation of Shakespearean drama is very well served by an understanding of this crucial intellectual and cultural context. We can see the plot of a play as representing the different sides of a particular classroom exercise, as Neil Rhodes has argued for *Measure for Measure* (Rhodes 2004: 105–10). In this respect, rhetorical training provides the material for complex dramatic plots. However, drama can also provide rhetorical training. The capacity of drama to unravel arguments through the manipulation and the development of a plot informs Shakespeare's interest in training his audience to become careful and sceptical auditors of rhetorical display throughout his drama. I am thinking of the gradual revelation of the King of England's deceit in act 2 scene 1 of Shakespeare's early history play, *The Life and Death of King John* (c. 1595/6). This is the odd scene in which the inscrutable 'Citizen' of Angiers repeatedly fails to choose between King John of England and young Arthur Plantagenet, a proxy of King Philip of France, both of whom demand that he and his city show allegiance to the rightful king. His arrival in France, King John argues, has deterred the French from laying siege to the city, though he warns the Citizen to beware of their shift to a posture of negotiation:

> And now instead of bullets wrapped in fire
> To make a shaking fever in your walls,
> They shoot but calm words folded up in smoke
> To make a faithless error in your ears.
>
> (2.1.227–30)

In a way, King John is right. King Philip's calm words are a smoke screen for the aggressive intentions of the French, and this becomes clear when, given the opportunity to speak, he offers the citizens an ultimatum: 'if you fondly pass our proffered offer, / 'Tis not the roundure of your old-faced walls / Can hide you from our messengers of war' (2.1.258–60). Yet, the battle that ensues after this failed debate vindicates the Citizen's reluctance to resolve the dispute because this also ends in stalemate. In fact, there is not much to decide between the dubious 'virtue' of either compromised claimant, and this is underscored in the decision they agree upon by excluding the Citizen, to attack the city, laying it waste, and then to fight 'who shall be king of it' (2.1.399–400). The proposal is put forward by the Bastard, the illegitimate Plantagenet promoted by King John, and it exposes brilliantly the interest of his benefactor: 'Now, by the sky that hangs above our heads, / I like it well' (2.1.397–98). If nothing else, the agreement reached prompts us to consider how King John's calm words masked his aggressive intentions. He depicted his presence as a chivalric defence of the chastity and honour of a maiden city from the treacherous French. Now we know better.

This is not to say that Shakespeare is undermining or abandoning the idea of rhetoric. *King John* also includes a powerful counter-defence of the importance of emotive persuasion in Prince Arthur's successful appeal to Hubert to imagine the physical consequences of his planned assault upon him (4.1). Shakespeare's evaluation of rhetorical argument is as many sided as we might expect and it includes awareness of how different political cultures can be gauged through their attitude to and deployment of rhetoric. In *Julius Caesar* (1599) we see a particularly striking example of this as the play explores the transition from republic to empire, and does so, moreover, by representing one of the most famous debates in antiquity, between the republican Brutus and the power-hungry Antony. This play also stands as another example of how 'rhetoric' extends the 'sphere of literature'. On the one hand, Shakespeare depicts the failure of rhetorical culture lamented by Tacitus: as power passes to Antony the possibilities for debate are inhibited. On the other hand, this 'loss' is redressed by the very play that captures its effects. Shakespeare distinguishes between republican and imperial rhetoric and presents admiringly the possibilities of the former in the frank engagement between Brutus and Cassius in act 4 scene 2. Such openness may not find its way into the rhetorical handbooks of Shakespeare's day, as we noted above, but it is given great theatrical vitality in this tragedy. Let us now turn our attention to this work.

Julius Caesar contains one of the most famous, and most problematic, orations of antiquity, Antony's speech in the forum over Caesar's body. We tend to think of this speech as a stunning rhetorical success because Antony achieves a political victory against the odds, destroying the attempt of Brutus and Cassius to preserve the traditional republican constitution of Rome by killing Caesar. Through the power of words alone he dissolves the trust of the citizens of Rome in the honour of the republicans; he transforms understanding of them from tyrannicides to assassins. By the end of this scene we learn that the co-conspirators Brutus and Cassius 'Are rid like madmen through the gates of Rome' (3.2.262). We may regard Antony's speech as a great success; after all, he wins. Yet, we could rather see it as a failure. Antony's success represents the end of rhetoric and the values and practices it should embody. I am not calling Antony a failed orator. In act 3 scene 2 he defeats his honourable opponent, Brutus, and he does so by using many of the rhetorical strategies advised in the Roman handbooks. However, his success represents the beginning of the end of the republic. In this scene we watch him turning the citizens into a mob, and a mob is something to be cowed by fear and moved by spectacle, not to be addressed as fellow citizens capable of rational deliberation.

We can see this passing of republican rhetorical culture just by comparing the rhetorical styles of Brutus and Antony. Brutus appeals to the reason of his audience, and the persuasiveness of his argument depends on their knowledge of his integrity, on his *ethos*: 'Believe me for mine honour, and have respect to mine honour, that you may believe' (3.2.14–16). More specifically, it depends on their recognition of his fairness, his reasonableness. This is emphasized also by the figures of speech on which he relies: *isocolon*, clauses of equal length, and *antithesis*, contrasting words and ideas placed in a parallel construction. These are used in the sentence just cited, but also throughout the speech. Here are some other examples: 'not that I loved Caesar less, but that I loved Rome more', and then immediately following this, 'Had you rather Caesar were living, and die all slaves, than that Caesar were dead, to live all free men?' (3.2.21–24). What is so effective about Brutus' use of these figures, is that they present his reasons in a fair and balanced way: he acknowledges Caesar's greatness, and emphasizes his love for him, but he also indicates the dangers he posed to the republic that led the republican conspirators to destroy him. This was no easy decision, he is telling them. Brutus also assumes the 'reasonableness' of his fellow citizens. Because they are 'Romans' and have the freedom to debate, he assumes they are unwilling to be subjected to a man, Caesar. This assumption is clarified forcibly towards the end of his speech with the figure *epimone*, the frequent repetition of a phrase or question dwelling on a point:

> Who is here so base that would be a bondman? If any, speak, for him I have offended. Who is here so rude that would not be a Roman? If any, speak, for him I have offended. Who is here so vile that will not love his country? If any, speak, for him have I offended. I pause for a reply.
>
> (3.2.29–34)

This is a powerful oration, and the response to Brutus' final question is categorical: 'None, Brutus, none' (3.2.35). Nonetheless, the support that Brutus wins will be quite dashed by Antony's different theatrical display. This is despite the fact that Antony initially faces a hostile audience. "Twere best he speak no harm of Brutus here!' says one plebeian; 'This Caesar was a tyrant', says another, while a third concludes 'We are blessed that Rome is rid of him' (3.2.68–71). So how does Antony change their minds? To begin with, he echoes Brutus at the start of his oration, achieving the same sense of balance: 'I come to bury Caesar, not to praise him' (3.2.75). However, his much longer oration also deploys a broader range of devices, and these begin to undermine his antagonist's *ethos*: Caesar has been brutally murdered, Antony reminds his audience, and so Brutus and his co-conspirators are *not* honourable men. However, he makes this argument indirectly, never openly accusing Brutus. One of the key figures he uses to achieve this is *paralepsis* or *occupatio*, which draws attention to an issue even as it is passed over: 'Have patience, gentle friends, I must not read it. / It is not meet you know how Caesar loved you' (3.2.141–42). This figure emphasizes an issue discreetly, so that Antony does not seem to be publicly confrontational, but it also arouses suspicion. In addition, Antony also very quickly renders his assertion 'Brutus is an honourable man' ironic just by repeating it, even as he offers evidence to counter the accusation that Caesar is ambitious. Most strikingly, and in stark contrast to Brutus, however, Antony arouses the violent emotions of his audience (*pathos*) with a range of theatrical devices so as to affect their final judgement. These include *apostrophe*, 'Judge, O you gods, how dearly Caesar lov'd him', and more dramatically still, the production of Caesar's bloodied cloak; this is the very gesture which Quintilian commended because it 'made the image of the crime so vivid that Caesar seemed not to have been murdered, but to be being murdered there and then' (6.1.31):

> You all do know this mantle. . . .
> Look, in this place ran Cassius' dagger through.
> See what a rent the envious Casca made.
> Through this the well-belovèd Brutus stabbed;
> And as he plucked his cursèd steel away,
> Mark how the blood of Caesar followed it.
>
> (Shakespeare 2005: 3.2.168–76)

This speech is a stunning rhetorical triumph, but it also represents a tragic defeat: Antony wins, but Rome loses. This loss is clarified in the scenes immediately following. In act 3 scene 3, the plebeians lynch the poet Cinna for no good reason, and then in act 4 scene 1, the three triumvirs, Antony, Octavius and Lepidus, proscribe their enemies and plot their next move. Particularly chilling is Antony's discussion of Lepidus as soon as he leaves their company, because it exposes his instrumental view of political relationships and his unwillingness to share power: 'This is a slight, unmeritable man, / Meet to be sent on errands', and then again, 'Do not talk of him / But as a property'. Antony shares power with Lepidus, he explains, only 'To ease ourselves of diverse sland'rous loads' (4.1.12–13, 20). Compare Antony's deceit with the open friendship between Cassius and Brutus depicted in act 4 scene 2, and we get a good sense of what has been lost.

Julius Caesar envisions the collapse of this 'spacious field' in which orators 'expatiate without let or hindrance' (Tacitus 1914: 39). There is a sense that Brutus' and Cassius' frank exchange is not to be repeated. The final collapse of this republican tradition is embodied in the diminished figure of Pompey the Great's son in *The Tragedy of Antony and Cleopatra* (c. 1606). His revolt against the triumvirate in the early part of the play makes a richly emotive appeal to the cause of 'all-honoured, honest, Roman Brutus' and those 'courtiers of beauteous freedom' who, like Pompey's father, had died defending the republic (Shakespeare 2005: 2.6.16–17). Yet the younger Pompey's oddly chosen term 'courtiers', in the sense of 'wooers', betrays that he is an uncertain, even a specious, exponent of these values. In the event, Pompey appears more exercised over Antony's possession of his father's house than the restoration of the republic and he accepts meekly enough a negotiated settlement in return for his own small piece of empire in Sicily and Sardinia.

I opened this section by questioning how the rhetorical training of the Tudor grammar school could possibly have shaped the flourishing of vernacular literature at the end of the sixteenth century. It is hard to see, I suggested, how the practice of collecting moral 'sentences' might contribute to this. Except that the process of selection and collection is just one aspect of this training; it was supported, in the classroom, with another exercise, 'declamation', or argument on different sides. This exercise is often deemed responsible for the ambiguity of much Shakespearean drama; as we have seen, it underpins the probing examination of moral and political issues in his plays. The question I want to raise now is whether this practice can be seen to complicate the rather exclusive view of rhetoric with which we ended our discussion of the Renaissance art in the last section, and even to structure writings by those who are excluded from this masculine tradition. Is the practice of declamation, argument on different sides, the foundation only of the kind of macho debate that Quintilian describes?

We are used to describing rhetoric as a male privilege, and identifying how women are disadvantaged by it (Hutson 1994). However, male authors might also use their rhetorical training not only to confirm sexual difference but also to debate the relationship between the sexes more probingly, or at the very least, to recognize the possibility of dissent. In *Of Domesticall Duties* (1622), William Gouge may advise that wives remain silent in the company of their husbands. However, he also offers a more complex reflection on the significance of female silence. Not only does he acknowledge the objections voiced by his rather vocal female parishioners to much of his advice in his preface (Gouge 1976: N3v), but he also offers a more varied account of what female silence might mean. Gouge may recall that 'the Apostle enjoyneth *silence* to wives', but he also understands that this should not be taken too literally: 'for silence in that place is not opposed to speech, as if she should not speake at all, but to loquacity, to talkativenesse, to over-much tatling'. Moreover, silence may in fact represent not submission, but 'stoutnesse of stomacke, and stubbornesse of heart' (281–82; Luckyj 2002: 58–62; Richards and Thorne 2006: 12). This second possibility is dramatized very successfully in one of the few published, female-authored plays of the period, Elizabeth Cary's closet drama *The Tragedy of Mariam* (1613). The possibility that female silence may signify 'stoutnesse of stomacke, and stubbornesse of heart' is represented by the protagonist Mariam, who refuses to answer the accusations of her mother and other onlookers as she walks to the scaffold. In response to cat calls she offers nothing but a 'scornful smile' (Cary 2002: 5.1.52). This play is also preoccupied with the inscrutability of female silence: for example, when Pheroras complains of his beloved Graphina's failure to respond to his declaration of love, and argues that 'silence is a sign of discontent' (2.1.42), she corrects him very quickly, offering different interpretations of its significance:

> If I be silent, 'tis no more but fear
> That I should say too little when I speak.

> (2.1.49–50)

Moreover, she argues, the many favours Pheroras has bestowed on her require her thought and attention if she is to requite them properly; and study needs silence:

> Then need not all these favors study crave,
> To be requited by a simple maid?
> And study still, you know, must silence have.
> Then be my cause for silence justly weighed.

(636)

Perhaps surprisingly, too, argument on different sides can inform the structural ambiguity of a more recent literary form, the novel, prompting us think again not just about the gender of rhetorical agents but also about the assumed narrative of this tradition's decline. My final example is a text that would appear to be at a substantial remove in literary kind and concerns from the rhetorical tradition, Mary Shelley's gothic novel *Frankenstein* (1818, 1831). Despite this distance, we can identify her close engagement with writings that were produced out of it. An obvious example is the influence of John Milton's *Paradise Lost*, which informs both the series of contrasts Shelley uses to structure the novel and its preoccupation with 'eloquence'. Just as in the first two books of *Paradise Lost* the reader is invited to engage critically with the fiery speeches of the fallen angels, so in this novel, we are invited to view the 'untrustworthy' eloquence of its contrasting narrators Dr Frankenstein and his Creature.

Frankenstein is organized as a series of letters written by an Arctic adventurer, Captain Walton, to his sister in England; these relate the narrative of Dr Frankenstein, a Genevan scientist who defies the laws of nature by creating a monster from the parts of the dead. Frankenstein is an eloquent narrator, and it is this quality that recommends him to the lonely Walton, who is trapped with his crew on the ice. Walton discovers in Frankenstein the companion and confidante for whom he has yearned: 'He is so gentle, yet so wise' Walton rhapsodizes, 'his mind is so cultivated, and when he speaks, although his words are culled with the choicest art, yet they flow with rapidity and unparalleled eloquence' (Shelley 2003: 29). Frankenstein's eloquence distinguishes him as a sensitive soul, a suitable companion for Walton who feels isolated even though he is surrounded by his crew in the little commonwealth of his ship. Frankenstein's moving self-representation leads Walton to trust and admire him. The reader's trust of Frankenstein, however, is compromised; it is compromised in part because of his inescapable egoism which inflects the personal narrative he tells to Walton, but also because we are offered a second competing narrative from a character who likewise speaks with 'unparalleled eloquence': Frankenstein's unnamed monstrous creation. This raises a difficult question. If Walton discovers in Frankenstein's eloquence evidence of his gentleness and cultivation, why should we not attribute the same qualities to the monster? Quite simply, which eloquent speaker should we be persuaded by, if any?

It is not until the second volume of *Frankenstein* that we experience this Creature's eloquence, although at two removes: his story is reported by Frankenstein to Walton, and then relayed by Walton to the reader. In volume 1, all we know about this Creature is that he has been constructed from the limbs and organs of the dead, and that he is horribly disfigured and morally corrupt. He is the suspected murderer of William and, indirectly, of Justine, who is executed for this crime. In volume 2, however, our sympathies suddenly shift when we are given the opportunity to reflect instead on the Creature's innate goodness and the cause of its corruption. In this volume, the Creature relates to Frankenstein the story of his awakening and education, his secret co-existence with his 'protectors', the De Lacey family, how he learns to speak and read, and of his longing for a companion. This longing is sharpened by his unequivocal rejection by the De Lacey family once they discover this malformed creature living in their midst. Their rejection prompts his first 'feelings of revenge and hatred' (140). By telling this story of his fall from anticipated grace, the Creature is seeking to persuade Frankenstein to create for him a fellow companion. The force of this plea rests on the argument that his vices 'are the children of a forced solitude', and the promise that his 'virtues will necessarily arise when I live in communion with an equal' (150). Frankenstein is persuaded, and he gives his reasons thus:

I paused some time to reflect on all he had related, and the various arguments which he had employed. I thought of the promise of virtues which he had displayed on the opening of his existence, and the subsequent blight of all kindly feeling by the loathing and scorn which his protectors had manifested towards him. His power and threats were not omitted to my calculations: a creature who could exist in the ice-caves of the glaciers, and hide himself from pursuit among the ridges of inaccessible precipices, was a being possessing faculties it would be vain to cope with. After a long pause of reflection, I concluded that the justice due both to him and my fellow creatures demanded of me that I should comply with his request.

(150)

The Creature's argument is quite persuasive, so too is Frankenstein's concluding explanation of why he is persuaded, at least at first glance: 'I concluded that the justice due both to him and my fellow creatures demanded of me that I should comply with his request'. But there is another, less laudable reason why Frankenstein accedes to the Creature's request: as he acknowledges, his 'power and threats were not omitted to my calculations'. Though Frankenstein is persuaded, he comes to regret this, and offers a sustained and, arguably, a convincing attack on the Creature's 'eloquence'. Frankenstein's reasons for agreeing to the Creature's request in the first place are directly contradicted later in the novel, when he explains to Walton his decision to renege on his promise thus:

During these last days I have been occupied in examining my past conduct; nor do I find it blameable. In a fit of enthusiastic madness I created a rational creature, and was bound towards him, to assure, as far as was in my power, his happiness and well-being. This was my duty; but there was another still paramount to this. My duties towards the beings of my own species had greater claims to my attention, because they included a greater proportion of happiness or misery. Urged by this view, I refused, and I did right in refusing, to create a companion for the first creature. He showed unparalleled malignity and selfishness, in evil.

(219–20)

In one sense, this represents Frankenstein's moral growth, for he is thinking, at last, of protecting his fellows from his dangerous creation. Moreover, his fear of the Creature's 'unparalleled malignity' is proved right: this monster murders Frankenstein's closest friend, Clerval, and his bride, Elizabeth. Of our two contrasted characters, then, it is perhaps the self-correcting Frankenstein who we might choose to trust, especially late in the novel when he has learned to resist the dangerous eloquence of his creation. His sense of this danger is shared with Walton when, dying, he begs his friend 'to undertake my unfinished work', the destruction of the Creature. Yet, he warns, if Walton is to complete this task, he must avoid making the mistake of listening to the Creature: 'He is eloquent and persuasive; and once his words had even power over my heart: but trust him not. His soul is as hellish as his form, full of treachery and fiendlike malice. Hear him not' (212). Frankenstein makes this request at what he describes as a moment of lucidity, 'when I am only induced by reason and virtue' (220), and this contrasts sharply with his representation of the Creature. The Creature is not to be trusted; he is malignant and selfish, and he possesses a 'satanic' eloquence. In this representation Frankenstein is merely developing the Creature's own misguided reading of *Paradise Lost*, which shapes his autobiography: it leads him to identify with the despairing and anguished Satan, although without recognizing his egoism: 'I, like the archfiend, bore a hell within me, and finding myself unsympathised with, wished to tear up all the trees, spread havoc and destruction around me, and then to have sat down and enjoyed the ruin' (138).

What is so interesting about *Frankenstein*, however, is that Shelley manages to make the reader suspicious of eloquence, and yet also cast a critical eye on reasonable men like Frankenstein who warn us to resist its appeal. Shelley makes much of the ambiguity of *Paradise Lost* to inform her own narrative, imitating Milton's representation of persuasive but untrustworthy characters; she invites the reader to supplement for Walton's naivety. In contrast to Milton's epic, though, Shelley's novel has no authorial narrator; there is no guiding voice that we might trust. Frankenstein's warning that we should be wary of the Creature's eloquence is very problematic, not only because he is representing it but also because his own account of it is then told by the partial Walton. So untrustworthy are this novel's narrators that it is never obvious who we are 'meant' to be persuaded by. And yet, I would argue that it is the Creature who ultimately requires our sympathy, though not our trust. This is not a story in which the 'good' changes sides with the 'bad': the Creature remains a disturbing and troubling character. Yet, the satanic orator of this novel is shown in the end to be Frankenstein himself. Repeatedly, he cites his compassion and sense of responsibility or duty to rhetorical effect. Always such citations obscure his self-interested motivations. This is apparent, for instance, when he appeals to the mutinous crew on the Arctic ship. The crew have approached Walton, requesting that the ship be turned back if the ice melts. Frankenstein steps forward to dissuade them and assert his interest thus:

> 'What do you mean? What do you demand of your captain? Are you then so easily turned from your design? Did you not call this a glorious expedition? And wherefore was it glorious? Not because the way was smooth and placid in a southern sea, but because it was full of dangers and terror; because, at every new incident, your fortitude was called forth, and your courage exhibited; because danger and death surrounded it, and these you were to brave and to overcome. For this was it a glorious, for this was it an honourable undertaking. You were hereafter to be hailed as the benefactors of your species; your names adored, as belonging to brave men who encountered death for honour, and the benefit of mankind. And now, behold, with the first imagination of danger, or, if you will, the first mighty and terrific trial of your courage, you shrink away, and are content to be handed down as men who had not strength enough to endure cold and peril; and so, poor souls, they were chilly and returned to their warm firesides.' ...
>
> He spoke this with a voice so modulated to the different feelings it expressed in his speech, with an eye so full of lofty design and heroism, that can you wonder that these men were moved? They looked at one another, and were unable to reply.
>
> (217–18)

This deliberative oration emphasizes the glory of the mission, but this means nothing when the personal motivation of the venture and the risks posed to the crew are taken into consideration. Moreover, in this speech we can see very clearly the coerciveness of Frankenstein's rhetoric: the rapid series of rhetorical questions which leave the crew no time to think, a technique which echoes Satan's temptation of Eve in book 9 of *Paradise Lost* (Milton 1998: 9.679–732). At this moment Frankenstein could be mistaken for one of the ancient sublime orators revered in the Enlightenment, Cicero or Demosthenes. This is certainly how Walton regards him. Yet Walton, as we have already noted, is foolishly partial. His eloquent companion is in fact a feverish and obsessed man, while his crew's apparent assent should rather be read as shocked silence. In the event, they do indeed rebel.

Frankenstein warns us of the dangers of eloquence, noting its misleading effects both on naive auditors like Walton, and also on characters such as Frankenstein who are persuaded of their own moral rightness. But it also illustrates the dangers of a failure to listen to others who do not possess the 'authority' of this novel's indulged and privileged male narrators, Walton and Frankenstein. The unheard characters of this novel include Walton's menial crew and Frankenstein's childhood sweetheart Elizabeth, whose eloquence *should* have saved the innocent Justine, if only she had carried authority in the male-dominated court room. They also include the Creature. We might read *Frankenstein* as a response to the argument of Rousseau's 'Essay on the Origin of Languages': that enlightened 'modern' citizens have lost the capacity to be moved. The Creature's eloquence fails to move his sought-after 'protectors', the very civil De Laceys and the privileged Frankenstein, to recognize the humanity he shares with them beneath his monstrous appearance. However, in contrast to Rousseau, Shelley's novel is not simply lamenting the loss of eloquence but rather arousing our capacity to sympathize; she invites recognition of the need to be affected by moving speech but also to engage critically with it. In the manner of Milton's *Paradise Lost*, which she insistently recalls throughout *Frankenstein*, Shelley invites us to read her text 'rhetorically', to engage with and assess the eloquence of its juxtaposed characters. In so doing, she offers a compelling case for the notorious Romantic sympathy with Milton's Satan. She encourages us to engage with the *other* side. In short, she makes us listen and judge.

'RHETORICAL DIDACTICS': POST-ENLIGHTENMENT

The modern or 'post-Romantic' separation of rhetoric and poetry is suggested by W.B. Yeats in the 1920s: 'We make out of the quarrel with others, rhetoric, but out of the quarrel with ourselves, poetry' (Yeats 1959: 331). For Yeats, rhetoric and poetry are incompatible. Poetry is produced by self-confrontation; its language is purged of evasiveness or of a desire to please or to challenge others. Rhetoric, in contrast, is advantage seeking; it is not only shaped by confrontation with others but misshaped by that antagonism. Yeats' observation is memorably terse but far from original. Rhetoric may have shaped the development of vernacular poetry, prose and drama in the Renaissance, but since the early nineteenth century, the renewal of literature has often been perceived as only becoming possible by breaking from rhetoric. Rhetoric is too combative; it inhibits self-exploration and self-expression.

It is also too prescriptive. In the last section I explored a different way of thinking about the relationship between rhetorical training and literary composition, noting that it is the exercise of arguing on different sides that informs the structural ambiguity of much Renaissance writing. Nonetheless, rhetoric is more usually understood as an art, a body of rules, and the categorical rejection of this as an approach to *creative* practice shapes modern literary history. The foundational moment in literary culture's revolt from rule-bound rhetoric can be located in William Wordsworth's *Preface* and the 'Appendix' to the 1802 edition of the *Lyrical Ballads*. Wordsworth's assault on poetic diction and all forms of artifice is an attempt to liberate the poetic from the dead hand of formal rhetoric. Wordsworth recognizes that the figures of speech were, in their origin, natural and vivid ways of conveying passion and emotion. However, he holds that the practice of imitation, the cornerstone of education in the liberal arts, soon led to these becoming merely conventional formulations. The figures were learned by rote and reproduced mechanically. This substituted for a direct confrontation with experience. This artificial language meant that poets ceased to rely on 'language which the Poet himself had uttered when he had been affected by the events which he described, or which he had heard uttered by those around him' (Wordsworth, 'Appendix' 1992: 89). In short, through the doctrine of imitation and through the cultivation of inherited figures of speech, rhetoric succeeded in separating the language of poetry from common life. It became an artificial system of representation, remote and unreal, demanding that the poet sacrifice his or her own sensibility and rendering him or her indifferent to 'the real language of men in *any situation*' (Wordsworth, 'Appendix' 1992: 88).

Wordsworth's epigraph to *The Ruined Cottage* perhaps sums up his attitude towards a culture still dominated by neoclassicism: 'Give me a spark of nature's fire / 'Tis the best learning I desire' (Wordsworth 1979: 42). The only hope for poetry, in his view, is to abandon rhetorical convention completely. Poets must reject the temptation to satisfy a conventional taste for refinement and return instead to the 'real language of men in a state of vivid sensation'. This 'real language' is to be found among the uneducated, within a rural life that Wordsworth saw as fast disappearing. He believes that the primary laws of nature are best identified in the speech of those who 'hourly communicate with the best objects from which the best part of language is originally derived'. 'Low and rustic life was generally chosen,' he explains, 'because in that condition the essential passions of the heart find a better soil in which they can attain their maturity, are less under restraint, and speak a plainer and more emphatic language' (Wordsworth, *Preface* 1992: 61, 60). Ordinary people using ordinary language do not conform to the conventions instilled by education: 'they convey their feelings and notions in simple and unelaborated expressions'. It was only by attending to language spoken simply and honestly without any attempt to persuade or manipulate that poetry could regain its power to move and to discover the permanent truths of our nature. In lives shaped by experience and unimproved by rhetorical training, the poet could observe common life in all its unadorned authenticity. This returned poetry to a more natural condition as 'the spontaneous overflow of powerful feelings', allowing poetic language 'to follow the fluxes and refluxes of the mind when agitated by the great and simple affections of our nature' (Wordsworth, *Preface* 1992: 61, 62, 63). What might poetry look like when it abandons rhetorical forms of expression? As Wordsworth sought to demonstrate in his *Lyrical Ballads*, it should be simple, expressive, and immediate:

> A slumber did my spirit seal;
> I had no human fears:
> She seemed a thing that could not feel
> The touch of earthly years.
> No motion has she now, no force;
> She neither hears nor sees,
> Rolled round in earth's diurnal course
> With rocks and stones and trees!

> (Wordsworth 1992: 246)

There is an additional aspect of Wordsworth's poetic practice which has been identified as a further solvent of the rhetorical tradition: the sublime. In *The Prelude*, the poet recounts his experience as a child when he clung to a cliff-face while trying to reach a raven's nest:

> Oh! When I have hung
> Above the raven's nest, by knots of grass
> And half-inch fissures in the slippery rock
> But ill sustained, and almost (so it seemed)
> Suspended by the blast that blew amain,
> Shouldering the naked crag, oh, at that time
> While on the perilous ridge I hung alone,
> With what strange utterance did the loud dry wind
> Blow through my ear! The sky seemed not a sky
> Of earth – and with what motion moved the clouds!

> (Wordsworth 1970: I. 341–50)

This is one of the recurrent limit experiences in the poem where language struggles to convey the awesome, disorientating force of the natural world. In this passage, nature seems both to sustain and threaten the poet, to speak to him, but in an inhuman language he cannot understand or convey. Unlike the language of men, the 'language' of nature is unfathomable, provoking wonder at its strangeness and power.

In the late twentieth century, this conception of the 'sublime' has been identified as a further example of the revolt against rhetoric. Language is not infinitely flexible and capable of observing, addressing and conceptualizing every situation. Some experiences defy any capacity to define them and this diminishes our faith in traditional resources and methods to categorize them or, rather, to make safe their 'otherness'. This is not necessarily a loss or an impoverishment. It can, as this astonishing extract from *The Prelude* demonstrates, release new forms of creativity, stretching language into new shapes and allowing it to cast off outworn conventions. Thus, in his essay 'The Sublime and the Avant-Garde' Jean-François Lyotard celebrates the 'sublime' as a counter to what he terms 'rhetorical didactics', and equates the decline of rhetorical practice and analysis with a consequent release of energy and creative freedom. This foregrounds a problem that the classical art of rhetoric cannot explain: that the classification and analysis of linguistic effects does not make language a tool of representation. Lyotard wants us to value work that 'dismantles' and 'deposes' consciousness, and which expresses or struggles to express 'what consciousness cannot formulate, and even what consciousness forgets in order to constitute itself' (Lyotard 1993a: 245). This approach contrasts a regimented neoclassicism with more experimental and 'modern' ways of thinking and working creatively:

> Between the seventeenth and eighteenth centuries in Europe this contradictory feeling – pleasure and pain, joy and anxiety, exaltation and depression – was christened or re-christened by the name of the *sublime*. It is around this name that the destiny of classical poetics was hazarded and lost; it is in this name that aesthetics asserted its critical rights over art, and that romanticism – in other words, modernity – triumphed.
>
> (246)

Paradoxically, Lyotard notes, the term 'sublime' derives from the attempt of a rhetorician to classify the inexpressible. The term is introduced, he notes, by 'one of the most dogged advocates of ancient classicism', a teacher of 'oratorical devices' whose essay 'On the Sublime', written in the first century AD, appeared in a French translation by Boileau in 1674 (247). 'Longinus', or whoever actually wrote this treatise, understands the sublime as 'a consummate excellence' (Longinus 1927: 1.3), an expression of genius rather than technical know-how. This mode expresses lofty emotion and nobleness of spirit, all of which are qualities that characterize the grand style. Longinus argues that the effect of the sublime is 'wonder' rather than conviction (1.4). Nonetheless, he still attempts to anatomize it by identifying the figures of speech that describe its effects and contribute to its production. Yet Longinus' analysis falters because 'the sublime, the indeterminate' destabilizes the 'didactic intention' of his essay (247). Indeed, the sublime resists straightforward exposition. It represents the 'unrepresentable' and the 'indeterminate'; it exists outside the linearity of traditional, rule-bound academic disciplines which are constrained by the logic that something must always follow: '"After" a sentence, "after" a colour, comes another sentence, another colour' (245). The temporal shift from rhetoric to the sublime supports a modern resistance to *technè* or skill. Artists are no longer regulated by the classical models of the academies or the tastes of their aristocratic audiences; they no longer need to focus on the mechanics of creation, but are free to reflect instead on a more profound question, 'What is it to experience an affect proper to art?' (249–50).

For Lyotard, the sublime bears witness to the inexpressible and the indeterminate. It confronts what defies reason and our expressive powers to master it, what no form of tradition prepares us for: 'The art object no longer bends itself to models, but tries to present the fact that there is an unpresentable' (252). Indeed, art gains rather than loses expressive power by its refusal to follow rules and its destabilizing of inherited ways of conceiving the world. Consequently, the sublime cannot be conveyed within a 'well-made' or perfected work; it is intensified within works which can be fragmentary or which lapse into silence. In contrast, 'figuration by means of images is a limiting constraint on the power of emotive expression, since it works by recognition' (251). The sublime engages with what a work refuses to mean and produces astonishment at a culture's model for understanding experience.

This is a persuasive argument in defence of creative and imaginative work unshackled from a prescriptive neoclassicism. Nonetheless, we might also ask: what has been lost with the demise of rhetoric? Disdain for 'rhetorical didactics' can diminish awareness of the choices we make, often semi-consciously, when we write or speak 'spontaneously', as well as the interests other speakers conceal, inadvertently or deliberately. Some of the contradictions that inform Wordsworth's rejection of rhetoric allow us to examine this. Although a detailed consideration of Wordsworth's Romantic ideology or its legacy is beyond the scope of this chapter, we can identify some of the key problems that pertain to the separation of the literary from the rhetorical especially as these have become important features of modern poetic composition and of postmodern aesthetics. Wordsworth had received a rhetorical education and although he disavows any attempt to address the reader by 'reasoning him into an approbation' of his *Lyrical Ballads*, his *Preface* is a forceful instance of anti-rhetorical rhetoric: we *are* being reasoned into an approbation. It might be added that Wordsworth's rejection of refinement and of educated tastes and experience is an enduring feature of the rhetorical tradition as it is embodied in georgic, the poetry of agricultural life; this had insistently valorized the plain style. Finally, Wordsworth's aim to observe the most potent and illuminating instances of common speech is entirely cognate with a central axiom of the rhetorical tradition: to learn from actual usages of speech in the world around one. Hence, the argument of his *Preface* – that it is only by attending to language spoken simply and honestly without any attempt to persuade or manipulate that we can renew poetry – begins to look like rather good 'rhetorical' advice. In essence, his revolt against rhetoric seems to involve and conceal some important rhetorical principles.

Wordsworth and Lyotard discard 'rhetorical didactics' in very different and equally illuminating ways. In response, I do not propose simply to embrace again what they reject, rhetoric as a body of rules, but rather to call attention to the subtle understanding of creative composition within this tradition. It is only fair to note that Lyotard had arrived at this conclusion well before me. For despite his dismissal of 'rhetorical didactics' in 'The Sublime and the Avant-Garde', he was happy to commend himself as a rhetorician in a different text, a conversation with Jean-Loup Thébaud in 1975, published in *Just Gaming* (*Au Juste*) in 1979. In this, Lyotard is responding to Thébaud's observations on the difficulty of his book-length study, *The Libidinal Economy* (1974), a passionate attempt to introduce desire into philosophical discourse. The 'few' readers of this book, Lyotard recognizes, 'generally accepted the product as a rhetorical exercise and gave no consideration to the upheaval it required of my soul' (cited in Lyotard 1993b: xx). In this conversation with Thébaud, he is given another opportunity to reflect on the 'rhetoric' of this text. The style and form of *The Libidinal Economy*, Thébaud notes, does 'not allow for any negotiating' (Lyotard and Thébaud 1985: 3). Lyotard admits that he did not intend in its writing to invite the kind of negotiation that Thébaud seems to expect; he was refusing to theorize or rationalize a position or argument that might constitute him as an authority. That is, he was deliberately rejecting the role of the 'classical' author who anticipates and clarifies the misunderstandings of his addressee. In the spirit of the avant-garde, he was experimenting to elicit new readers. This means that he did not adopt or assume received standards or criteria but attempted to invent them; this is the challenge of this passionate book to its readers. This sounds like the argument of 'The Sublime and the Avant-Garde', only this time Lyotard is describing himself as a rhetorician, and he claims the title in two respects. He is a rhetorician in the sense that he 'seeks to produce effects upon the other, effects that the other does not control' (4) but also, perhaps more importantly, because he engages in the ongoing creation of the 'rules' of debate. This is an unexpected change of position. In this conversation, 'rhetoricians' are recognized as:

> people for whom prescriptions are subject to discussion, not in the sense that the discussion will lead to the more just, but rather to the extent that a prescription cannot be founded.

(17)

The idea that rhetorical prescription cannot be founded is evident from the way in which the description of key tropes and figures changes over time: *licentia* means one thing in republican Rome and another in monarchical England. However, this insight, I want to emphasize, is also understood within the rhetorical tradition, and shapes very different advice on how to prepare for creative composition. I want to underscore the difference between rhetoric conceived as an 'art' and as a 'practice' by comparing Wordsworth's *Preface* to a treatise on poetry written some two hundred years earlier by a writer who had survived Tudor rhetorical training; this is Philip Sidney, and the treatise is his *A Defence of Poesy* (*c.* 1579). In contrast to Wordsworth, Sidney has a broader understanding of the rhetorical tradition, partly informed by his careful reading of Cicero's *On the ideal orator*. He understands that the rejection of 'rhetorical didactics' is integral to the art of persuasion anyway, and he shows us how important practise is to the composition of eloquent poetry. More importantly, this understanding shapes the critical content of his poetic treatise; in contrast to Wordsworth, it leads Sidney to the view that knowing the 'truth' of human 'nature' depends on understanding its conventionality

Initially it might seem as if Sidney has a common cause with Wordsworth. Like Wordsworth he insists that the poet should follow 'nature' rather than a set of rules or examples. Sidney complains, for example, of love poets who 'apply fiery speeches, as men that had rather read lovers' writings ... than that in truth they feel those passions' (Sidney 1989: 246). Like Wordsworth, too, he berates contemporaries who slavishly imitate the rules propounded in manuals or fill their 'paper-books' with collected 'figures and phrases' (246). He is attacking a faddish 'Ciceronianism', the attempt to reproduce exactly the style of Cicero, and which was supported by handbooks such as Marius Nizolius' popular *Thesaurus Ciceronianus* (1533). Such imitation leads to awkward and unpersuasive expression. For example, there are many poets who over-use the rhetorical 'figure of repetition' (*conduplicatio*), which is advocated by Cicero for the expression of anger 'when it were too too much choler to be choleric' (247). These poets fail to convince their readers that they are angry because they have misjudged the effect of the figure. They have followed the rules of rhetorical theory rather than the example offered by experience; the latter advice is closer to what Cicero intended.

Yet, there is an important difference between this and Wordsworth's rejection of rhetorical study. Sidney is not rejecting rhetoric, but exploiting the tension between rhetoric and eloquence to reflect critically on the writing of expressive poetry. In contrast to Wordsworth's *Preface*, Sidney's *Defence* is self-consciously rhetorical. The *Defence* is organized as a five-part oration (Myrick 1935: 46–83). Although we do not hear the other side of the debate, we do not really need to. Not only does Sidney rehearse it anyway, but his argument is intrinsically two-sided: the narrator of the *Defence* returns to arguments which have been confidently asserted only to qualify or cast doubt on them. In part he does this by drawing out the different senses of key terms and, in so doing, advances a more nuanced understanding of an argument, complicating his starting point. For instance, Sidney uses the term 'nature' to describe an original point or source, as in divine Nature or mother Nature, but significantly, also to connote a convention or custom, as in the case of this rather complicated example which we explored in Chapter 1, and to which I will return yet again: 'the courtier, following that which by practice he findeth fittest to nature, therein (though he know it not) doth according to art, though not by art' (247).

Sidney's attack on servile imitators appears in the part of the *Defence* often identified as the 'digression'. Usually an opportunity to entertain the audience, Sidney's digression offers instead a serious defence of a more sophisticated *rhetorical* approach to the composition of poetry, and this immediately complicates our understanding of natural expression. Sidney is not advising, for example, that only men or women who are head over heels in love can write decent love poetry. On the contrary, he believes that this passion 'may be bewrayed by the same forcibleness or *energia* (as the Greeks call it) of the writer' (246). Sidney is referring to *enargeia*, the rhetorical device described by Quintilian as '*illumination* and *actuality*', and which involves a vivid imagining of a scene or experience. Such imagining means that 'our emotions will be no less actively stirred than if we were present at the actual scene' (6.2.32).

Enargeia is, paradoxically, a rhetorical technique which enables a poet to experience the very emotions he wants to represent, and to do so sincerely. However, a poet can also achieve natural expression by a different route, just by imitating the right models. For Sidney, this means imitating the courtier rather than the scholar on the grounds that the former, 'following that which by practice he findeth fittest to nature, therein (though he know it not) doth according to art, though not by art' (247). This is a difficult sentence to unpack, but it connects with Sidney's understanding of the complex relationship between art and nature. Sidney is advising the poet to follow expression that has been copied from the everyday practice of the best poets and *practised*. This argument derives from Cicero's *On the ideal orator*, which berates the mechanical study of rhetoric, arguing instead that the orator should learn from 'practice': that is, the study of everyday linguistic usage but also exercise in writing, reading and, most importantly, debate and conversation with friends. In the *Defence* Sidney is not rejecting rhetorical tradition, but rather engaging more confidently with it; he is encouraging his compatriots to renounce their habits of mechanical imitation since these leave vernacular poetry underdeveloped, a poor copy of venerated classical models. He wants his fellow poets to follow the example of the ancients, not their writings exactly, but the 'practice' which enabled them to internalize linguistic strategies so that they became 'second nature'.

Sidney *is* offering practical advice on how to write better poetry, though the *Defence* is not a manual, a 'how-to' book. The sentence I have just quoted, which advises the poet to follow what is 'fittest to nature', is curiously artful; it calls attention to itself and so halts the reader, prompting her to pause for reflection. As I noted in Chapter 1, the repetition of the word 'art' at the end of each clause is an example of the figure *epistrophe*. The sentence also presents a paradox: how can you do something by art, but not by art, at the same time? This narrator's artfulness perhaps implies the kind of tricky sophistry we can expect of a 'courtier', a view encouraged by Sidney's recollection in the lines immediately preceding of the advice offered by the two famous speakers in Cicero's *On the ideal orator*, Antonius and Crassus:

> the great forefathers of Cicero in eloquence, the one (as Cicero tes-tifieth of them) pretended not to know art, the other not to set by it, because with a plain sensibleness they might win credit of popular ears (which credit is the nearest step to persuasion, which persuasion is the chief mark of oratory).

(247)

Yet, the artfulness of this sentence in conjunction with the allusion to Cicero's two speakers is particularly suggestive; it draws attention to, and advances our understanding of, the complex relationship between art and nature that he is exploring. Cicero's *On the ideal orator* is not advising orators to deceive their audiences exactly. This dialogue is unique among the Roman rhetorical manuals in refusing to divulge straightforwardly the rules of this art because, as Crassus and Antonius argue, their careful study does not make us *eloquent*.

This is not so different to Wordsworth's invitation to the poet to imitate the speech of uneducated people, though we might note that in his *Preface* the social status of the model has shifted, from courtier to rustic labourer. And yet, because Sidney has a more nuanced understanding of the relationship between art and nature, he is also able to reflect more probingly than Wordsworth on the conventionality of social status. That is, his flexible sense of the congruence between art and nature affects how we under-stand the relationship between 'nature' and 'custom'. Sidney's insistence that the ear is the 'fit and natural place' for earrings is, in the context of this debate, calculatedly absurd. What we assume to be natural expression turns out to be artful and prac-tised. By the same token, what we assume constitutes a natural condition, for example, that the best poets are aristocrats since they display 'many things tasting of a noble birth, and worthy of a noble mind' (242), turns out, on closer inspection, to be an assumption that is open to challenge or modification. In fact, you do not need to be either passionately in love or nobly born to write good poetry. The *Defence* offers a plea to scholars for the development of a national poetry with a proper understanding of a rhetorical culture of debate and conversation, at the same time that it holds out to them the promise of fulfilling their social aspirations. Sidney is giving away one of Nature's secrets. If Sidney had had the opportunity to read Wordsworth's *Preface*, I think it highly likely he would have thought of him as akin to the ironic speakers of Cicero's *On the ideal orator*, or the courtier-poet admired in his own *Defence*, all of whom are expert at hiding their art.

3

FROM RHETORIC TO
RHETORICALITY

The concern of this chapter is with the revival of rhetoric in the
twentieth century. By 'revival' I do not mean to suggest that this
involves a second Renaissance. Training in the classical system,
or some version of it, was central to school and university curricula in the West for hundreds of years, at least until the mid-
nineteenth century. The only students likely to receive an introduction to this scheme now are those attending classes in Classical studies and, in North America, classes in Rhetoric and
Composition. Engagement with the classical art continues to
play an important role in its teaching in many institutions.
Thus, Edward P.J. Corbett's *Classical Rhetoric for the Modern Student*, first published in 1965, and reissued in 1971, 1990 and
1999, repackages Aristotle's rhetoric for those engaged in the
composition of academic writing as well as those who just want
to improve their communication skills. Corbett defends the
'complicated, formalized system' that has come down to us
because he recognizes rhetoric as 'an inescapable activity in our
lives'. 'Every day', he notes, 'we either use rhetoric or are exposed

to it. Everyone living in community with other people is inevitably a rhetorician. A parent constantly uses rhetoric on a child; a teacher, on his or her students; a salesperson, on customers; a supervisor, on workers' (Corbett 1990: 29). Knowledge of the classical system equips 'us to respond critically to the rhetorical efforts of others in both the oral and written forms'; it will also make us more persuasive in turn (30). However, while the evident popularity of this book suggests that its practical digestion of the classical system still has a significant role to play in the modern academy, at least in the USA, Rhetoric and Composition struggles for disciplinary recognition in some quarters. As Jasper Neel observes wryly, Rhetoric and Composition is 'low-class grunt work' within departments of English Literature; it represents the kind of work that the true literary scholar does not do (Neel 1995: 62, 75).

The decline of formal rhetoric as a key discipline seems irrevocable. There are several reasons for this, some of which we considered in the previous chapter: the complexity of the system; the veneration of imaginative work unshackled from the constraints of formalist training; and distrust of the orator's emotive manipulation of linguistic effects. A further reason for its dramatic decline is that since the beginning of the twentieth century, the art of rhetoric has also been studied as a theory of language, and in this respect it has been found wanting. The traditional account of rhetoric as an art of persuasion, its critics complain, does not tell us how language works. Given such disillusionment we may well wonder how rhetoric could be revived. This chapter explores several different ways in which this did happen, starting with I.A. Richards' attempt in the 1930s to renew rhetoric by providing a more accurate 'theory' of one trope, metaphor; it then explores the fate of rhetoric in the 1960s, when linguistics promised to provide a more scientific theory of language. In the 1960s, Roland Barthes argued that rhetoric was only an object of critical and historical interest; just a few years later, though, rhetoric was revived again as the attempt to establish a science of language foundered. Paradoxically, it was valued again, however, because it failed as a theory of language. With this revival it also received its most far-reaching redefinition. Rhetoric was no longer regarded as a resource, which could be called upon by the skilled speaker or writer to affect others. On the contrary, it was understood that language is so profoundly and pervasively figurative that the tropes and figures cannot be rationalized and controlled at all: that is, rhetoric could not be reduced to an 'art'. A new term, 'rhetoricality', has been coined to describe this extension of rhetoric (Bender and Wellbery 1990: 25).

Critics and historians of rhetoric are divided in their response to these developments, but one thing is certain: the call for a return to *classical* rhetoric is unpersuasive, even impossible, once our confidence in linguistic possession is exposed as a problem. Nonetheless, we should not be overly preoccupied with the figurative description of language at the expense of recalling the critical possibilities offered by rhetoric conceived as argument on opposite sides. In my final section, I will consider why rhetoric will not go away, and I will explore the attempt of one thinker, Kenneth Burke, to extend its traditional conception, moreover, to include undeliberate acts of persuasion. Burke was writing in the 1940s and 1950s, but his work on rhetoric underwent a revival at the end of the last century as critical thinkers sought to adapt the new emphasis on the rhetoricality of language in order not to lose the possibility imagined in classical rhetoric of speaking from a position of opposition, a position of difference.

I.A. RICHARDS: THE ART RENEWED

One of the earliest philosophers of language to test rhetoric as a theory of language was I.A. Richards, a founder of 'Practical Criticism' in the 1920s and early 1930s and the author of a ground-breaking series of lectures at Bryn Mawr College, later published as *Philosophy of Rhetoric* (1936). In these lectures Richards renews an art that has become 'the dreariest and least profitable part of the waste that the unfortunate travel through in Freshman English!', and he does so, he explains, in order to support 'a study of misunderstanding and its remedies' (Richards 1936: 3). One reason for the dreariness of this subject, according to Richards, is that its theorists have mistaken the 'art' of persuasion for a 'science' of language. Richards illustrates this problem by deferring to the somewhat obscure figure of Archbishop Whately (1787–1863), 'who wrote a treatise on Rhetoric for the *Encyclopædia Metropolitana*' planned by Samuel Taylor Coleridge (5–6). In his treatise, Richards notes, Whately argues that the study of rhetoric 'must go deep, must take a broad philosophical view of the principles of the Art' (cited in Richards 1936: 7). Yet, nothing like this is ever attempted by Whately. Instead of the promised philosophical view he offers:

> a very ably arranged and discussed collection of prudential Rules about the best sorts of things to say in various argumentative situations, the order in which to bring out your propositions and proofs and examples, at what point it will be most effective to disparage your opponent, how to recommend oneself to the audience, and like matters.
>
> (7)

That is, he offers his readers 'the usual postcard's-worth of crude common sense' that has been typical of the handbook tradition since the eighteenth century:

> be clear, but don't be dry; be vivacious, use metaphors when they will be understood not otherwise, respect usage; don't be long-winded, on the other hand don't be gaspy; avoid ambiguity; prefer the energetic to the elegant; preserve unity and coherence.
>
> (8)

No-one is going to learn anything from this text that they did not already know, Richards complains.

It is, of course, a little unfair to single out Whately, as Richards recognizes. Really, the problem begins more than a thousand years earlier, with the formation of the 'art' of rhetoric. Or, as Richards suggests, Whately's misconception of 'rhetoric' begins with Aristotle's failure to recognize the deeply ambiguous character of language, and more specifically, to understand the nature of metaphor itself and its omnipresence in language. Aristotle argued that 'metaphor is something special and exceptional in the use of language', and that having a command of it requires an eye for resemblances. The result is that throughout its history:

> metaphor has been treated as a sort of happy extra trick with words, an opportunity to exploit the accidents of their versatility, something in place occasionally but requiring unusual skill and caution. In brief, a grace or ornament or *added* power of language, not its constitutive form.
>
> (90)

The influence of this idea is apparent from Quintilian to Adam Smith, as we have seen. The problem is compounded by the definition of metaphor that this emphasis supports: a comparison between two things which involves the substitution or transference of a word from one context to another. Though Richards does not dispute this definition, he views it as too narrow. Traditional rhetoric 'noticed only a few of the modes of metaphor', and it is overly preoccupied with metaphor as 'verbal matter'. In fact, he argues, metaphor is 'fundamentally':

> a borrowing between and intercourse of *thoughts*, a transaction between contexts. *Thought* is metaphoric, and proceeds by comparison, and the metaphors of language derive there-from. To improve the theory of metaphor we must remember this. And the method is to take more note of the skill in thought which we possess and are intermittently aware of already. We must translate more of our skill into discussable science. Reflect better upon what we do already so cleverly. Raise our implicit recognitions into explicit distinctions.
>
> (94–95)

As this quotation suggests, Richards is not only extending our understanding of metaphor, he is also redesigning the 'art' of rhetoric as a 'philosophy' of language. On the face of it, what he is proposing to do, perhaps, recalls the methods by which rhetoric is already constituted as an art; the rules for composition that we find in traditional handbooks are merely observations of what works persuasively 'everyday'. Only the focus of Richards' analysis is not 'verbal matter', but our thought processes. When we ask about how language works, he suggests, we are really asking 'about how thought and feeling and all the other modes of the mind's activity proceed' (95), only we do not have a method of analysis that allows us to address this. Richards' proposed method of rhetorical analysis focuses on a single trope, metaphor. To refine our understanding of it he introduces two new technical terms: 'tenor', which refers to the 'underlying idea or principal subject' of a metaphor, and the 'vehicle', for what the 'figure means' (96–97). This is not to reintroduce the idea that a figure decorates content, that the vehicle adorns 'the plain meaning, the tenor', which 'alone really matters'. On the contrary, as Richards argues, meaning is derived from the 'co-presence of the vehicle and the tenor'; the two constitutive parts of a metaphor are essential. Moreover, he explains, a 'modern theory would go on to point out that with different metaphors the relative importance of the contributions of vehicle and tenor to this resultant meaning varies immensely' (100). This approach allows Richards to challenge some of the assumptions that emerged out of the eighteenth-century renewal of rhetoric, namely the view that metaphors should be used sparingly and that there should be a proper resemblance between the objects being compared. The latter assumption is challenged by Richards in a reading of the following line from *Othello*, which is cited by Henry Home, Lord Kames in his *Elements of Criticism* (1762):

> Steep'd me in poverty to the very lips.

> (104)

About this line, Lord Kames has nothing positive to say. The combination of ideas does not make any sense. 'The resemblance is too faint to be agreeable', Kames argues; 'Poverty must be conceived to be a fluid which it resembles not in any manner.' And yet, argues Richards, if we look at the speech from which this line is taken, '[w]e shall find that it is not an easy matter to explain or justify that "steep'd"'. The line comes from a speech in which the tormented Othello confronts Desdemona for the first time:

> Had it pleas'd heaven
> To try me with affliction, had he rain'd

All kinds of sores, and shames, on my bare head,
Steep'd me in poverty to the very lips,
Given to captivity me and my utmost hopes,
I should have found in some part of my soul
A drop of patience; but alas! to make me
The fixed figure for the time of scorn
To point his slow and moving finger at;
Yet could I bear that too; well, very well.
But there, where I have garner'd up my heart,
Where either I must live or bear no life,
The fountain from the which my current runs,
Or else dries up; to be discarded thence!
Or keep it as a cistern for foul toads
To knot and gender in!

(cited in Richards 1936: 104–5)

It is not that there is too little resemblance, Richards argues. In fact, there is none at all: the tenor of this metaphor, 'Poverty', constitutes 'a state of deprivation, of desiccation; but the vehicle – the sea or vat in which Othello is to be steeped – gives an instance of superfluity'. The speech is full of such 'liquid images', though none of them 'helps *steep* out'; indeed, 'one of them, "a drop of patience" makes the confused, disordered effect of *steep* seem much worse'. And yet, despite these problems, the mismatch between tenor and vehicle works dramatically very well, if only to give expression to the disorderliness of Othello's mind. Othello has been persuaded by a mere image of Desdemona committing adultery. He '*is* obsessed with images regardless of their fittingness' (105–6).

I pause over Richards in this introductory section not just because he offers a distinctive challenge to how the 'art' of rhetoric is formulated as a method of analysis, but also because he was the end-point of my predecessor's comprehensive volume on *Rhetoric* in the first Critical Idiom series. Peter Dixon was concerned with rhetoric as a technical art, and in his book he explained the nuts and bolts of the classical system and traced its subsequent history, from the Renaissance to the Enlightenment. Richards provided a fitting conclusion to this narrative because his lectures offered one of the more probing challenges to traditional rhetoric at the time of Dixon's writing. In particular, Dixon commended Richards' attempt to over-rule the combative nature of the 'old rhetoric', and to reformulate its theory of figurative language so as to support 'a study of misunderstanding and its remedies' (Richards 1936: 3). Richards is valued because he aimed to *clarify* ambiguity. Nonetheless, the renewal of rhetoric that Richards sought in 1936, and which Dixon commended in 1971, has not really been fulfilled. Richards has been superseded by other theorists of language in the late twentieth century. Indeed, had Dixon written his book just a few years later it might have ended rather differently, by including within its survey the yet more probing contributions of the post-structuralist Paul de Man (1919–83), among others. Richards' argument that metaphor is the constitutive principle of language proved prescient; this also defines the post-structuralist return to rhetoric in the late twentieth century among Francophone writers. Only, this later interest in metaphor takes a different turn. The omnipresence of tropes such as metaphor, it is argued in this tradition, complicates our attempts to communicate, to control meaning and, indeed, to persuade. In contrast to Richards, de Man is not attempting to renew the art of rhetoric in order to support 'a study of misunderstanding and its remedies' (3). De Man certainly knew Richards' work, and he is responding, in part, to American 'Practical Criticism', but his return to rhetoric is more obviously a response to the attempt of his structuralist predecessors such as Roland Barthes who relegated the 'old rhetoric' to history, thinking to replace it with a yet more systematic study of how language works, one that is born out of the new science of linguistics.

THE DEATH OF RHETORIC

Rhetoric and linguistics represent two contrary ways of thinking about and analysing language. Traditionally, rhetoric is concerned with the affective power of language, and with describing and classifying the devices that produce emotion, or develop a logical proof, and so sway the judgement of an audience. Central to this is the conception of the orator as an individual skilled in the 'art' of persuasion, as someone who can deploy, at will, a range of devices. The theory of language developed by the Swiss founder of modern structural linguistics, Ferdinand de Saussure (1857–1913) revolutionized linguistic and literary study. This was outlined in lectures he delivered at the University of Geneva between 1906 and 1911, and which were later published post-humously as the *Course in General Linguistics* (1916). In these Saussure described language as a system of conventional signs, 'conventional' in the sense that they relate to their signifiers 'by convention'. Meaning or signification was recognized as depending, in the first place, on phonic difference. There is no natural relation between a sign, a word, and its signified. Rather, the meaning of a sign is recognized primarily by its difference from another sign: a sign and signifier coexist by convention to produce a meaning ('cat'), and do so by virtue of their 'difference' from other combinations ('bat'). In short, the relationship of the 'sign' to a signifier is arbitrary; there can be no appeal to some notion of the 'real' to explain differences. But signs are also related to one another, linked in a chain which can be either 'linear' or *syntagmatic*, 'composed of two or more consecutive units (e.g. French *re-lire* "re-read," *contre tous* "against everyone" . . .)', or *associative*, connected by association in our memory: for example, 'the French word *enseignement* "teaching" will unconsciously call to mind a host of other words (*enseigner* "teach," *reseigner* "acquaint," etc.)' (Saussure 1966: 123). This theory broke new ground by asserting that language is not primarily concerned with refer-entiality, that it does not correspond with the real world, and moreover, that it functions as a self-determining and self-contained system. Meaning is not inherent in words, Saussure insisted, but rather is constituted by systematic patterns of similarity and difference.

The negative impact of this theory on the study of rhetoric is not hard to guess. Saussure's linguistic theory presents an alternative way of seeing language, one which has little place for the resource-fulness of the trained orator. However, the main problem for historians of rhetoric is not the theory itself, but the way in which it has been used to appropriate a reduced rhetorical terminology.

The main offender in this respect is the Russian formalist Roman Jakobson (1896–1982). In his study of the linguistic disorder *aphasia*, written in 1956, he distinguished between two kinds of aphasiac, those with 'similarity disorder' and those with 'contiguity disorder'. To explain this, he appropriated two key tropes, metonymy and metaphor, although redefining them in terms of Saussure's distinction between the *syntagmatic* and *associative* relations. He understood the speech of aphasiacs experiencing 'contiguity disorder', for instance, as metonymic: '*Fork* is substituted for *knife*, *table* for *lamp*, *smoke* for *pipe*, *eat* for *toaster*', While the speech of those suffering from 'similarity disorder' was understood metaphorically, as depending on associational substitutions: '*Spyglass* for *microscope*, or *fire* for *gaslight*' (Jakobson 1956: 69, 72). There are different objections that can be made to this from the viewpoint of standard rhetoric. Are Jakobson's examples of contiguous substitutions, for example, really metonyms? The key objection raised, however, is that his pilfering of a rhetorical vocabulary is reductive in the extreme (Vickers 1988: 442–45).

Nonetheless, even as theorists of language and literature turned away from rhetoric as a practical theory of how language works, preoccupation with it continued, although in perhaps unexpected ways. A less well recognized outcome of the linguistic turn has been the attempt to defend a need for a fuller understanding of the rhetorical system, although the aim is not to revive it but to avoid reproducing its errors.

We can find the first defence of this in the work of the French structuralist Gérard Genette, in particular his key essay 'Rhetoric Restrained' ('La Rhétorique restreinte') (1970). This essay explores the history of the diminution of rhetoric and its modern culmination, represented, for Genette, by the Belgian Liège group, whose representatives include Michel Deguy and Jacques Sojcher, and who published a *General Rhetoric* (*Rhétorique générale*) in 1969. However, there is nothing 'general' about their rhetoric, Genette complains. Aristotle's *Rhetoric* is a 'general' rhetoric. In this manual the figures do not 'merit any particular attention'; they constitute an 'out-of-the-way region, lost in the immensity of an Empire'. 'Nowadays', however, 'we call general rhetoric what is in fact a treatise on figures', as the example of the Liège school suggests (Genette 1982 [1970]: 103–4). There is a need to 'fill out and correct this more than cavalier approach', Genette argues, though his own essay does not constitute a 'historical investigation' as such (104). It offers the beginning of such an investigation, enabling us to understand how the linguistic return to rhetoric entails the establishing of the 'absolute, undivided rule of metaphor' (117), and also what this means.

Genette argues that Deguy and Sojcher represent the culmination of a long tradition of decline which began in the Middle Ages, when rhetoric was 'crushed between grammar and dialectic' in the *trivium*, and gathered momentum in the eighteenth century, when 'pride of place' was given to literary authors, and attention turned to figurative expression: 'Homer and Vergil (and soon Racine) supplanted Demosthenes and Cicero' (104). The trajectory of this modern reduction of rhetoric is described by Genette as having three distinct phases: it begins with César Dumarsais' conflation of metonymy and synecdoche as figures of 'relation' or 'connection' in his *Des Tropes* (1730); it proceeds, one hundred years later (1818), with Pierre Fontanier, who restores the difference between synecdoche and metonymy, retains metaphor but excludes the trope irony. '[A]ll that was needed now', Genette notes, was the merging of these two theories to leave us with the 'irreplaceable bookends of our own modern rhetoric: metaphor and metonymy'. This reduction came via Russian formalism, with Jakobson's pairing and opposition of metaphor and metonymy, and their 'overly bold assimilation' to the linguistic oppositions of Saussure (106–7). The 'one last reductionist movement', however, comes courtesy of the Liège group: in their texts, metaphor absorbs 'its ultimate antagonist', metonymy, to become the '"trope of tropes" (Sojcher), "the figure of figures" (Deguy), the kernel, the heart, and ultimately the essence and almost the whole of rhetoric' (113).

Genette has a very good understanding of what has been lost with this reduction. He understands that the rise of metonymy and metaphor, and the subsequent, exclusive rule of metaphor, 'frozen in its useless royalty' (115), entails the occlusion of a diverse range of tropes and figures associated with contiguity on the one hand and analogy on the other. However, Genette is not proposing that critics return to a more general rhetoric. Such a return, he argues elsewhere, would be a 'sterile anachronism' (Genette 1982 [1966]: 58). Rather, his self-confessedly limited 'historical investigation' aims to bring to light the *centrocentrism* of the process of reduction that he is describing. 'Central', he notes:

> is the result of a deliberate movement of valorization, which recalls irresistibly Gaston Bachelard's remark on Buffon's animal hierarchies: 'The lion is king of the animals because it suits an advocate of order that all creatures, even animals, should have a king.' Similarly, no doubt, metaphor is 'the central figure of all rhetoric' because it suits the mind, in its weakness, that all things, even figures, should have a center.
>
> (Genette 1982 [1970]: 114)

The 'profound desire' within contemporary poetics to 'establish the absolute, undivided rule of metaphor' (117), involves the 'valorization of the analogical' (119), which is also a mode of thinking, or rather, the unthinking discovery of similarity when we are confronted with dissimilar things. For Genette, an example of this is the 'spontaneous belief in the resemblance of words and things'. As he concludes, a 'rational semiotics', a more scientific rather than poetic study of language and signification, 'must be constituted in reaction against this primary illusion' (120).

'What is needed', Genette writes in the opening paragraphs of 'Rhetoric Restrained', 'is an immense historical investigation'. This is 'well beyond' his 'competence', he adds, but a 'sketch' of this has already been provided by Roland Barthes (104). In 'The Old Rhetoric: an aide-mémoire,' Barthes composed a 'history' of rhetoric at a transitional moment in the science of language. In the first half of the essay, titled 'The Journey', Barthes offers a chronological overview of rhetoric, from its birth in antiquity to its 'rebirth' in Renaissance France and, finally, to its decline in modernity. In the second half, he provides a careful and well-informed overview of rhetoric as a system or 'Network'. In both of these respects, Barthes seems to offer a rather conventional contribution to the field of rhetorical studies, one which easily rivals surveys offered by this art's traditional historians and analysts. However, he also departs from standard treatments of this subject. 'The Old Rhetoric' is a rhetorical manual which is sensitive to the 'internal variations' of the system it details (Barthes 1988: 15), and yet does not attempt to teach its reader how to be persuasive. His aim, Barthes explains, is to 'confront the new semiotics', the new scientific study of language and signification, with the system that preceded it (11), but also to mark the departure, finally, of the 'old' rhetoric, the system that 'has taken three centuries to die, and [which] is not dead for sure even now' (15). That is, Barthes intends to reduce rhetoric to 'a merely historicized object' (93).

Barthes is offering a distinctive defence of rhetoric. For someone who is not interested in rhetoric as a *living* system, it is curious that he gives rhetoric so much attention, that he takes the time to write a manual which, he admits, 'I should have liked to find ready-made when I began to inquire into the death of Rhetoric' (11). This 'manual' does not offer a nostalgic return to a forgotten discipline, despite Barthes' admission that he has 'often been moved to admiration and excitement by the power and subtlety of that old rhetorical system, and the modernity of certain of its propositions' (12), and his recognition that rhetoric 'has been the only practice (with grammar, born subsequently) through which our society has recognized language's sovereignty' (15). Indeed, Barthes insists on the importance of knowing 'thoroughly . . . the rhetorical code which has given its language to our culture' (92), but only so that we understand why it has 'died', so as to establish, to borrow his metaphor, a less imperialistic system. At the heart of this essay is Barthes' articulation of a distinctive critical purpose, to recognize rhetoric as a 'glamorous object of intelligence and penetration, [a] grandiose system which a whole civilization, in its extreme breadth, perfected in order to classify'. He conceives rhetoric anew, as 'an ideological object, falling into ideology at the advance of that "other thing" which has replaced it, and today compelling us to take an indispensable critical distance' (47). The advance of a new science of language, yet to be fully defined, has made it both possible and imperative to study rhetoric as ideology: a 'science' of literary language which has endowed the ruling elite with power, but which has also behaved like an imperial force, colonizing academic curricula and repressing the possibility of other kinds of linguistic study.

How does Barthes achieve 'critical distance' from this vast 'rhetorical empire', a system of language that has been all-encompassing for centuries, and whose rule has been 'greater and more tenacious than any political empire in its dimensions and its duration' (14)? Barthes works with the system, painstakingly exploring its complex self-definition, but always with a view to highlighting its possessive origins, its servicing of power. Rhetoric is a technique, a science, an ethic and a social practice, he explains. It is an 'ethic' in the sense that its role is 'to supervise (*i.e.* to permit and to limit) the "deviations" of emotive language', and it is a social practice in the sense of being a 'privileged technique', one which 'permits the ruling classes to gain *ownership of speech*' (13–14). This emphasis informs Barthes' telling of the story of the origins of rhetoric as a self-conscious practice. As I have already noted, the rhetorical tradition is believed to have originated as a self-conscious practice in Sicily in the fifth century BC, after the overthrow of the tyrant Thrasybulus. In standard histories this is understood as the proto-democratic origins of the art; in Barthes' retelling, in contrast, the focus is very much on the link between the inception of this system and the first attempts to defend the ownership of property. Rhetoric begins 'not from a subtle ideological mediation,' he remarks, 'but from the baldest sociality, affirmed in its fundamental brutality, that of earthly possession: we began to reflect upon language in order to defend our own' (17).

Barthes also achieves 'critical distance', though, by exploring rhetoric in terms of what he calls 'the play of the system', that is, 'the structural interplay' between rhetoric and 'its neighbours (Grammar, Logic, Poetics, Philosophy)' (46). He is interested in how rhetoric came to dominate the other arts. Genette tells the story of rhetoric's gradual diminution; Barthes, in contrast, tells a story of intellectual colonization. By the second century AD, he remarks, rhetoric 'encompasses everything' and is well on its way to becoming a 'national education' (28). From the early Middle Ages, rhetoric is rivalled by grammar and rhetoric; it remains a downtrodden art. It is in the Renaissance, however, that rhetoric comes to dominate the curriculum. In the universities of seventeenth-century France, the:

> only academic prizes are the prizes for Rhetoric, for translation, and for memory, but the prize for Rhetoric, awarded at the conclusion of a special contest, designates the first pupil, who is henceforth called (and the titles are significant) *imperator* or *tribune*.
>
> (44)

Other theories of language are lost upon the way. In the early sixteenth century, the Dutch humanist Desiderius Erasmus dismissed as barbarians the Modistae, a group of grammarians mainly from Scandinavia; these are the forebears of modern structuralists because they understood that language begins, not with the 'word-sign', but with 'relation, at the inter-sign', and privileged syntax and 'structuration' (37–38).

This represents a significant critical engagement with rhetoric. Many of Barthes' insights are applied, independently, in studies of Renaissance rhetoric (Parker 1987). This is important remedial work; it challenges critical discussions of rhetoric that are perhaps too easily persuaded by the 'rhetoric' of the handbooks, with their promise of the civilizing power of eloquence. Nonetheless, as I have also suggested in Chapter 2, with this approach we easily lose sight of the way in which 'rhetoric' might facilitate 'critical distance', an understanding not just of the 'how-to' persuade others to serve our interests, but also of the 'how-to' resist being persuaded. This oversight is especially apparent in Barthes' essay. In 'The Old Rhetoric', Barthes is remembering and resisting an oppressive system, and he does so in order to ensure that the linguistic theory that replaces it, 'the text which does not yet exist', does not reproduce its strategies of domination. But he is only interested in rhetoric as a *system*, and the emphases he privileges in his retelling of its history are unremarkable. All rhetoric, he argues, is fundamentally Aristotelian; 'all the didactic elements which feed the classical manuals come from Aristotle' (20). Aristotle independently theorized rhetoric for himself, and this is later 'practiced by Cicero', and 'taught by Quintilian' (21). Cicero in particular is treated dismissively by Barthes. Of the several manuals he wrote, according to Barthes, the best is 'the driest and least ethical', the *Partitiones*, because it is the most systematic: 'it is a complete elementary rhetoric, a kind of cate-chism which has the advantage of giving the entire scope of rhetorical classification'. The least successful is *On the ideal orator*, in which Cicero 'moralizes rhetoric' and turns 'against speciali-zation'. In general, Cicero displays a 'fear of "system"', the de-intellectualization or 'destructuring' of Aristotle which was to reach its apex in the second century AD with St Augustine's *On Christian doctrine* (*De doctrina Christiana*), which insists that the Christian 'need only be clear' (23–24).

However, as I noted in Chapters 1 and 2, the recognition that rhetoric exceeds its rationalization as 'system' already informs classical and Renaissance rhetorical theory, while the process of arguing on different sides underpinned critical reflection in quite profound ways, contesting the tendency to domination that Barthes perceives as an inevitable aspect of this tradition. Recognition of this double potential of rhetoric, as a tool of power and a critical method, must inform any attempt to renew it. However, before we consider an example of such an attempt at the end of this chapter, in the work of Kenneth Burke, I want to consider whether 'the text which does not yet exist' did in fact come into being. Barthes was teaching and writing about rheto-ric in the mid-1960s at the height of 'structuralism', with its imperative to develop systems for the analysis of cultural 'signs'. All of this, though, was about to change.

POST-STRUCTURALIST RHETORIC

Roland Barthes predicted that there could be no return to rhetoric, to the art or 'science' of language which had endowed the ruling elite with power. Consequently, the only future for rhetoric was to be as a subject of historical interest. This is because the linguistic theory of Ferdinand de Saussure had paved the way for a different science of language, and a 'new semiotics of writing'. Barthes is aware of being 'on the horizon' of something new, of the 'modern text, i.e., the text which does not yet exist' (Barthes 1988: 11). Nonetheless, despite this confidence, rhetoric was returning even as Barthes was writing 'The Old Rhetoric: an aide-mémoire'. It returned just as the linguistic certainties of Saussure gave way to a different conception of language as unstable, and of meaning as something always deferred. Structuralism was succeeded by post-structuralism, by the linguistic play of Paul de Man, and of course of Barthes himself.

The distinction between the 'structuralist' phase of critical thought, dedicated to the study of linguistic and literary *systems*, and its successor, 'post-structuralism', is usually conceived in linguistic terms. For Saussure, as we have noted, the relationship between a 'sign' and what it 'signifies' is arbitrary. A sign and signifier coexist by convention to produce a meaning ('cat'), and do so by virtue of their 'difference' from other combinations ('bat'). Post-structuralism, writes Terry Eagleton, took this insight one step further, dividing the sign from the signifier, and recognizing a plurality of meanings: '"Cat" may mean a furry four-legged creature, a malicious person, a knotted whip, an American, a horizontal beam for raising a ship's anchor, a six-legged tripod, a short tapered stick, and so on' (Eagleton 1983: 128–29). For Eagleton, Barthes is one of the key contributors to this shift. In an essay published in 1966, *Critique et vérité*, Barthes describes 'critical discourse ... as a "second language" which "floats above the primary language of the work"'. However, as Eagleton notes, the 'same essay' also 'begins to characterize literary language itself in what are now recognizably post-structuralist terms: it is a language "without bottom", something like a "pure ambiguity" supported by an "empty meaning"' (137).

This contrast represents a familiar and concise way of explaining this critical shift in the 1970s. However, this same shift, from structuralism to post-structuralism, can also be elaborated rhetorically. Post-structuralists are not interested in replacing an outdated and oppressive system with a more 'scientific' conception of language as a signifying practice, and thereby reducing rhetoric to an 'ideological object' (Barthes 1988: 47). Rather, they contribute to a new recognition of the instability of language, which 'penetrates to the deepest levels of human experience' (Bender and Wellbery 1990: 25). Rhetoric, in a broad sense, is both the beginning of this problem and a means to focus attention on it. For example, in the 1970s, Paul de Man invited students of language and literature to develop a greater understanding of how the rhetorical dimension of language interrupts the cognitive functions of grammar (de Man 1982). To put this another way, he draws attention to the value of rhetoric as a metalanguage which takes as its object the epistemological instability of language. Tropes and figures are not within our control; rather, they are constitutive of language, and they interrupt our attempts to communicate clearly. The omnipresence of the tropes, on this view, makes achieving 'critical distance' difficult (Barthes 1988: 47). Quite simply, rhetoric will not stay in place as an 'ideological object'; it cannot be rationalized. This is quite a revival. A new term has been coined retrospectively to represent both this instability and shift in critical emphasis, 'rhetoricality'. As Steven Bender and David E. Wellbery explain:

> The classical rhetorical tradition rarified speech and fixed it within a gridwork of limitations: it was a rule-governed domain whose procedures themselves were delimited by the institutions that organized interaction and domination in traditional European society. Rhetoricality, by contrast, is bound to no specific set of institutions. It manifests the groundless, infinitely ramifying character of discourse in the modern world. For this reason, it allows for no explanatory metadiscourse that is not already itself rhetorical. Rhetoric is no longer the title of a doctrine and a practice, nor a form of cultural memory; it becomes instead something like the condition of our existence.
>
> (Bender and Wellbery 1990: 25)

This new term 'rhetoricality' is difficult to grasp because, as Bender and Wellbery recognize, it has no 'explanatory metadiscourse'; one cannot position oneself outside this conception of rhetoric to rationalize its rules. However, we can come closer to understanding this conception and its implications for a practice of rhetorical analysis that does not allow the critic or commentator to step outside or transcend linguistic uncertainty by engaging with its formulation in the early work of Friedrich Nietzsche (1844–1900), the 'paradigmatic philosopher of modernity and postmodernity' and the figure whose rereading in the twentieth century came to set 'the agenda for the modernist reconceptualization of rhetoric' (Bender and Wellbery 1990: 26).

Nietzsche is well known as a philosopher of nihilism but his training as a skilled philologist and classicist also involved him in the teaching of rhetoric at the University of Basel in 1872–73. His 'Lecture Notes on Rhetoric', probably written in 1874 for a later course which he never taught, offer a startling new defence of rhetoric as 'the essence of language' (106). Traditionally, we call 'a style "rhetorical" when we observe a conscious application of artistic means of speaking' (Nietzsche 1983: 107). For example, Quintilian explains that the emphasis in the line 'Alas! for these are degenerate days!' can only be given the name of *exclamation* and included 'among Figures of Speech' when it is 'feigned and artificially produced', rather than expressed automatically, without design (Quintilian 2001: 9.2.27). Nietzsche, however, insists that 'what is called "rhetorical" as a means of conscious art, had been active as a means of unconscious art in language and its development' (106). That is to say, tropes and figures are not only artful adornments of everyday language. Nor are they only a means to communicate vividly the thoughts of a speaker. Rather, *all* words are tropes. 'What is actually called language', Nietzsche argues, 'is actually all figuration', and he demonstrates this by exploring the figural basis of words whose literal meaning is taken for granted: for example, Latin 'serpens' (snake), which literally means 'that which crawls' (107–8).

Nietzsche's 'Lectures Notes' discuss a range of tropes, including metonymy and synecdoche. However, it is his account of metaphor that can best enable us to understand how he coincides with and departs from the advice given in classical handbooks. Like Quintilian, Nietzsche understands metaphor as involving the transference of words from one context to another in such a way as to give 'new meaning to them' (108). He also acknowledges that a distinction is generally drawn between 'conscious pre-sentation' and 'inartistic metaphors'. The 'popular tropes,' he summarizes, 'originated from embarrassment and stupidity, the rhetorical tropes from art and delight' (123). Yet, as soon as this hierarchical distinction is drawn by Nietzsche, it is qualified. He insists that the distinction between the conscious and inartistic use of this trope is 'entirely false' (123). Moreover, he rejects the assumption that the tropes more generally are deviations from the literal use of words (Quintilian 2001: 9.1.2); that is, he rejects the distinction between literal and figurative meaning. Though he may accept the basic definition of metaphor, he also extends it to describe any kind of 'transference' that takes place from one realm to another. This informs his conception of language more generally. The naming of things, in his view, involves a three-stage process of transference: a nerve stimulus is transferred into an image, which is then transferred into a sound image. Words, or sound images, recall a prominent feature, an image, of the thing they represent: for example, the crawling of a snake (107). So accustomed are we to these 'literal' words that we have forgotten their figurative basis. Calling a snake a snake is no less 'rhetorical' than calling a person a snake.

The consequences of this emphasis on 'rhetoricality' for the possibility of knowledge are far-reaching. If language represents things figuratively rather than literally, how can we ever grasp their truth or 'essence'? This problem is posed in Nietzsche's essay 'On Truth and Lies in a Non-moral Sense' (1873), which is contemporaneous with the 'Lecture Notes'. In 'On Truth and Lies', Nietzsche argues that our lives are organized around a tissue of lies and that humanity is intrinsically self-deceiving, so much so that we can never gain a clear understanding of the 'truth' of things. In one sense, such deceit is necessary. The social fictions we create ensure stability; they prevent us from acting aggressively towards one another. In another sense, though, they are inescapable because they are endemic to language itself, which is the only tool we have to comprehend our world. Nietzsche is sceptical of the idea of 'enlightenment' because any attempt to understand the essence of a thing is always dependent on language, which is never adequate to the expression of its reality. There is no pure philosophical language. We have tricked ourselves into thinking that a language divested of tropes and figures can lead us to the truth when in fact the 'drive to truth' is necessarily a 'drive to metaphor' (Nietzsche 1979: 79–97).

Nietzsche is overturning the distinction emphasized by Enlightenment rhetoricians between literal and figurative language. As we have seen in Chapter 2, this distinction underpinned the rejection of rhetoric in the seventeenth and eighteenth centuries and paved the way for the imagined cultivation of a 'plain' language of commerce and science, a conception of language that is outside or beyond the emotive and duplicitous practices of the orator. Language is 'pruned' of tropes and figures to provide a resource or tool for communication and instruction. In Nietzsche's view, however, language is fundamentally figurative and duplicitous; it can never represent exactly what we mean, or what we think we mean. Challenging this move to escape from or evade the rhetoricality of language is important because it is also a challenge to the process of discrimination and the creation of hierarchies: the assumption, for example, that literal language is better than figurative language in the sense that it is clearer or, more insidiously, less 'primitive'.

This is a far-reaching revision to classical rhetoric, though one that develops clearly from it. We can see the influence of this reconception of language in post-structuralist writing, perhaps notably in the work of Paul de Man, as I will explain in the next section. But before we turn to de Man, and consider how this perception of the 'rhetoricality' of language shapes his understanding of and approach to literature, I want to consider one further revision to traditional rhetoric and the telling of its history. This is offered by Jacques Derrida (1930–2004) in his substantial essay 'Plato's Pharmacy', published in *Dissemination* (1972), a detailed study of Plato's *Phaedrus* and its translation history. This essay is important because it offers an early exposition of Derrida's deconstructive method, which is in turn an attempt to formulate a critical mode of analysis that can clarify rather than obscure the 'rhetoricality' of language. It is important, too, because it clarifies the long reach of Derrida's engagement with the problematic relationship between philosophy and rhetoric. Deconstruction develops out of the 'old rhetoric'. As Patricia Parker notes, its development was impelled 'by an education which included classical rhetoric' (Parker 1987: 5), and this claim is reiterated by Derrida: 'I was trained in those very classical norms. And probably people who read me and think I'm playing with or transgressing norms – which I do, of course – usually don't know what I know that all of this has not only been made possible by but is constantly in contact with very classical, rigorous, demanding discipline in writing, in "demonstrating," in rhetoric' (Derrida in Olson 1990). Nonetheless, Derrida is not seeking to defend this tradition though, like Barthes, he recognizes its historical importance. Rather, in 'Plato's Pharmacy' he invites us to conceive differently the opposition between rhetoric and philosophy that is the well-established origin of its history, and which has structured its defence for centuries. Derrida is not just reminding us that the language of philosophy is also rhetorical, as Nietzsche had insisted; he is also exploring how the opposition to rhetoric in the writings of Plato established that entrenched attachment in Western thinking to binary opposition.

Jacques Derrida

'Plato's Pharmacy' unravels what Derrida describes as the 'supplementary thread' of *Phaedrus*, its easily missed 'whole last section (274*b*ff.)', which ties together the dialogue (Derrida 2004: 72); this is Socrates' attack on writing. Derrida is concerned not just with this attack, however, but also with the language of its representation: in particular the shifting depiction of it as a *pharmakōn*, a term which is rendered from the Greek, 'without mistranslation', by a range of related and contradictory terms, '"remedy", "recipe", "poison", "drug", "philater" etc.' (77). The word *pharmakōn* is first introduced indirectly at the beginning of the dialogue when Socrates and Phaedrus reflect on the choice of location for their conversation, a riverbank where, according to myth, the god Boreas seized and killed Orithyia while she was playing with Pharmacia. Derrida cites the note for 'Pharmacia' in a French translation by Léon Robin: 'A fountain, "perhaps with curative powers,"' that 'was dedicated to Pharmacia' (75). Pharmacia,

Derrida also notes, is 'a common noun signifying the adminis-
tration of the *pharmakōn*, the drug: the medicine and/or poison'.
A 'little further on' in *Phaedrus*, he notes, this ambiguous term is
used to describe the written text. Thus, Socrates remarks that
Phaedrus has discovered a 'drug (*pharmakōn*)' which can draw
him away from the city; this is the copied-out speech by Lysias
that Phaedrus has hidden under his cloak (75–76). However, it is
not until the 'supplementary' section towards the end of the
dialogue that this association between writing and the *pharmakōn*
in its different senses is firmly established.

In this supplementary section, also known as the myth of
Theuth, the argument against writing is articulated by the king
of Egypt. The god of writing, Theuth, presents his invention to
the king, describing it as a *pharmakōn*, meaning by this 'remedy'.
In response, the king of Egypt reveals the second meaning of
pharmakōn, conceiving it as a 'poison'. Writing, it turns out,
harms memory and wisdom. Writing only *seems* to be good, the
king argues, and this makes it doubly pernicious and dangerous.
The argument develops a further complication. It is not just that
writing is a *pharmakōn* in one or other of its senses; it also
embodies the ambivalence of the term used to represent it.
Writing shares in the dangerous slipperiness of the *pharmakōn*, its
forgetting of clear-cut distinctions between good and bad,
remedy or poison. For instance, writing forgets the distinction
between 'inside' and 'outside'. Writing is outside memory in the
sense that it substitutes for it: we jot down things that we want
to remember. At the same time, however, it 'affects memory and
hypnotizes it in its very inside', by serving as a substitute for the
activity of remembering (113). In brief, writing is bad because it
makes us forgetful and careless thinkers, reliant on signs when
we should be trying to think our way back to the original forms,
to ideas rather than their representation. This attack on writing
is closely associated with Socrates' diatribe against the sophists,
the defendants in the 'interminable trial instituted by Plato' in
Phaedrus and his other writings 'under the name of philosophy'
(108). Indeed, like the speech-writer, with whom he is inex-
tricably linked, the sophist 'sells the signs and insignia of science';
he sells 'memorials', not 'memory' (109).

So far 'Plato's Pharmacy' does not seem to be saying anything out of the ordinary. We already know that *Phaedrus* constitutes an attack on both sophistic rhetoric and the art of writing. Yet, Derrida's focus on the language of its representation provides a very different starting point. In standard histories, the response to this attack, as we have seen, is attributed to Aristotle's *Rhetoric* which offers a defence of the art of rhetoric as pragmatic discourse. However, Derrida, in contrast, is interested rather in understanding Plato's attempt to remedy the slipperiness of the *pharmakōn*. Plato does this, Derrida explains, by transforming its dangerous ambivalence into opposition, 'by inserting its definition into simple, clear-cut oppositions: good and evil, inside and outside, true and false, essence and appearance' (105). For instance, as the example of the myth of Theuth demonstrates, Plato manages the ambiguity of *pharmakōn* by clarifying and separating its two oppositional meanings: Theuth claims it is a remedy, the king of Egypt insists it is a poison. The significance of this split should not be under-estimated; it is in this way, through this antagonism, that Plato establishes the logic of binary opposition: good versus bad, speech versus writing and philosophy versus rhetoric. In so doing, Plato establishes the dialectical method of the philosopher, which involves distinguishing carefully between 'good' and harmful things, as a remedy for the poisonous confusion or mixing of these categories by the sophists.

This is a significant change of focus, though it is not Derrida's close analysis of the 'rhetoric' of Plato's text, his management of the slipperiness of the term *pharmakōn,* that has caught critical interest, but rather how his sensitivity to the linguistic dexterity of Socrates begins to undermine the clear-cut distinction Plato has established between the philosopher and the sophist. Thus, Derrida notes the unexpected proximity of Socrates to the sophists. 'Contrary to what we have indicated earlier', Derrida suddenly notes, 'there are also good reasons for thinking that the diatribe against writing is not aimed first and foremost at the sophists. On the contrary: sometimes it seems to proceed *from* them' (111). For, like Socrates, the sophists also reject the art of writing and value the exercise of memory, although they do so 'in order to enable themselves to speak without knowing, to recite without judgement' (115). Like Socrates, too, the sophists 'extolled the force of living *logos*', but unlike Socrates, they do so because its powers of infiltration are greater than those of writing: that is, they understand that the 'infiltration' of speech, in contrast to writing, is 'more profound, more penetrating, more diverse, more assured' (117). This point is made by Gorgias in *The Encomium to Helen* when he attempts to exonerate Helen of Troy by arguing that she was 'persuaded' to abandon her husband, and then explains this as an excuse by noting the forcefulness of persuasive speech. In Derrida's translation (and in Barbara Johnson's rendering of this): 'Speech is a powerful lord, which by the means of the finest and most invisible body effects the divinest words' (118). It 'is comparable to the power of drugs (*tōn pharmakōn taxis*) over the nature of bodies'. For Gorgias the *pharmakōn* is *logos* or speech rather than writing, and he draws attention to the wildness, the 'ambiguous animality' of speech from which its '"pharmaceutical" force' derives (118). Socrates deplores this dimension in writing, and values the greater control of the spoken word. However, arguably, he also speaks like a sophist in the sense that his attempt to control the *pharmakōn* involves exploiting its ambiguous reversibility. Socrates is also a conjuror with words. He is able to persuade us that writing, which is deemed a cure on one view, is in fact a poison, and inversely, that a poison, the hemlock that the historical Socrates was forced to drink as a punishment for his supposed impiety, is in turn a cure. Socrates would have us believe that his dialectical method, which involves distinguishing carefully between good and harmful things, is a remedy for the poison of the sophists. But it is also to be conceived as an 'exorcism', a 'counter-spell' to a form of linguistic wizardry that seems dangerous and uncertain (124). This counter-spell is only possible because 'the pharmako-logos' already contains 'within itself that complicity of contrary values' (128). 'The Socratic *pharmakōn*', Derrida writes, 'acts like venom, like the bite of a poisonous snake', provoking 'a kind of *narcosis*, benumbing and paralyzing into aporia', so lithely has it organized our way of thinking, leading us away from a complex understanding of how language works (120).

This challenging engagement with Plato's sophisticated anti-rhetorical dialogue does not constitute a defence of traditional rhetoric, even though Derrida is sometimes regarded as one of the 'major rescuers' of rhetoric in the twentieth century (Booth 2004: 77). Indeed, Derrida was rather circumspect about how 'Plato's Pharmacy' might be understood as contributing to such a defence. In an interview in 1990 with Gary A. Olson, a teacher of Rhetoric and Composition, he expressed his discomfort with the label 'rhetorician', articulating his suspicion of the emphasis on what he calls 'rhetoricism' in writing courses: the 'thinking that everything depends on rhetoric as simply a technique of speech'. In this interview, he argues against the teaching of Rhetoric and Composition when this is understood as instruction in verbal techniques irrespective of disciplinary expertise. Derrida appears to be rehearsing the argument of Socrates in *Phaedrus* against the technical teachers of rhetoric, the sophists, who supposedly disseminate an empty formalism, even though in his critique of this dialogue, 'Plato's Pharmacy', he seems to side with the sophists against Socrates. Olson spots a contradiction: 'In your deconstruction of the *Phaedrus* in "Plato's Pharmacy," you seem to offer support for a sophistic stance towards rhetoric and philosophy. Yet, at times you seem to retreat from a full-fledged endorsement of the sophists'. Derrida responds by noting that deconstructionists are often misrepresented as 'modern sophists', and asserts some sympathy with Plato: 'I've resisted the way Plato attacked or imprisoned the sophists, captured the sophists, in the figure of the sophists. To that extent, it's as if I were simply counter attacking Plato from the position of the sophists.' Yet, he adds, he is not in favour of the sophists, at least not if the portrait of them in Plato carries any weight (Derrida in Olson 1990).

This hesitant negotiation with Olson is in fact an extension of the approach that Derrida adopts in 'Plato's Pharmacy'. Though Derrida's reading of *Phaedrus* is 'rhetorical' in the sense that he is attentive to the way in which its argument is represented through a series of metaphors, he not exposing Plato as a rhetorician who has cunningly concealed his artistry so as to argue against the very skill he practises. On the contrary, he exposes how Plato is struggling to tame the ambiguity of language. This makes Derrida cautious in 'Plato's Pharmacy' about how much, or how little, authorial control he ascribes to Plato. On the different meanings of the word *pharmakōn*, he observes how it is 'caught in a chain of significations', and that though these seem 'systematic', and thus potentially exploitable by a skilled speaker and writer, the play on it that appears in *Phaedrus* 'is not, simply, that of the intentions of an author who goes by the name of Plato' (Derrida 2004: 98). Later on he acknowledges more explicitly that 'it would be impossible to say to what extent he manipulates [the chain of significations] voluntarily or consciously, and at what point he is subject to constraints weighing upon his discourse from "language"' (131–32). Derrida is not just showing us that Plato's writing is rhetorical by bringing into view the metaphors that he is using. Rather, he is showing us why it cannot be anything but rhetorical.

Paul de Man

Paul de Man's new rhetoric marks a radical departure from the 'old' rhetoric criticized by Barthes. Its success is perhaps evident from the broad attacks on it presented by critics who seek to protect the classical tradition. Brian Vickers' *In Defence of Rhetoric* (1988) defends the traditional authority of the plain-speaking and technically competent critic. On his view, post-structuralist verbal play should not be dignified as rhetoric because it has abandoned the classical conception of rhetoric as an art of persuasive communication, along with its demanding requirement to command tropes and figures and to master rules for the composition of orations. This attack is directed principally at Paul de Man, who he holds singularly responsible for the most serious reduction of rhetoric to date. De Man published a series of books which include 'rhetoric' or rhetorical terms in their titles: *Blindness and Insight: Essays on the Rhetoric of Contemporary Criticism* (1971), *Allegories of Reading: Figural Language in Rousseau, Nietzsche, Rilke and Proust* (1979) and *Rhetoric of Romanticism* (1984). Despite this, Vickers doubts that he is fully cognisant of the classical tradition given his imprecise use of its vocabulary

(Vickers 1988: 457). These criticisms apply particularly to the opening essay of *Allegories of Reading*, 'Semiology and Rhetoric' (458), which lays out de Man's new conception of rhetoric most completely. According to Vickers, de Man erroneously defines rhetoric in this essay as 'the study of tropes and of figures', rather than as the art of 'eloquence and persuasion' (de Man 1979: 6). Other criticisms include that he confuses figures with tropes, and that he displays a basic misunderstanding of one key figure in particular, the rhetorical question. With regard to this last mistake, Vickers notes that de Man tells an implausible anecdote about a man named 'Archie Bunker', who responds to a query from his wife about whether he wants the laces of his bowling shoes to be tied under or over with another question: 'What's the difference?' What Archie Bunker means by this, de Man explains, is: 'I don't give a damn what the difference is' (9). The frustration he expresses when his wife then proceeds dutifully to explain the difference 'reveals his despair when confronted with a structure of linguistic meaning that he cannot control' (10). Vickers is not happy. The proper definition of this figure is 'a question posed without expectation of a reply'. However, de Man 'says that a question "becomes rhetorical ... when it is impossible to decide by grammatical or other linguistic devices which of the two meanings [literal or figurative] prevails"' (Vickers 1988: 458).

We might understand the basis for this attack *and* its limitations if we take a closer look at Vickers' own style of 'rhetorical criticism'. *In Defence of Rhetoric* aims to correct this misguided but influential view by providing careful analysis of the rhetorical devices used in a variety of literary writings in different periods, and by preserving their precise definition. That is, it defends rhetorical criticism as 'the analysis of texts in terms of specific rhetorical devices', the tropes and figures of the classical art (Vickers 1988: 306). De Man uses the terms trope and figure interchangeably, Vickers complains. In contrast, in his own reading of the long and intensely rhetorical episode set in the office of two Dublin newspapers, 'Aeolus', in James Joyce's modernist epic *Ulysses* (1922), Vickers follows 'systematic treatments' of classical rhetoric by distinguishing between these, and then by identifying their application and effect (315). The point of this exercise is to recover the expressive function of the tropes and figures, the capacity of these devices to represent thought and to communicate 'real-life emotional states' (300). More generally, Vickers wants to recover the potential of classical rhetoric to function as a civic art which shapes relationships between people and which values 'public debate in a society guaranteeing free speech, a debate in which both sides of the case are heard and those qualified to vote come to a decision binding on all parties' (Vickers 1988: viii).

Vickers does make a convincing case for the importance of Joyce's knowledge of the classical art. In *Ulysses*, Joyce draws on a seventeenth-century French translation of Aristotle's *Rhetoric*; he also uses examples from the *Oxford English Dictionary* for three figures of speech, and an unidentified rhetorical manual (388). Notably, the 'Aeolus' episode deploys an array of classical tropes and figures and Joyce's friend, Stuart Gilbert, who published a commentary on the novel in 1930, advises that 'Aeolus' includes some ninety-five rhetorical devices (388). These are deployed to create and evaluate characters and to convey the experience of the newspaper office. For example, the trope *onomatopoeia*, when a word imitates a sound, is used to represent the noise of the printing presses, and the figure *tmesis*, the dividing up of words, to represent the typesetter's process of proof-reading: for example, 'It is amusing to view the unpar one ar alleled embarra two ars is it?' (Vickers 1988; 395–96; Joyce 1980: 154). Another figure used by Joyce is *antimetabole*, the repetition and inversion of words; this serves in the sentence cited below to communicate the difficulty of a drayman's labour by making us 'live through the activity' of moving barrels 'twice':

> Grossbooted draymen rolled barrels dullthudding out of Prince's stores and bumped them up on the brewery float. On the brewery float bumped dullthudding barrels rolled by grossbooted draymen out of Prince's stores.
>
> (Vickers 1988: 401; Joyce 1980: 148)

Vickers conveys how important the expressive function of these figures was to Joyce and, more broadly, to literary tradition, but whether we can or, indeed, should return comprehensively to this style of rhetorical criticism is a different matter. Vickers' trope-spotting is not for all tastes. 'Joyce uses so many different figures', he notes, 'that it becomes difficult to synthesize them into any coherent sequence. One gets the impression, if not of a thesaurus then of a display-piece or demonstration of verbal skills' (Vickers 1988: 400). Attention to Joyce's use of these figures allows us to appreciate his linguistic dexterity. Missing here, though, is any sense that Joyce's technical knowledge of rhetorical devices might inform, say, a critique of the pomposity of amateur classicists or, indeed, that his verbal play is 'tinged by the pathos of the inexpressive' as well as 'the energies of verbal invention' (Sherry 2004: 98–99).

Moreover, it misses the possibility that Joyce may be engaging with the classical art critically, using it to satirize the admiration of the newspapermen in 'Aeolus' for the arts of language. This can be illustrated by his use of the three rhetorical genres. First comes Dan Dawson's 'display' on 'Erin, Green Gem of the Silver Sea', which is read out aloud by Ned Lawson. Then we have Seymour Bushe's comparison of Roman justice with Mosaic law, excerpts of which are recalled by J. J. O'Molloy; this is an example of forensic oratory. The third is an example of deliberative oratory: Professor MacHugh's recitation of John F. Taylor's speech at a college historical society meeting. The first cliché-ridden oration is all pomp and swagger, 'shite and onions' as Mr Dedalus calls it (Joyce 1980: 160). It evokes a romantic, nostalgic memory of pastoral Ireland. The second speech, with its 'polished periods', fares better, so that Stephen Dedalus, who is 'wooed by grace of language and gesture, blushed' on being asked if he likes it (176–77). Meanwhile, the final speech, the work of 'a finished orator', is described by MacHugh as 'full of courteous haughtiness' and 'chastened diction', 'pouring the proud man's contumely' on a new movement, the revival of the Irish language (179). Joyce is not, however, displaying his appreciation of these three genres, leading us finally to the last speech, the one which 'receives most space and most adoration', and which 'is, appropriately, in the deliberative genre, which Aristotle pronounced the noblest' (Vickers 1988: 391–93). There is a satirical side to the representation of all three, a suspicion that they are all hot air, governed by the god of winds, Aeolus, much like the characters in the office themselves. The characters' progressive appreciation of the different genres is part of that debunking. 'Enough of the inflated windbag,' Professor MacHugh shouts at Ned Lawson as he reads out Dawson's oration (159). However, despite their varied critical reception, all of the speeches are inflated. Moreover, the intellectual and classicizing aspirations of the newspapermen and MacHugh, the professor of Latin down on his luck, are juxtaposed with reminders of their material, physical presence. Burke is praised for his 'divine afflatus' (from Latin *afflare*, to blow) while MacHugh's recitation of high oratory is interrupted by a 'dumb belch of hunger' (177, 181). When J. J. O'Molloy reflects on the nobler sound of '*Imperium romanum*' over 'British or Brixton', MacHugh wisely advises 'We musn't be led away by words, by sounds of words' (166). But that is exactly what will happen. MacHugh identifies the Irish with the ancient Greeks who created the 'empire of the spirit' (Joyce 1980: 169), rather than with the commercial Romans and English; later, the Irish will be compared to God's chosen people, the Jews. However, such ambitious analogies must be set against the treatment of the Jewish outsider in this episode, Leopold Bloom. The self-indulgent linguistic camaraderie of the newspaper office does not include him. Indeed, Bloom is the one character to retain some integrity because his speech is not 'rhetorical'; he is not blown away by 'words, by sounds of words'.

There are other problems with Vickers' defence of rhetoric. His hostility to de Man suggests that rhetorical study is really the preserve of those who understand and seek to explain the classical system; everyone else is engaging with 'poetics', issues of form and verbal ingenuity. Yet his insistence on a standard rhetoric, which originates with the rule-bound classical manuals, obscures the longstanding complexity of debate about this 'art'; it reduces it to a fixed system that has to be mastered and then applied. *In Defence of Rhetoric* has drawn criticism from within the classical tradition it seeks to recover and defend. Jakob Wisse, the most recent editor with James M. May of Cicero's *On the ideal orator*, accuses him of, among other things, an 'anachronistic' account of the liberalism of Greek politics and of misrepresenting the art as 'one static edifice, instead of something which developed over centuries' and which 'kept changing in form and emphasis' (Wisse 1992: 538, 542). Moreover, despite Vickers' interest in the early history of rhetoric and the ongoing relevance of the classical system, his critical interest, like de Man's, focuses on one aspect of rhetoric, the tropes and figures. Vickers commends the link between ancient Greek democracy and its rhetorical culture of 'free speech', represented by the cut and thrust of debate in the law-courts. However, he does not offer reflection on the processes of argument in modern literary and critical writing, including his own. He writes as if he were composing a judicial oration, setting out to win his case in public by refuting his opponents' evidence. His style of argument is combative; it involves, among other things, expressing mock disbelief at the folly of his opponents. This is perhaps why he does not catch the nuances of de Man's argument, or value his attempts to negate his own critical authority.

Indeed, Vickers does not catch the nuances of de Man's argument. On Vickers' summary, de Man's description of Archie Bunker's rhetorical question does suggest that he has misused an established vocabulary to defend his singular opinion that communication is unstable. However, it is important to recognize that this departure is careful and deliberate. In 'Semiology and Rhetoric', de Man does not ignore the correct definition of the rhetorical question. Rather, such definition is the starting point not the end point of the process of interpretation. Using the example of Archie Bunker, in fact an allusion to the befuddled bigot played by Carroll O'Connors in the popular 1970s American sitcom 'All in the Family', de Man explores how a grammatically correct sentence can give rise to two contradictory meanings. He follows 'the usage of common speech in calling this semiological enigma "rhetorical"' (de Man 1979: 10). The adjective 'rhetorical' applies both to linguistic devices and also to the verbal effect of ambivalence that he calls a 'semiological enigma'. This 'enigma' is created by the tension between a literal (grammatical) and a figural (rhetorical) structure, neither of which is privileged over the other. Figural play is not superior to grammatical clarity, or vice versa; it is the interchange between them that is ambivalent and meaningful. In the Archie Bunker example the wife's literal response to the question 'What's the difference?' is as valid as its intended meaning, 'I don't give a damn what the difference is'. This might be seen as a creative rather than an irresponsible departure from a traditional rhetoric which thrives on the interplay between different viewpoints.

Moreover, once de Man's different use of the term rhetoric is clarified it is possible to understand how he is contributing to contemporary rhetorical and literary debate. De Man is responding, on the one hand, to a resurgence of context-led literary criticism in the wake of American New Criticism. Literary critics have become tired of the restrictions of close readings which attend to the form of literary writing and 'cry out for the fresh air of referential meaning' (4). This has given rise to a 'metaphorical model of literature as a kind of box that separates an inside from an outside', and content from its form, while establishing the authority of the critic 'as the person who opens the lid in order to release in the open what was secreted but inaccessible inside' (5). On the other hand, he is responding to a quite separate development in literary studies which turned to linguistics for its model of language, French semiotics or Semiology. The title of this essay, 'Semiology and Rhetoric', may seem to confirm the suspicion that de Man is contributing to the wayward subordination of the rhetorical tradition to 'an alien enterprise', linguistics. Yet, de Man's return to rhetoric is in fact a critical response to the linguistic turn in literary scholarship; it signals his movement away from 'structuralism', which attempts to systematize the study of literary language, to the preoccupation with its ambiguity and play generated by the interplay between figurative and grammatical utterances.

De Man values the work of earlier structuralists such as Barthes and Genette because their emphasis on the conventionality of meaning 'explodes the myth of semantic correspondence between sign and referent' (6). In so doing, it frees linguistic analysis from the 'the authority of reference' which context- and content-led Anglophone literary critics have started to turn back to, and it shifts attention to the 'literary dimensions of language' which a preoccupation with referentiality obscures (5). Yet, he is also concerned with the way in which Barthes and Genette collapse the difference between rhetorical and grammatical structures in their literary analyses 'without apparent awareness of a possible discrepancy between them' (6). De Man maintains the distinctiveness of grammatical and figurative language, and of linguistics and rhetoric. Both 'arts' represent the systematic study of language, but this is about as far as the similarities go. For instance, rhetoric is usually described as an 'art' or 'practice', whereas linguistics is defined as a 'science'. In these contrasting self-definitions there lies a world of difference. Grammar underpins logic: no statement is logically true unless it is grammatically correct. Rhetoric, in contrast, is perhaps better understood, de Man suggests, in terms of Kenneth Burke's 'deflection': 'any slight bias or even unintended error'. Rhetorical figures subvert the 'consistent link between sign and meaning that operates within grammatical patterns' (8).

Addressing this problem does not mean returning to the 'old rhetoric'. Rather, for de Man it means extending our conception of rhetoric to take account of the advance of linguistics; hence, his conception of rhetoric in terms of a 'semiological enigma'. To argue that rhetoric is an art of persuasion is to assume a linguistic model in which someone acts upon someone else. De Man has no confidence in the intrinsic communicability of language or in our ability either to express ourselves unambiguously or to discover the final meaning of a text. In spite of our best efforts, he argues, we cannot control meaning. Attending to rhetoric as 'semiological enigma' realizes this; moreover, it enables de Man to place rhetorical and grammatical meaning in productive tension.

Let us consider his second, more challenging example of this tension. De Man's first example of a rhetorical question undermines our confidence in the meaning of a grammatical sentence. His second example reveals how an unplanned literal reading can interrupt an intended metaphorical reading which privileges 'unity' between sign and content, image and reality. This example of a rhetorical question is the final line of 'Among School

Children', a late poem by W. B. Yeats (1865–1939): 'How can we know the dancer from the dance?' (Yeats 1990: 261–63). This line is 'usually interpreted', he remarks, 'as stating, with the increased emphasis of a rhetorical device, the potential unity between form and experience, between creator and creation'. In this respect, he adds, it 'could be said that it denies the discrepancy between the sign and the referent from which we started out' (11). De Man does not offer to explain 'Among School Children', though he does assume his reader's familiarity with it or, at the very least, their access to it; and for this reason I shall outline the poem so we can understand the significance both of its usual interpretation and of de Man's disagreement with that.

The setting for this poem is a convent school in Ireland which the poet visited in 1926 in his role as senator, as 'A sixty-year-old smiling man public man.' In the first stanza, a nun takes him around the school, explaining the curriculum, while the children stare at this unfamiliar guest 'In momentary wonder' (261). The sight of these children sitting at their desks prompts him to recall vividly and nostalgically a memory of his beloved, who experienced readers of Yeats would be aware was Maude Gonne. He recalls her 'Ledaean body, bent / Above a sinking fire' as she in turn remembers some 'trivial event / That changed some childish day to tragedy', and he is led to wonder whether this magnificent woman once experienced something of the lives of the ordinary children before him: 'For even daughters of the swan can share / Something of every paddler's heritage' (261–62). 'Among School Children' is not just about memories of a sweetheart; it also reflects on the distance between the past and the present, between nostalgic ideals and material reality. The narrator's proud and idealistic remembering of the young woman ('Did Quattrocento finger fashion it?'), and, indeed, of his own youthful 'pretty plumage' is abruptly interrupted in the fourth stanza when he turns his attention back to the school children, back to the present:

> Better to smile on all that smile, and show
> There is a comfortable kind of old scarecrow.

(262)

This brings about a shift in the poem, and the stanzas that follow offer melancholy tribute to the distance between what we recall or desire and what we experience. The narrator is led to wonder, for instance, whether a mother would deem her birth pangs worthwhile if she could see ahead into the future, picturing her baby 'With sixty or more winters on its head' (262). Meanwhile, nuns, like mothers, are alike in that they 'worship images', and even though their images are made of 'marble' or 'bronze', they 'too break hearts':

> –O Presences
> That passion, piety or affection knows,
> And that all heavenly glory symbolise–
> O self-born mockers of man's enterprise

> (263)

It is in this context that critics have made sense of the final stanza, and its last line in particular, as stating the 'potential unity between form and experience, between creator and creation':

> Labour is blossoming or dancing where
> The body is not bruised to pleasure soul,
> Nor beauty born out of its own despair,
> Nor blear-eyed wisdom out of midnight oil.
> O chestnut-tree, great-rooted blossomer,
> Are you the leaf, the blossom or the bole?
> O body swayed to music, O brightening glance,
> How can we know the dancer from the dance?

> (263)

The last line is read figuratively, as a rhetorical question: no answer to this question is required because the dancer and the dance, creator and creation, are one and the same. This is a credible reading, de Man acknowledges, because the poem has already established the principle of unity with a parallel question in the lines directly preceding the final line which also serves as a synecdoche, in which the parts of a tree represent the whole:

O chestnut-tree, great-rooted blossomer,
Are you the leaf, the blossom or the bole?

The rhetorical question-cum-synecdoche of these lines becomes in turn 'the most seductive of metaphors', conveying 'organic beauty'. In the same way, the final rhetorical question, 'How can we know the dancer from the dance?', becomes a metaphor conveying the 'convergence' between 'erotic desire' and 'musical form'.

This reading is responsive to the figures and tropes that Yeats has created to convey the unity of form and experience. However, it is also 'equally possible', de Man argues, 'to read the last line literally rather than figuratively', in which case we might foreground in our reading not the convergence of form and content, of sign and referent, but rather the opposite: the impossibility of making 'distinctions that would shelter us from the error of identifying what cannot be identified'. This is not a simpler reading than the figurative one preferred by many critics. On the contrary, the figurative reading which interprets the final line only as a rhetorical question 'is perhaps naïve'; it is the literal reading that 'leads to a greater complication of theme and statement':

> For it turns out that the entire scheme set up by the first reading can be undermined, or deconstructed, in the terms of the second, in which the final line is read literally as meaning that, since the dancer and the dance are not the same, it might be useful, perhaps even desperately necessary – for the question can be given a ring of urgency, 'Please tell me, how *can* I know the dancer from the dance' – to tell them apart.
>
> (de Man 1979: 11–12)

De Man's style of rhetorical criticism is distinguished by his fluid treatment of key tropes and by the attention he gives to the interplay between literal and figural reading, between grammar and rhetoric. It is possible to see how his method of close reading can reveal the interrelationship between different figures and tropes and also, how individual tropes can change their shape, so that a rhetorical question reads also as a synecdoche and as a metaphor. De Man urges readers to be aware of such figural slipperiness. However, it is his focus on the tension between literal and figural reading that inspires an awareness of the error-prone process of interpretation. De Man does not resolve this dilemma by privileging one kind of reading over another, or by implying that meaning is denied; on the contrary, he argues that these two readings 'have to engage each other in direct confrontation' (12). To opt for one reading over the other is to suppress the complexity of the text and to cling to false conclusions.

De Man's emphasis on the interplay between literal and figurative meaning counters the criticism that all he has produced is an empty circular rhetoric. This criticism can be countered again, in a different way, by turning to a later essay in *Allegories of Reading*, 'Rhetoric of Tropes', which engages critically with one of the key sources of post-structuralist rhetoric, Nietzsche's 'Lecture Notes on Rhetoric'. In this essay, de Man identifies two key innovations of these 'Lecture Notes': first, that 'Nietzsche moves the study of rhetoric away from techniques of eloquence and persuasion ... by making these dependent on a previous theory of figures of speech or tropes' and, second, that he reveals how 'figurative structure is not one linguistic mode among others' but that 'it characterizes language' more generally (105). Vickers disputes the accuracy of de Man's account of the 'Lecture Notes', complaining that de Man ignores Nietzsche's 'well-balanced account of the art' (Vickers 1988: 460–61). It is true that de Man has nothing to say about the comprehensive account of classical rhetoric in the 'Lectures Notes', but it is also fair to say that he has grasped what is original and innovative in them. Moreover, he understands that this new emphasis on the 'intralinguistic resources of figures', rather than their 'extralinguistic' meaning, is a central concern of Nietzsche's philosophy (de Man 1979: 106)

'Rhetoric of Tropes' explores the philosophical implications of Nietzsche's rhetoric rather than the specific techniques of persuasion that he employs (103). De Man recognizes that Nietzsche is not usually regarded as a rhetorical thinker. Because the rhetorical vocabulary so visible in his earlier works disappears in later writings, it appears as if he 'had turned away from the problems of language to questions of the self' (106). De Man tests this assumption by citing one brief passage in *The Will to Power* (1888) in which Nietzsche reflects on a widespread tendency to describe mental events in terms of physical experience. Nietzsche is interested in the *'chronological reversal'* by which we misunderstand a conscious event as a response to an external stimulus, rather than vice versa. That is, our failure to recognize that 'what was assumed to be the objective, external cause is itself the result of an internal event' (107). De Man discovers that the 'substitution and reversal' of cause and effect noted in this canonical philosophical text of Nietzsche's is conceived 'as a linguistic event' (108). That is, it is described in the same terms that Nietzsche reserved for the trope metonymy in the 'Lecture Notes': 'the exchange or substitution of cause and effect' (108).

De Man's work is valued by many critics because it deconstructs the opposition between literary (rhetorical) and philosophical discourses. Like Nietzsche, he reminds us that there is no privileged discourse and that we need to regard with suspicion the claim to communicate in a lucid and straightforward fashion. Like Nietzsche too, he argues that an exploration of the relationships established between tropes undermines the traditional emphasis on rhetoric as an art of persuasion. De Man is steeped in the critical tradition of the anti-Enlightenment represented by the work of Nietzsche, and he values rhetoric because it reveals the unstable condition of language. His emphasis on the rhetoricality of language is a response to the attack of Enlightenment thinkers on what they saw as the misleading, rabble-rousing rhetoric of the Renaissance, not a wilful departure from a venerable tradition. It is a response, that is, to the attempt by Enlightenment thinkers to divest their language of deceptive and emotive tropes and figures, and to create a 'science' of polite communication. He is emphasizing the futility of this project since he recognizes that even plain speech is rhetorical. On this account de Man, like Nietzsche, can be fairly described as a 'conceptual rhetorician, one who perceives the linguistic (or tropological) blocks in the way of conceptual understanding' (Norris 1988: 111).

Yet de Man is not to be confused with Nietzsche. The latter's argument that all language is figurative is often seen to authorize the postmodern 'move into rhetoric'. Thus, Bender and Wellbery argue that the shift to rhetoricality is nowhere 'more forcefully evident' than in the writings of Nietzsche, for whom rhetoric is no longer a doctrine, a set of rules to be mastered and applied but 'a kind of immemorial process – an *a priori* that thought can never bring under its control precisely because thought itself is one of the effects of that process' (Bender and Wellbery 1990: 27). This is just as de Man argues in 'Rhetoric of Tropes'. 'We are now living in a postmodern epoch', writes Christopher Norris, 'where all claims to truth have been finally discredited, where language games circulate without any epistemological warrant' (Norris 1988: 77). All the more important, then, that de Man was reluctant to identify his work as 'postmodern' because, as Norris argues, he cannot 'conceive of language without taking account of its cognitive and referential aspects' (78). This is why the emphasis in his opening essay 'Semiology and Rhetoric' lies on the interplay between literal and figurative meaning, between grammar and rhetoric. It explains why he supports a return to the school *trivium*, the traditional grouping of the disciplines of rhetoric, grammar and logic.

So far I have been defending de Man from criticism. Yet it is important to recognize that attacks on de Man's work are also not easily dismissed. In part, this is a problem of his style of close reading. Though he may set out to undermine the authority of the context-led critic who would establish him- or herself 'as the person who opens the lid in order to release in the open what was secreted but inaccessible inside' (de Man 1979: 5), arguably he also recreates this. In *Allegories of Reading* his assertions are admirably tentative and carefully supported; his critical reading intends to create not to resolve ambiguity, but the crucial question we are left pondering is this: does this openness constitute an invitation to debate, or are we required only to admire the subtle close reading that has discovered so capably the impossibility of settling meaning?

There are other problems too. Vickers' complaint that de Man betrays the potential of rhetoric as a mode of political intervention is echoed by other critics who, nonetheless, are troubled by the confident commitment to linguistic agency on which this is founded. For Terry Eagleton, for example, de Man's engagement with rhetoric represents a failure of 'ideological nerve'. 'Mocked and berated for centuries by an abrasive rationalism, rhetoric took its terrible revenge'. Thanks to Nietzsche and de Man rhetoric has assumed 'the Fool's function of unmasking all power as self-rationalization, all knowledge as a mere fumbling with metaphor' (Eagleton 1981: 108). Eagleton argues instead for a fuller sense of this tradition which recognized that 'speaking and writing' were not just 'textual objects, to be aesthetically contemplated or endlessly deconstructed' but were rather 'forms of *activity* inseparable from the wider social relations between writers and readers, orators and audiences, and as largely unintelligible outside the social purposes and conditions in which they were embedded' (Eagleton 1983: 206). When we forget this tradition we lose sight of the transformative potential of 'utterance'.

Equally provocative, however, is the refusal of de Man's deconstructive theory to allow that language has 'any power to refer to events or objects or experience outside itself' (Vickers 1988: 467); this criticism, too, is echoed by those who remain open to the broad problems of communication that de Man describes. De Man's hermetic preoccupation with linguistic detail remains a concern because it deliberately evades the circumstances outside the text. 'Semiology and Rhetoric' begins by lamenting the return in literary-critical work of a belief that 'valid interpretation is possible' and that 'writing and reading' constitute 'potentially effective public speech acts'. However, de Man's evasion of extralinguistic meaning has become all the more controversial since the discovery of his wartime journalism in a Belgian collaborationist newspaper. Because of this discovery, his linguistic scepticism looks like a failure to take responsibility for language. It underscores the failure of his rhetorical criticism to address the relationship between language and power in social and political contexts. As Frank Lentricchia puts it, de Man 'has nothing to say about the social work that representation can and does do' (Lentricchia 1983: 50). For instance, he has nothing to say about how figurative language may 'work' to naturalize relationships of power, as we saw in Chapter 2, or, conversely, how it can be used, self-consciously, to expose the injustice of the operations of power. In the following quotation from a speech delivered in Rochester, New York by a former slave, writer and activist, Frederick Douglass (*c.* 1815–95), the question form is used repeatedly and emphatically in its rhetorical capacity as described by Quintilian: 'not in order to acquire information but to emphasize a point' so as to prompt indignation and amazement (Quintilian 2001: 9.2.7). Douglass is using it very effectively to draw attention to the lie posed by the co-existence of a constitution that protects the liberty of a people while tolerating slavery. This speech was delivered on Independence Day, 4th of July 1852, a decade before the American Civil War:

> Would you have me argue that man is entitled to liberty? that he is the rightful owner of his own body? You have already declared it. Must I argue the wrongfulness of slavery? Is that a question for republicans? Is it to be settled by the rules of logic and argumentation, as a matter beset with great difficulty, involving a doubtful application of the principle of justice, hard to be understood? How should I look today, in the presence of Americans, dividing and subdividing a discourse to show that men have a natural right to freedom? speaking of it relatively and positively, negatively and affirmatively? To do so would be to make myself ridiculous and to offer an insult to your understanding. There is not a man beneath the canopy of heaven that does not know that slavery is wrong for him.
>
> (Douglass 1996: 262)

Of course, these rhetorical questions can also be read literally, as a request for information, but what would be the point? To read these as grammatical questions would be to diminish the intellectual and moral force of the speech.

This excerpt helps to emphasize what is lost when a reading ignores context. De Man focuses on 'the formal analysis of linguistic entities as such, independent of signification' (de Man 1986: 56). Thus, in 'Semiology and Rhetoric' he argues that Yeats' poem 'Among School Children' 'is not explicitly "about" rhetorical questions but about images or metaphors, and about the possibility of convergence between experiences of consciousness such as memory or emotions – what the poem calls passion, piety, and affection – and entities accessible to the senses such as bodies, persons, or icons' (de Man 1979: 12). But we might note that it is not *only* 'about' such images and metaphors; or, rather, that the 'experiences of consciousness' that matter in the poem are very limited ones. De Man has nothing to say about the context of 'Among School Children'. He turns away from readings that would see it, for example, as a melancholy testimony to the feelings of loss and isolation experienced by the Anglo-Irish in post-independence Ireland. He is closed to the possibility that, in this context, the poem may reflect on the desire for a union between myth and experience but yet acknowledge its impossibility. The pathos of this unappeased want might be better seen not as issuing from abstract reflection but from a particular historical conjuncture and from a very specific form of disenchantment. Along with many of his Anglo-Irish circle Yeats felt uneasy and even adrift from an Irish state which had achieved a new kind of 'unity' but also one in which they had lost power and in which their own experiences and aspirations had become more difficult to voice. This context, perhaps, matters, not least because it complicates the formal playfulness of the poem, enabling us to read its final stanza in terms of a different figure: irony. On this reading, the poet does not so much yearn for a mystical unity, but invites us to reflect on how this poem, with all its contradictions, could not have been written without the pain of his sixty years. Its final aspiration, that 'Labour is blossoming or dancing where / The body is not bruised to pleasure soul,' is as unreal and unrealizable as the images that mothers and nuns create (Yeats 1990: 263).

RHETORIC EXTENDED

In 1983 Terry Eagleton defended a return to rhetoric in order to recover a way of engaging with language as an *activity* or as a 'concrete performance' in response to the post-structuralist emphasis on the rhetoricality of all language. In so doing, however, he was not advocating that we 'revive the whole range of ancient rhetorical terms and substitute these for modern critical language' (Eagleton 1983: 206), a reticence echoed by other critical thinkers. There are several reasons why such a return to ancient models is unwelcome. One of these is that defences of classical rhetoric often fail to address why this art has so often been rejected in our own time. As Roland Barthes understood, those who mourn the squandered persuasive resources of traditional rhetoric do not usually acknowledge how its practice emerged from profoundly stratified and exclusionary societies.

This is as true for those for whom a return to rhetoric constitutes a critical engagement with the conditions of modernity as it is for those who simply value the emotional range of the old system. Hannah Arendt's *The Human Condition* (1958), for example, contrasts conformist 'mass' society with the vibrant rhetorical culture of the Greek *polis*. She laments how modern social and political spheres have become intertwined; we all now live in one unhappy family, the state or nation, sharing pretty much the same interests and the same opinions. Politics is nothing more than 'a function of society', while 'action, speech, and thought are primarily superstructures upon social interest' (Arendt 1998: 39, 33). In the ancient Greek *polis*, the political and social spheres remained distinct. The realm of the household was dedicated to the necessities of life and it was organized hierarchically, whereas the political sphere, the *polis*, remained the 'realm of freedom', fostering debate between equals (30). To function in the *polis* was to live out the idea of *being* political; it was to coexist in a realm where 'everything was decided through words and persuasion and not through force and violence' (26). It was to live as an individual in negotiation with others rather than as just another face in the crowd. The *polis* was 'permeated by a fiercely agonal spirit', Arendt explains, 'where everybody had constantly to distinguish himself from all others, to show through unique deeds or achievements that he was the best of all'. The *polis* was a realm 'reserved for individuality' (41).

Nonetheless, we need to be wary of such nostalgia for rhetoric and the world that brought it into being, and find a different way of engaging with this problem rhetorically. For instance, though Arendt's vision is a compelling one, it glosses over how separating the political from the domestic sphere in ancient

Athens also allowed a coercive system of inequities and exclusions to be maintained. Thus, historians of rhetoric also warn against romanticizing Greek democracy (Schiappa 1999: 62). The democracy of ancient Athens was very different from its modern conception. It may have 'pioneered the practice of a self-ruling citizenry' in which each citizen was given the 'chance and duty to participate in the decisions and practices that framed their lives', but citizenship was not extended to women, foreigners or slaves (Honohan 2002: 16, 29). Indeed, the competitive debate that allowed Athenian men to develop as individuals depended on their being propertied, married and slave-owning: they needed to be freed from the necessities of everyday life to engage in public decision-making. Only a citizen who had properly ordered his household had the time to take part in such debate. This might demand, as Lorna Hutson suggests, persuading your wife and your slaves to serve your interests more willingly (1994: 30–41). Perhaps modernity looks a little less callow and confused in the light of this. In short, we need to be aware of how idealizing the origins of rhetoric informs a narrative of cultural loss and political debasement. For some, the collapse of the social into the political was an opportunity for emancipation.

One way of addressing this problem is not to abandon classical rhetoric or its ideals but to *extend* the opportunities it offers for participation to subjects, or rather agents, who were normally precluded from doing so. Rhetoric is usually conceived as 'action'. We could say that 'oratory is nothing if it is not language that makes things happen', Michael Edwards and Christopher Reid argue; indeed, an oration is invariably 'judged by its success or failure in achieving definite legal, political, or broadly ideological outcomes' (Edwards and Reid 2004: 7). However, the contexts for such speech action, law courts and parliament, have traditionally been preclusively male: some actors are more visible than others. We might consider extending what we understand as 'action' to include emotive and moral appeals to social duty which affect the conduct of husbands, servants, neighbours and friends, as well as some '"milder", less agonistic types of persuasion' usually attributed to women in earlier periods, such as supplication or petition (Richards and Thorne 2006: 15).

Recovering the persuasiveness of female interlocutors, or other marginalized speakers, undoubtedly matters in a tradition that has tended to particularize its agents and which has also conceived of rhetoric as primarily agonistic. However, there are limits to this kind of historical analysis too. Extending our understanding of the range of people who have become rhetorical agents is insufficient as a way of restoring faith in its possibilities. This is because our understanding of how language works has changed profoundly. Rhetoric cannot be called upon simply to replace rhetoricality. It is not just a problem of the interpretation of speech acts, the difficulty of knowing, say, whether to understand a question rhetorically or grammatically. It is also a problem of recognizing rhetorical 'motives' where they seem obsolete. How can we speak of an *art* of persuasion when we cannot understand how we are being systematically *acted* upon? The challenge to rhetoric in our own time is not so much a problem of the 'aberrant will', the deployment of rhetoric for 'bad' ends by the wrong kind of people, but of 'structural relations' (Kastely 1997: 221). There is recognition that individuals can only become conscious and persuasive within particular linguistic *and* social and ideological constraints. That is, modernity has intensified understanding of how power is not always explicitly disseminated or experienced, but is 'ideological' in that our values, beliefs, feelings, and how we express these, are shaped by political structures and the relations of economic exchange which organize our social lives.

Any attempt to revive rhetoric must take account of 'the inescapable ideological basis of our identities' (Kastely 1997: 255), though what form this might take is a matter of debate. Eagleton remains hostile to de Man, whose work, he argues, reveals 'all knowledge as a mere fumbling with metaphor' (Eagleton 1981: 108). And yet, despite this, he also argued that a revived rhetoric must take account of the practice of deconstruction, at least when this is concerned with how we organize our lives. In contrast to de Man, for example, Derrida always understood his 'rhetorical' method as a mode of ideology critique because it involves 'an attempt to dismantle the logic by which a particular system of thought and behind that a whole system of political structures and social institutions maintains its force' (Eagleton 1983: 148).

Eagleton's emphasis on the practical effects of the linguistic devices offers a useful counterweight to their unreadability in much post-structuralist work (Eagleton 1983: 206). Yet, his conception of the way in which any new rhetoric should also take stock of the critical methods of deconstruction remains frustratingly vague. His work calls for a new rhetoric that combines these different emphases but does not detail it. How can we accommodate the emphasis in 'old' rhetorics on the agency of the speaker to the linguistic dispossession described, in different ways, by de Man and Derrida? How can we recognize the 'rhetoricality' of language and yet avoid what is often regarded as the debilitating circularity of deconstructive reading, realizing the potential of rhetoric as a tool to critique 'ideology', to understand how we are persuaded to organize ourselves in ways that often run against our interests?

Eagleton never formulated a practice of rhetorical criticism as such. On the contrary, his thinking is indebted principally to the Marxist thinker Louis Althusser, who poses the rhetorician with a particular problem. Althusser refined the conception of ideology as it is formulated by Karl Marx and Friedrich Engels in *The German Ideology* (1845): 'as pure illusion, a pure dream, i.e. as nothingness' that is 'manufactured by who knows what power' (Althusser 1971: 150–51). An ideology, Althusser argues, is not an illusory set of ideas that conceals the real structure of our material relations; rather, it has a 'material existence' (155). It 'exists in an apparatus' such as the school or the church, and in 'its practice or practices' (156). This means that an individual's beliefs need to be understood as *material actions inserted into material practices governed by material rituals*'; they are not independent of ideological state apparatuses. An individual 'acts' only insofar that he or she is already 'acted on' (158–59). The problem with this extension of ideology to every aspect of our lived experience *and* conscious existence, however, is that it makes it impossible to find any position of opposition; it makes it impossible to argue on the opposite side. As Althusser explains:

what seems to take place outside ideology (to be precise, in the
street), in reality takes place in ideology. What really takes place in
ideology seems therefore to take place outside it. That is why those
who are in ideology believe themselves by definition outside ideology: one of the effects of ideology is the practical *denegation* of the
ideological character of ideology by ideology: ideology never says, 'I
am ideological'.

(163–64)

A more substantial basis for the extension of rhetoric, one
which realizes its potential as a tool to critique 'ideology', is
suggested by those critics who, dismayed by the post-structuralist
rhetoric of de Man and the social determinism of Althusser, have
turned to a neglected theorist writing about rhetoric in the
1940s and 50s: Kenneth Burke (1897–1993) (Lentricchia 1983;
Kastely 1997).

Kenneth Burke

'Why go back to the work of "this man without tenure, a PhD.,
or even a B.A., who writes books that cannot be touched by
conventional academic definition"'? (Lentricchia 1983: 119; Biesecker 2000 [1997]: 9). This is an important question to ask
because Burke is writing about rhetoric in the early years of the
Cold War, and he is very evidently a product of his times. But it
is also an important question for other reasons, one of which is
that Burke is an especially difficult figure to pin down. He was a
prolific writer and publisher throughout his lifetime, but his best
known texts, *Grammar of Motives* (1945) and *Rhetoric of Motives*
(1950), were written when he was teaching part-time at Ben-
nington College in Vermont. During this time he also completed
the manuscript for a third book that was meant to complete this
trilogy, 'A Symbolic of Motives', but this remains unpublished.
He is mainly remembered now as a 'thirties Marxist' (Bygrave
1993: 8), though he was rejected by his contemporaries as a
theorist of Marxism because of his seemingly compromising
engagement with Western capitalism. Attempts to define or
locate Burke are also obstructed by the complexity of his writings.

With its 'false starts, delays, fissures, and detours', *Rhetoric of Motives* can test 'the patience of the most virtuous readers among us' (Biesecker 2000: 15–16). Indeed, so difficult is this text, notes Barbara A. Biesecker, that the many critical studies over the last sixty years 'have not produced an incremental series of readings that, strictly speaking, collectively and progressively develop and refine our understanding of Burke's work'. In fact, scholarship on Burke is itself 'riddled by an oftentimes hostile "conflict of interpretations"' (10).

None of this seems very promising. However, Burke was an important figure for critics on the left at the end of the twentieth century who recognized the advance of post-structuralist thinking, namely, that there can be no resurrection of 'self-proximate subjects' (Biesecker 2000: 3), and yet who were uncomfortable with the accompanying emphasis on the ineffectiveness of rhetoric. This is because, in contrast to de Man and Derrida, Burke's engagement with rhetoric is distinguished by his admission of 'the role of human agency in the making and unmaking of social structures and history, without resurrecting the sovereign subject of Enlightenment philosophy' (Biesecker 2000 9). We could say that his value lies in his contribution to a different conception of 'rhetoricality' to the one outlined earlier in this chapter. Central to this is Burke's claim that 'man' is 'a symbol-using (symbol-making, symbol-misusing) animal' (Burke 1989: 70). Admittedly, the emphasis on 'representation' here may recall Nietzsche. For Bender and Wellbery, Burke in fact comes 'close to the Nietzschean definition of man as the imperfect animal, as a being whose only nature is the unremitting nonnaturalness of his symbolic-rhetorical self-constitution' (Bender and Wellbery 1990: 37). Yet, in contrast to Nietzsche and his successors who, arguably, draw attention to the figurative nature of language, and then leave us there to contemplate the impossibility of escaping this, Burke understands language as symbolic action. Language is a resource that can be drawn upon by individuals to act on or persuade others, just as traditional theorists of rhetoric argued. But it also shapes our values and beliefs in ways that we are not always aware of. Burke is keen to alert us to the rhetorical effect of terms that we accept as part of our everyday vocabulary:

positive 'merger' terms such as 'community', which conceal the divisions that structure the terms of our engagement with others. In this respect, his rhetorical project is an act of demystification, and this explains, in part, his interest in Marx. Yet, Burke was not recognized as a Marxist by his contemporaries on the left, and here is the reason why: he sought not to expose and over-throw the material conditions that are hidden by a language that is intensely ideological, but to engage with and exploit the flex-ibility of language so as to allow for those conditions to be *thought* differently. Burke delivered a paper titled 'Revolutionary Symbolism in America' at the first American Writers' Congress in 1935. In this, Lentricchia notes, he argued that 'Collective coherence is no psychic reflex of the economy but the effect of an active, fusing work of cultural production, that organizes "social cooperation".' Consequently, his proposal for overcoming this requires 'symbolic' rather than social and economic revolution. Burke argues that we need 'to move inside and infiltrate the duplicitous but powerfully entrenched language of liberty' that persuades us to cooperate in the first place (Lentricchia 1983: 23–25). And 'he looked so *honest*', one disappointed delegate at this conference is reported to have said (22).

For Burke, we are constituted in language, but we are not determined by it. Language is flexible, re-definable, re-usable. For example, the term 'class' fits us into a way of aligning our-selves with others that is fixed; people are ranked against one another according to their profession, tastes and, often, financial standing. Yet, if we address a more abstract term that underlies this, 'hierarchy', then we can begin to unfix 'class'. Linguistically, a hierarchy is symbolically reversible; it is only in its material expression that it becomes fixed as a particular order, a 'class'. We need to return to the 'idea' or 'principle' of order so as to contest its material manifestation. For Burke this return must be repe-ated; it must become a habit. This is because he recognizes the inevitability of the impulse to order and to hierarchize. We must seek always to unsettle this impulse rather than to overcome it otherwise it is reconstituted without our realizing it. Burke's confidence in the flexibility of language to unsettle deeply held assumptions about how our social experience is organized *and* his commitment to this as an ongoing process, goes some way to explaining his difficult style, both his addiction to paradox and the dizzying moves he makes in his argument. For it is only with such moves that Burke is able to challenge his own impulse to order and prioritize. It is in this way that he is able to honour the ethical obligation within idealist rhetorical practice, to construct a just society. In his terms, though, this means adjusting 'to the demands of variety and separateness, identity and difference, persuasion and refutation' (Kastely 1997: 236).

It is time that we gave *Rhetoric of Motives* some closer attention. From the beginning of this book it is evident that Burke aims to extend rather than overturn the classical tradition. *Rhetoric of Motives* offers, in part, a general defence of 'rhetoric'. One of his aims, he explains in the preface, is to 'rediscover rhetorical elements that had become obscured when rhetoric as a term fell into disuse', that is, when this art was replaced by 'other specialized disciplines', aesthetics, anthropology, psychoanalysis and sociology. He wants us to recognize what we can no longer readily see, the rhetorical motives that structure our everyday social interaction. In particular, he aims to draw attention to the way in which terms that emphasize association or 'community' serve rather to mystify the divisions that underlie and inform our social experience. In order to reveal this, though, he recognizes the need to extend the study of rhetoric beyond its 'traditional bounds' (Burke 1969: xiii).

What does this mean? Classical rhetoric is concerned with deliberate acts of persuasion. Burke accepts this, but also extends this account to include 'an intermediate area of expression that is not wholly deliberate, yet not wholly unconscious', and which 'lies midway between aimless utterance and speech directly purposive'. Such utterances also fall within the sphere of rhetoric, he argues, though they can no longer be understood in terms of its traditional definition as an 'art of persuasion'; quite simply, this definition is 'not an accurate fit, for describing the ways in which the members of a group promote social cohesion by acting rhetorically upon themselves and one another' (xiii–xiv). According to his new rhetoric, acting rhetorically encompasses deliberate attempts to elicit the cooperation of companions, colleagues, customers and so on; however, it also includes moments of self-persuasion of which we may not even be aware. For example, when we believe that we are working for the good of the community, though we are, in fact, satisfying our self-interest at the expense of others. One aim of *Rhetoric of Motives*, then, is to elucidate those persuasive acts of which we are barely conscious, especially those which reaffirm our place within the established social order, and by which we discreetly manage our antagonistic relationship with others. To underscore this development Burke substitutes the term 'persuasion' with a new keyword, 'identification'.

'Identification,' for Burke, is keyed to its conventional associations, meaning something like empathy, affinity or association. In classical rhetoric it is understood as a means to persuasion: 'You persuade a man only insofar as you can talk his language by speech, gesture, tonality, order, image, attitude, idea, *identifying* your ways with his' (55). Traditionally, an orator facilitates identification by noting and articulating an audience's opinions, usually with the help of the 'topics' which offer 'a survey of the things that people generally consider persuasive' (56). But 'he' might also draw upon a range of 'formal patterns' or figures in order to 'awaken an attitude of collaborative expectancy'. For example, the formal structure of the figure *antithesis* leads us to assent: *'we* do *this*, but *they* on the other hand do *that*; *we* stay *here*, but *they* go *there*; *we* look *up*, but *they* look *down'*. As Burke notes, we find ourselves 'swinging along with the succession of antitheses, even though [we] may not agree with the proposition that is being presented in this form' (58). Such devices prompt identification in a twofold sense. They induce 'the auditor to participate in the form, as a "universal" locus of appeal' but they also 'include a partisan statement within this same pale of assent' (59).

Let us take Cicero as an example of a rhetorical thinker who might be subjected to a Burkean reading, demonstrating how this approach undermines the idealist strain in the old rhetoric. Cicero values the orator's ability to facilitate identification because this sustains a just society; on his view, the rhetorician realizes our natural propensity to collaborate with others. The 'unnatural' alternative to this state is tyranny. In contrast, Burke recognizes not only that identification is often achieved without rational assent, but that its realization in turn comes at a cost. The identification that rhetoricians pursue conceals the competitiveness integral to all human exchange. It does not overcome it. When individuals identify with one another, divisions still exist, although in ways that are now hidden. Identification, Burke argues, is 'compensatory to division'. If we were not already divided there would be no need for the rhetorician to 'proclaim' our 'unity' (22). Identification is the 'ironic counterpart' of division because it conceals the antagonism that characterizes all human relationships (23), and it does so very well:

> When two men collaborate in an enterprise to which they contribute different kinds of services and from which they derive different amounts and kinds of profit, who is to say, once and for all, just where 'cooperation' ends and one partner's 'exploitation' of the other begins?
>
> (Burke 1969: 25)

Burke makes us routinely and deeply suspicious.

How might we read this back into Cicero's treatment of rhetoric? Michelle Zerba calls upon Burke to help us understand that the 'emphasis on harmony and consensus in human communities' conceals the fact that 'a politics of intense competition and personal rivalry has inhabited the humanist vision since antiquity' (Zerba 2004: 219). For example, the fact that Cicero's *On the ideal orator* (*De oratore*) offers rhetorical advice in the form of a dialogue, and emphasizes the camaraderie between its two interlocutors, Antonius and Crassus, demonstrates the close relationship between the social virtues and eloquence. Indeed, much of the advice that Antonius gives in book 2 is concerned with winning goodwill. It is easy, then, to miss the competitiveness that informs the relationship between this dialogue's two speakers. Zerba subjects Antonius' change of position on the second day of the dialogue to careful scrutiny, emphasizing his claim to have disagreed with his companion, Crassus, on the first day only to outdo him: 'It was my intention, if I had refuted you, to take these students away from you' (Cicero 2001: 2. 40). He 'can afford' to adopt Crassus' position on the second day, she suggests, because he has the attention of the audience; his 'envy has been allayed by his superiority – by his success in making his listeners want him' (Zerba 2004: 232–33).

So far so good: Burke is clearly providing a model of rhetorical criticism that enables us to resist the orator's techniques of 'identification'. However, this account now needs complicating. First, Burke's critical engagement with rhetoric seeks to expose structural and ideological 'persuasions', as well as the actions of an individual; second, the attempt to demystify, to reveal a rhetorical motive where none had been previously suspected, is itself subjected to critical scrutiny. Burke understands that such an act can, in itself, constitute a mystification. There is no limit to his suspicion. Importantly, though, this suspicion is creative; the attempt to critique demystification as well as to perform it can be understood, paradoxically, as the beginning of a new 'rhetoric of reconstruction' (Simons 2004: 160). Burke turns back on the act of critical demystification to discover *its* rhetorical motive, for he understands that criticism is, in turn, 'a persuasive activity' (Jasinski 2001: 381). At the same time he also com- pensates for this by discovering in the unlikeliest of places the possibility of what he terms 'pure persuasion', language that is not advantage-seeking. Like much of Burke's terminology, 'pure persuasion' sounds hopelessly idealistic and old-fashioned. In fact, Burke argues that pure persuasion is impossible. Yet, he sig- nificantly adds, it can be present as a motive 'in any rhetoric', in just the same way that self-interest can be easily discovered in speech or writing that is purportedly disinterested, outside the realm of rhetoric:

> we may think of social or literary courtship as pure persuasion, when we contrast it with a direct bid for sexual favors, or with commercial advertising. Similarly, education in contrast with debating might be called pure persuasion. And scientific and religious insemination may seem 'pure' when compared with the injection of the doctrinal seed through political ideologies. But all these modes of expression are 'impure,' and seek advantage, as compared with the absolute, and therefore nonexistent, limit we speak of. Yet, though what we

> mean by pure persuasion in the absolute sense exists nowhere, it can be present as a motivational ingredient in any rhetoric, no matter how intensely advantage-seeking such rhetoric may be.
>
> (Burke 1969: 268–69)

Not only is the language of sociability and unity often deeply interested, but explicitly self-interested language can also contain the seeds of something 'purer'. Arguably, we might understand these apparent contradictions in Burke's argument as an extension of the practice already noted in the 'old' rhetoric of debating on opposite sides. I do not mean arguing on opposite sides in the Aristotelian sense, when such debate is a way of discovering the strongest position, but rather in the manner demonstrated by Cicero in *On the ideal orator*, and which is associated with the philosophical position of academic scepticism. For the 'about turns' of this Roman dialogue reveal the competitiveness of seemingly collegial relationships, just as Zerba suggests, but they also discover similarity where division is assumed. Antonius demonstrates the rivalry between two orators, *and* within himself; after all, he also argues against himself. Ultimately, though, such contradictoriness also underscores the unexpected compatibility between the orator and the sceptical philosopher, who rely on the same method of argument on different sides of a question because they do not *know* the answer.

Let us consider an example of how Burke complicates the act of demystification. Central to his treatment of rhetoric is an engagement with Karl Marx as a rhetorical thinker. This is an unusual approach since Marx's critique of capitalism in *The German Ideology* is regarded as a contribution to the science of economics not to the art of rhetoric. Yet, because this critique intends to serve as an 'inducement to action', Burke argues, it is 'unsleepingly rhetorical'. Indeed, the polemical edge of Marxism might lead us to redefine its theory of rhetoric as 'the knack of speaking ill in civil matters' (101). Burke chooses this phrase 'speaking ill', a parody of Quintilian's definition of rhetoric as the 'science of speaking well', because he understands Marxism as a project of demystification: its critique of capitalism 'is designed to disclose (unmask) sinister *factional* interests concealed in the bourgeois terms for benign *universal* interests' (102). That is, Marx formulates a critical practice which can expose how 'traditions' which were once 'the pride of mankind', have been 'upheld' by a ruling class with the result that their 'factional interests' have been mistaken for 'universal interests' (103). Marx's critical project seeks to demystify the merger terms that conceal social division and antagonism in the interests of a ruling class.

The Marxist critique of ideology involves reversing the relationship between 'base' and 'superstructure'. *The German Ideology* argues that we need to grasp that social and economic change shapes our consciousness, not vice versa. The division of society into different social and economic classes follows the rise of private property and the division of labour. This reality, however, is obscured by a conception of history as the unfolding of a 'Universal Idea'; this 'Idea' encompasses our values and beliefs: positive terms or 'ruling ideas' such as honour, loyalty, liberty (106). Changes in our social experience are seen as deriving from the realm of ideas, not from a brutalizing reorganization of economic relations. Social conflict is 'rooted in *property*', yet whenever attention is drawn to this 'fact' we seek the explanation for it in 'theological anguish' or in vague, stock concepts such as the 'alienation' of humankind. 'At every significant point where there is an economic factor to be faced', Burke notes, paraphrasing *The German Ideology*:

> your 'ideology' introduces an 'illusion,' a purely spiritual 'appearance.' Where empires are striving for *world markets*, you are 'ideologically' inclined to ponder the ways of 'universal spirit.' Where classes within a nation are struggling for dominance, you are likely to confuse the issue by ideals that give a semblance of national unity.
>
> (108)

The German Ideology is valued by Burke as an example of rhetorical critique. It offers a brilliant critique of capitalist rhetoric: Marx and Engels call attention to the 'economic interests' that discreetly shape 'modes of expression', and which 'seem wholly to transcend the economic'. However, having approved of this insight, Burke then counters it in what could be seen as a regressive move. I want to follow this counter-move, and try to understand not only why he offers this apparent and unexpected backtracking, but also why it might, paradoxically, constitute a step forward. Primarily, this reversal is prompted by Burke's acknowledgement that 'Marxism' is also an example of rhetoric in action in the sense that, while 'analysing the hidden advantage in other terminologies (or "ideologies")', it also induces to itself 'advantages of a special sort' (103). Thus, while Burke follows approvingly Marx and Engels' ideological critique of class, he is also ready to subject *The German Ideology* to the same kind of critique. Or rather, he is ready to offer a further reversal of Marx and Engels' initial inversion of the genealogy of culture so as to present a quite different perspective on the relationship between base and superstructure, between economic interest and 'spirit'.

Burke accepts their conception of 'ideology' as an 'illusion' and 'mystification' which conceals the economic interests that structure our social experience (110). Yet, he also complicates this account of ideology, and he does so by questioning the relationship Marx establishes between base and superstructure. He considers the possibility that mystifying terms such as honour, loyalty, justice, freedom might once have been used in a way that 'summed up their *material* conditions' (111). In short, he complicates our understanding of what comes *first*. He complicates the assumption that material relations are reconstituted or disguised in ideology. He is not arguing, as Althusser did two decades later, that ideology permeates every aspect of our lived experience and beliefs. Rather, he is suggesting that any act of demystification can involve mystification; and in so doing, it can conceal the extent to which the material structure of our lives is already intuited.

To begin a critical reversal of Marx and Engels' view of ideology he steps back in time to question the rhetoric of a very different revolutionary, Oliver Cromwell. The English Civil War is a failed revolution: it did not lead to a permanent shift of power. The Stuart monarchy which was displaced in 1649 was restored in 1660. This revolution is deemed to have happened too early, before enlightened understanding of economic interest. Take, for instance, Cromwell's defence of this Revolution as 'God manifesting

Himself', which seems an example of 'mystification'. And yet, Cromwell also acknowledges, when addressing parliament, that 'the conflict did not begin with religious motives'. Burke adds: 'He is saying what his contemporaries knew, but what a *later* mystification might deny' *if* his defence were read literally, as spiritual justification (112). Then again, arguing against those who accuse him of 'having, in these great Revolutions, made Necessities', Cromwell offers:

> 'There is another Necessity, which you have put upon us, and we have not sought. I appeal to God, Angels and Men, – if I shall now raise money according to the Article in the Government, whether I am not compelled to do it!'
>
> (112)

Cromwell also pours scorn on the idea that he is individually responsible for this upheaval. 'You need but think of "God" or "Providence"', Burke insists, in a '"neutral" or "technical" sense, merely as a term for the universal scene, for the sum total of conditions' to 'make it perfect for Marxist thinking' (112–13). Burke explains that he is not trying to 'deny the obvious differences in motivation between the English protectorate and the Russian dictatorship', but that he wants only to 'indicate that, even the most "mystifying" of terms may subsume much materialistic relevancy' (113). Both historical materialism and the appeal to 'Providence' in Cromwell's parliamentary speeches can be understood as mystifying in the sense that 'necessity', the administrative or bureaucratic organization of revolution, is 'omitted'; in both, 'the bureaucratic, administrative details are "spiritualized"'. Yet, at the same time, neither one 'may be as "mystifying" or "general" as it seems, since it is used by people in specific social contexts, and in various unspecified ways derives meaning from such material conditions' (114).

Rhetoric of Motives is a difficult read. Yet, as I have already suggested, the frequent turns in Burke's argument, his confidence in the flexibility of language and, we might add, his lack of respect for the conception of 'enlightenment' as a progressive, historical phenomenon, are integral to his attempt to challenge the impulse to order and prioritize. Just as we think that Burke has successfully demystified a set of terms as advantage-seeking, he returns to complicate this very discovery. He may do so by exploring the act of demystification itself as an example of rhetoric in action, as a mystification, as we have just seen. However, he may also do so by effecting a yet more extreme reversal, by reclaiming the importance of rhetoric as mystification. This argument is defended at the end of *Rhetoric of Motives*, when Burke discusses the 'traditional function of rhetoric' as 'courtship'. For Burke, courtship can be understood as 'the use of suasive devices for the transcending of social estrangement' (1969: 208). This fits with his account of rhetoric as identification. Yet if we expect to find another attempt to expose the division concealed by identification at the end of the book, we will be sorely disappointed. For what we get instead is a defence of courtship when it is conceived as 'pure persuasion'.

I can best explain this by summarizing his treatment of a six-teenth-century Italian conduct book, which represents the 'Paradigm of Courtship'; this is Baldassare Castiglione's *The Book of the Courtier* (*Il libro del cortegiano*) (1528). The first three books of this text explore a range of persuasive devices designed to bring the Renaissance courtier to the attention of the prince, and so advance his interests. Paradoxically, *The Book of the Courtier* assumes the possibility of social mobility, yet at the same time, it strongly reaffirms hierarchy because the advance of the courtier entirely rests on his reverential wooing of his prince. However, in book 4 of Castiglione's text this hierarchy is reversed. It is not that the fourth book is 'less rhetorical than the other three', Burke argues, but that 'the advantages to which it would persuade transcend those of the preceding chapters' (228). Mainly, the role of the courtier becomes that of teacher rather than suitor; he aims to teach the prince how to be a good governor, how to court his people. He aims to initiate the prince into the mysteries of *his* code (229). As Burke remarks, in this book the courtier 'would be winsome for the advancement not of himself personally, but of human relations in general' (229). And he explains, 'the rhetoric of persuasion' leads in this book 'to an ultimate of pure persuasion', while the 'hierarchic principle of courtship sets a pattern of communication between "lower" and "higher" classes (or kinds)'. We can understand this change in general or 'universal' terms as a movement upwards, for example, from the body to the soul, from the senses to intellect, from the worldly to the spiritual. This sounds suspiciously like the kind of mystification that Marx and Engels sought to deflate. However, Burke is transforming this; we might also recognize, he argues, that 'the communication may be between merely "different" kinds, where the relevant grading is *not* established by general agreement' (231–32; emphasis added). Quite simply, there is no reason why courtship should be thought of as a one-way relationship. The point to emphasize here is that with any analysis of courtship 'one can also expect to find ambiguities whereby, even if a scale is recognized, the roles become reversed, the superior in one respect becomes the inferior in another, or the superior must court the underling' (232). This is exactly what happens in book 4 of *The Book of the Courtier*.

Why is Burke so preoccupied with courtship? Though he rejects the mystifications it gives rise to throughout *Rhetoric of Motives*, he also understands that it 'remains the mode of appeal essential for bridging the conditions of estrangement "natural" to society . . . with its reliance upon the devices of magic, pantomime, clothes, or pastoral' (211–12). This is a positive reversal of the opening concern of *Rhetoric of Motives* to expose 'identification' as mystifying. Courtship can be dangerously mystifying; it can conceal the antagonistic basis of our social experience. Yet it also remains integral to our social being; we cannot do without it. This insight helps to explain Burke's critical engagement with Marx, who sought an end to mystification:

> Believe, if you will, that social classes will be 'abolished.' Even so, at least grant that there will be a constant 'temptation' for them to again rise. And insofar as there are temptations, there are corresponding 'temptations' to the rhetoric of 'courtly intercourse' between classes.
>
> (212)

Burke is not a utopian thinker. He is not aspiring to a world beyond mystification because he does not believe that social relations can ever be fixed. Even if we reorder our material world to achieve a more equal distribution of resources, he suggests, the impulse to order and prioritize will return in a different form. Consequently, an ethical way of being requires constant rhetorical vigilance, not so much in the sense that we need continuously to represent our interests or resist being persuaded to actions in which we have no 'interest' in a dog-eat-dog world, but rather to engage always in the kind of checking or 'self-interference' (269) that resists the impulse to fix, to dominate. Not only does he seek to exemplify this in his own style of thinking and writing, but he also discovers it in places where we least expect it.

Burke's doubled-edged rhetoric, which is both critical and constructive, might be valued properly with a more contemporary example. This is taken from the work of the late feminist political theorist, Iris Marian Young, whose study *Justice and the Politics of Difference* (1990), as James L. Kastely has suggested, offers a timely grounding for Burke's new rhetoric (Kastely 1997). Young's attempt to formulate a politics that accommodates difference takes as its starting point a critique of the ideals of community and equality. These ideals do not enable social justice, in her view, because they 'direct attention away from difference'; as Burke would put it, they mystify and so perpetuate division. 'In a community persons cease to be other, opaque, not understood,' she argues, 'and instead become mutually sympathetic, understanding one another as they understand themselves' (Young 1990: 231). Yet the transparency assumed in this ideal is impossible not only because we cannot communicate without mishap with one another, but also because we are not even transparent to ourselves: 'I do not always know what I mean, need, want, desire'. 'The same difference that makes sharing between us possible', she argues, is also the basis for deep antagonism; it 'makes misunderstanding, rejection, withdrawal, and conflict always possible conditions of social being' (231). In response Young imagines a different ideal of the democratic city, a 'vast, even infinite, economic network of production, distribution, transportation, exchange, communication, service provision, and amusement' (238), in which strangers belong to social groups that 'overlap and intermingle' with one another without the 'borders and exclusions' that define contemporary urban life, and in which their 'interfusion' is encouraged in a variety of spaces, streets, parks, squares, bars and restaurants, which support a 'diversity of activities'. The 'public' which Young imagines is 'heterogenous, plural, and playful'; it is a place 'where people witness and appreciate diverse cultural expressions that they do not share and do not fully understand' (241). In the end this is still just an ideal, Young recognizes, but it is at least a different ideal. In a reversal worthy of Burke she both acknowledges its limits as an ideal and defends the possibilities it offers for critical engagement with our world; it allows us to think differently:

> I have tried to fill out the implications of a politics of difference by envisioning an ideal of city life as a being together of strangers in openness to group difference. This ideal cannot be implemented as such. Social change arises from politics, not philosophy. Ideals are a crucial step in emancipatory politics, however, because they dislodge our assumption that what is given is necessary. They offer standpoints from which to criticize the given, and inspiration for imagining alternatives.
>
> (256)

CONCLUSION

Rhetoric of Motives extends the traditional conception of rhetoric as an art of persuasion by exploring the ways in which we act on others and how we are, in turn, acted upon, inadvertently as well as deliberately. However, we can also understand Burke's 'new' rhetoric as an extension of the 'old' in a different way, as a restatement of the philosophical potential within this tradition that always enabled it to 'undo' as well as to perform the act of persuasion. Indeed, I would argue that the most valuable and under-rated legacy of the rhetorical tradition is not the rich technical vocabulary it has bequeathed, which allows us both to describe and emulate linguistic effects. Instead, its most valuable endowment lies in its flexible process of argument, which insists on the reversibility of all positions. Rhetoric is useful not only because it makes us 'persuasive' but also because it makes us self-reflexive. In this aspect, it represents the beginning of critical thinking.

Burke is valuable for another reason; he prompts us to take stock of the history of rhetoric that we have inherited. This history has long been influenced by Aristotle's defence of rhetoric as pragmatic discourse. Rhetoric is useful, it is argued, because it helps us to discover the stronger of two different viewpoints, and to arrive at a decision when matters are uncertain. But it is possible to trace a different tradition that counters this pragmatic motive, and which uses argument on different sides to unsettle positions that seem 'natural' and unquestionable. That there is a move to contest Aristotle's authority as the starting point of rhetoric is now well recognized. There has been a concerted effort to recognize an alternative tradition of arguing on different sides which forms the basis of what might be termed an 'interrogative rhetoric' or 'rhetoric of refutation' (Meyer 1994; Kastely 1997). As Michel Meyer writes, rhetoric is better understood as 'a discourse in which one can hold opposite judgements on the same question' so that what is 'problematic remains so through the displayed multiplicity of judgements' (Meyer 1994: 52). For Meyer, rhetoric is important because it generates rather than resolves questions.

> An answer can suppress the original question, but it can also pose it afresh for other questioners or suggest new questions, and even be contested in its very claim of being a solution. ... rationality begins with the formulation of problems, and it does not reduce itself to the adequacy of response.
>
> (Meyer 1994: 2–3)

Recognizing this alternative tradition is important if we are to 'check' ourselves in other ways, and perhaps especially in a book such as this one, which aims to trace the history and development of a 'critical idiom' across distinctive periods. It checks the tendency towards a narrative of enlightenment: from traditional art to postmodern play. The title of my last chapter, 'From Rhetoric to Rhetoricality', acknowledges that there is a marked break in the rhetorical tradition in modernity. Moreover, this chapter recognizes that it is not desirable to defend a return to the classical art of rhetoric once our control of language is identified as a problem. And yet the newness of the new rhetorics *and* their critical force depend in part on our acceptance of a narrow conception of rhetoric which establishes misleading oppositions. If we turn attention instead to Burke's method of argument then we are reminded of a broader conception of rhetoric, one which begins to 'check' a tendency to reaffirm the experience of modernity as a historical phenomenon.

To reinforce this I want to turn briefly to the French humanist Michel de Montaigne (1553–92). Montaigne may seem an odd choice for a conclusion to a study of rhetoric because he is often seen to present a 'radical critique' of this art. He borrows the practice of argument on different sides to structure his essays, but he does so, it is argued, only 'in order to suspend the possibility of judgement or persuasion to action altogether' (Kahn 1985: 116). Yet, this account only makes sense if we understand rhetoric primarily as a pragmatic art. I am suggesting, in contrast, that we see Montaigne as representing an alternative tradition of rhetoric that extends from Socrates to Burke, and which understands contrariness as integral to the process of reasoning. On this account, the reversals in an argument complicate their solution, initiating further questions rather than closing them.

Montaigne's *Essays* are autobiographical. They are 'attempts' or 'assays' at self-exploration and self-understanding; he is seeking to comprehend his values and habits of thought, but also to restore his power of judgement after suffering from melancholy or depression, brought on by his retirement from public life in the difficult years of the French Civil War. He is also exploring the process of reasoning itself in terms of contrary debate and we can see this in his late essay, 'The art of conversation' ('De l'art de conferer'). In this essay, 'conversation' means, literally, discussion between people. In its early stages, then, this essay functions as a conduct manual, advising on the 'art of conversation'. Montaigne gives sensible, practical advice on how to manage a conversation, noting, for instance, that we ought to welcome correction and also that we should not pursue our own opinions ruthlessly, or speak like 'scholars', using technical or rarified language. However, he is also championing the value of contrary thinking, of taking delight in the cut and thrust of debate for its own sake. As he repeatedly reminds us, he is willing to listen to all opinions so long as he can *just debate*: 'I care little about what we are discussing; all opinions are the same to me and it is all but indifferent to me which proposition emerges victorious' (Montaigne

1993: 1048). He is not recommending argument for the sake of argument exactly. Rather, this essay is objecting to stubborn thinking: to the kind of thinking that fixes viewpoints and establishes social hierarchies. This essay includes a devastating critique of the way in which speakers establish their *ethos* or credibility, basing this 'on the tokens of rank' (1059), or relying on argument culled unthinkingly from other sources (1061). In response, 'conversation' is called upon to serve as a metaphor for the kind of thought processes or internal reflection that Montaigne is attempting to defend, and which is represented in this very essay itself: 'My thought so often contradicts and condemns itself that it is all one to me if someone else does so, seeing that I give to his refutation only such authority as I please' (1047). Good reasoning is like a good conversation, because the authority of the speaker or thinker is always compromised, always challenged. For example, Montaigne reveals his contempt for 'blockheads', especially those of inferior status who assert 'their asinine excuses and daft defences'; then he pauses almost immediately to challenge and implicate himself in this criticism:

> Yes, but what if I myself am taking things for other than they are? That may well be: that explains first of all why I condemn my inability to put up with it, holding it equally to be a defect in those who are right and those who are wrong, since there is always an element of tyrannical bad temper in being unable to tolerate characters different from your own.
>
> (1052)

Montaigne is laying bare his thought process, exposing the false starts, the rambling, the contradictions, the lateral rather than logical connections that shape his thinking. But he also establishes the value of this; his argument does not move forward logically, but incorporates contradictions, although in such a way that he is always able to show us a different way of thinking that challenges an established position.

Glossary of rhetorical terms

Activities of the orator   These are sometimes also referred to as the stages of composition. For Aristotle there are three: **invention**, or the discovery of the available means of persuasion, **disposition**, or the arrangement of this material, and **style**, its presentation and adornment. The Roman rhetoricians add two further activities: **memory**, the memorization of a speech, and *pronuntiatio*, its 'delivery'.

Commonplaces   A commonplace is a general argument or observation. In the Roman handbooks, the commonplaces are lists of ready-made arguments organized according to types of legal defence. These overlap with, but are different to, Aristotle's **topics**.

Declamation   The classroom exercise of practising a speech; more specifically, the practice of arguing *pro* and *contra* any issue.

Deliberative rhetoric   *see under* **genres**.

Delivery (*pronuntiatio*)   The art of effective presentation, especially, the use of gesture and tone. Also one of the five **activities of the orator** in the Roman handbooks.

Demonstrative rhetoric   Also known as *display* or *epideictic*; *see under* **genres**.

Dialectic   The philosophical art of reasoning, of describing and ordering phenomena.

Digression (*digressio*)   *see under* **parts of a speech**. This division is usually an occasion to entertain the audience or beautify a speech.

Disposition (*dispositio*)   The organization of the material in a speech; also one of the **activities of the orator**.

Division (*divisio, partitio*)   *see under* **parts of a speech**. This is the part in which an orator outlines the structure of a speech and its key points.

Eloquence   The force or fluency of speech or writing. In the eighteenth century, eloquence denotes the grand or sublime style of classical oratory. Eloquence is the subject of the 'art' of 'rhetoric', which aims to explain what produces it.

Ethos   The mild or calm emotions that an orator enacts, often at the start of a speech, in order to affect an audience's impression of his or her trustworthy character.

Exordium The introduction to a speech or prologue; see under **parts of a speech**.

Figure This is a generic term for all figurative language, for linguistic effects which involve either a substitution of one word for another that affects meaning (**tropes**), or a change in syntactic structure for emphasis or ornament ('figure of speech' or 'scheme'). In contrast to tropes, figures of speech involve a change in the structure of a sentence or group of words. This category includes both grammatical figures and rhetorical figures. An example of a grammatical figure given in this book is parenthesis or *interpositio*, when we insert a remark in the middle of a sentence, modifying the original assertion or complicating it.

Examples of rhetorical figures of speech noted in this book include:

- *amplification*, the doubling of words
- *antithesis*, the opposition of contrary words or sentences
- *antimetabole*, the inverting of the order of repeated words
- *conduplicatio*, the doubling or repetition of a word or words in successive clauses
- *epimone*, the repetition of a phrase or question
- *epistrophe*, the repetition of a word at the end of several clauses or sentences
- *gradatio* or *climax*, the consecutive use of parallel words or sentences to convey gradation
- *isocolon*, the repetition of clauses or phrases of equal length, and often of a similar structure
- *onomatopoeia*, the use of a word of which the sound imitates what it names.
- *paradiastole*, when you redescribe a vice as a virtue, or vice versa.
- *paranomasia* or *adnominatio*, when we repeat a word, but 'with a deeper meaning'
- *periphrasis*, talking around something, usually through description.
- *tmesis*, the interjection of a word or phrase between parts of a word or between syllables of a word.

There is a separate category for the figure of thought, which is concerned with the conception rather than the presentation of a thought. Examples in this category include:

- *antithesis*, the conjoining of contrasting ideas (also a figure of speech)
- *apostrophe*, the interruption of a speech to address a person or a thing
- *dissimulatio*, pretending not to know what you already know; irony
- *licentia* or *parrhesia*, frank speech and accompanying gestures of palliation, for example, apologizing for one's frankness
- *rhetorical question*, a question posed not in order to acquire information but to emphasize a point

Genres Aristotle determined that rhetoric has three genres. *Judicial* or *forensic* rhetoric is concerned with past events; it is used primarily in law-courts to accuse or defend. **Deliberative rhetoric** is concerned with future events; its action is exhortation or dissuasion. **Demonstrative rhetoric**, also known as *display* or *epideictic*, is concerned with the present: its context is usually commemorative occasions and its function is praise or blame.

Identification Identification is the term Kenneth Burke chooses to distinguish his rhetorical theory from traditional rhetoric, conceived as the art of persuasion. Identification has long been important to the art of rhetoric: an orator facilitates persuasion by identifying with an audience. However, Burke recognizes that identification can be semi-conscious. He also recognizes that it comes at a cost: it can conceal the competitiveness integral to human exchange. For Burke, identification is essential to human communication, but it can also be abused, knowingly and unknowingly. By using the term identification Burke aims to make us understand how we often use language to create the impression of social cohesion where none exists.

Invention (*inventio*) The 'discovery' of the content of a speech by running through lists of **commonplaces**. This is one of the most important **activities of the orator** for Aristotle. In the reformed rhetoric of the Renaissance, however, invention is divided from rhetoric.

Judicial rhetoric Also known as forensic rhetoric. See under genres.

Logos This is usually translated as 'reason' or rational argument. *Logos* is also one of Aristotle's three means of persuasion or proof, comprising the example and the enthymeme. The example proves that something is so from a number of similar cases. The enthymeme demonstrates that if certain propositions are true then a second proposition must also consequently be true.

Memory (*memoria*) Roman orators relied on a good memory to recall the points of a case in the correct order; the arguments made by an antagonist in court so they can respond to them fully; and also their own speeches so that they could appear 'extempore'. To support this they deployed a range of visual techniques and images.

Metaphor The most straightforward definition of metaphor is offered by Quintilian, who describes it as the most beautiful of the **tropes**. A metaphor, on his definition, involves the transference of a verb or noun from a place where it properly belongs to another where 'the *transferred* is better than the *literal*' or, indeed, where there is 'no *literal* term'. However, this account of metaphor is subject to redefinition. In contrast to Quintilian, the nineteenth-century German philosopher Friedrich Nietzsche uses the term metaphor to describe any kind of transference that takes place from one realm to another; on this account, all language can be seen as metaphorical; all words as metaphors. In the early twentieth century I.A. Richards revised the classical definition of metaphor yet further, distinguishing between the tenor, the underlying idea of a metaphor, and vehicle, what the 'figure means'. This conception of metaphor shapes Richards' different approach to rhetoric. He is less concerned with speaking well, and the rules that underpin that, than with understanding our thought processes.

Mystification Kenneth Burke distinguishes between two kinds of mystification. The first is ubiquitous; it derives from the fact that language can be used to deceive. The second kind is ideological; it involves the obfuscation of the conditions of our existence. For example, terms that emphasize community often mystify division between people.

Narration (*narratio*) See under **parts of a speech**. In this division of a judicial oration the orator details what is meant to have happened.

Parts of a speech The divisions of a speech. Roman orations could have as many as seven parts: a prologue or **exordium**, in which the orator tries to win the goodwill of an audience by representing his character in the best light; then a **narration** of what is supposed to have happened; the **division** of the points that will be treated; the **proof** of the argument; the **refutation** of an opponent's arguments;

the **digression**, which is an occasion to entertain the audience or beautify a speech; and the epilogue or **peroration**, used to sum up the speaker's position and to arouse strong emotion.

Pathos This term refers both to strong emotions such as anger or pity, and the techniques used for their arousal, usually at the end of a speech.

Peroration (*peroratio*) The concluding part of a speech or epilogue; see under **parts of a speech**. The orator is encouraged to use devices that will arouse the stronger emotions of an audience (**pathos**) to affect judgement.

Proof (*confirmatio*) For Aristotle, the activity of 'invention' involves three kinds of proof which can be invoked at any stage in an oration: *ethos*, *pathos* and *logos*. Of these the discovery of *examples* and **enthymemes**, discussed under *logos*, is by far the most important activity. These are derived from Aristotle's lists of **topics**, lines of reasoning. In the Roman manuals, *logos* is restricted to the parts of speech identified as the proof and refutation, while the topics are '*loci communes*' or '**commonplaces**'.

Refutation (*refutatio, reprehensio*) See under **parts of a speech**. This division or part of a speech concerns the refutation of an opponent's arguments.

Rhetoricality Traditionally, rhetoric is defined as the art of persuasion, but many theorists have argued that rhetoric cannot be reduced to an art, that language is so profoundly and pervasively figurative that it is impossible to distinguish between natural or literal and rhetorical expression. A new term has been coined to represent this aspect of language: rhetoricality.

Sophists Itinerant teachers of rhetoric in fifth- and fourth-century BC Greece. They provided a broad liberal education for the elite, offering training in judicial oratory, usually through public lectures on a set theme.

Status-theory A theory which helped orators to identify the central concerns of a speech.

Style The fifth part or activity of classical rhetoric, and one of the three main activities for the Renaissance orator. It is concerned mainly with the adornment of speech and writing with the **tropes** and **figures**. There are four virtues of style: purity, clarity, decorum and ornament, and there are three types of style: the low or plain, the middle and the grand styles.

Symbolic action   Language is one of the ways that we act in the world, according to Kenneth Burke. We act on ourselves and others by using language which conveys our attitudes and beliefs.

Topics   These are lines of reasoning or patterns of inference that constitute the content of an oration. Aristotle distinguishes between 'common topics', the lines of reasoning which are 'common' to a range of questions, moral, scientific and political, and the 'special topics', which are particular to the **genres** of rhetoric.

Tropes   In contrast to the figures of speech, which concern the structural alteration of a sentence or a group of words, tropes affect meaning. Tropes involve the transference of a word or words from one context to another. The most common examples of these include:

- *metaphor*, see above
- *metonymy*, when one word is substituted for another
- *synecdoche*, when the term for a part of a thing is substituted for the whole, or vice versa

Bibliography

Althusser, Louis (1971) *Lenin and Philosophy and other Essays*, trans. Ben Brewster, London: NLB.

Altman, Joel B. (1978) *The Tudor Play of Mind: Rhetorical Inquiry and the Development of Elizabethan Drama*, Berkeley, CA: University of California Press.

Arendt, Hannah (1998) *The Human Condition*, Chicago, IL: University of Chicago Press.

Aristotle (1984) *Rhetoric*, trans. W. Rhys Roberts, in *The Complete Works of Aristotle: The Revised Oxford Translation*, vol. 2, ed. Jonathan Barnes, Princeton, NJ: Princeton University Press.

——(1991) *A Theory of Civic Discourse: On Rhetoric*, trans. George A. Kennedy, Oxford: Oxford University Press.

Astell, Mary (1986) 'Reflections upon Marriage' [1706], in *The First Feminist: Reflections upon Marriage and other Writings by Mary Astell*, ed. Bridget Hill, Aldershot: Gower Publishing.

Austen, Jane (1970) *Persuasion, with a Memoir of Jane Austen by J. E. Austen-Leigh*, ed. D. W. Harding, London: Penguin Books.

Barilli, Renato (1989) *Rhetoric*, trans. Giuliana Menozzi, Minneapolis, MN: University of Minnesota Press.

Baron, Hans (1938) 'Cicero and the Roman civic spirit in the Middle Ages', *Bulletin of John Rylands Library* (22): 72–97.

Barthes, Roland (1988) *The Semiotic Challenge*, trans. Richard Howard, Oxford: Basil Blackwell.

Bender, John and David E. Wellbery (eds) (1990) *The Ends of Rhetoric: History, Theory, Practice*, Stanford, CT: Stanford University Press.

Biesecker, Barbara A. (2000) *Addressing Postmodernity: Kenneth Burke, Rhetoric, and a Theory of Social Change*, Tuscaloosa, AL: University of Alabama Press.

Bizzell, Patricia (2003) 'Editing the rhetorical tradition', *Philosophy and Rhetoric* (36): 109–18.

Blair, Tony (2003) 'Prime Minister's Address to the Nation', www.number-10.gov.uk/output/Page3322.asp (20 March 2003), accessed 23 December 2005.

Blake, William (1980) *The Poems of William Blake*, ed. W.H. Stevenson and David V. Erdman, London: Longman Norton.

Booth, Wayne C. (2004) *The Rhetoric of Rhetorics: The Quest for Effective Communication*, Oxford: Blackwell Publishing.

Brathwait, Richard (1640) *Ar't Asleepe Husband? A Boulster Lecture*, London.

Brock, Bernard L. (ed.) (1999) *Kenneth Burke and the 21st Century*, Albany, NY: State University of New York.

Burke, Kenneth (1969) *A Rhetoric of Motives*, Berkeley, CA: University of California Press.

——(1989) *On Symbols and Society*, Chicago, IL: University of Chicago Press.

Burrow, Colin (2004) 'Shakespeare and humanistic culture', in Charles A. Martindale and A. B. Taylor (eds), *Shakespeare and the Classics*, Cambridge: Cambridge University Press: 9–27.

Butler, Samuel (1970) *Hudibras*, London: Scolar Press.

Bygrave, Stephen (1993) *Kenneth Burke: Rhetoric and Ideology*, London: Routledge.

Cary, Elizabeth (2002), *The Tragedy of Mariam*, in David Bevington, Lars Engle, Katherine Eisaman Maus and Eris Rasmussen (eds), *English Renaissance Drama: A Norton Anthology*, New York: W.W. Norton and Company.

[Cicero] (1954) *Ad C. Herennium de Ratione Dicendi (Rhetorica ad Herennium)* trans. Harry Caplan, London: William Heinemann; Cambridge, MA: Harvard University Press.

Cicero, Marcus Tullius (1939) *Brutus and Orator*, trans. G. L. Hendrickson and H. M. Hubbell, London: William Heinemann; Cambridge, MA: Harvard University Press.

——(1954) *De Inventione; De Optimo Genere Oratorum; Topica*, trans. H. M. Hubbell, London: William Heinemann; Cambridge, MA: Harvard University Press.

——(1961) *De officiis*, trans. Walter Miller, London: William Heinemann; Cambridge, MA: Harvard University Press.

——(2001) *On the Ideal Orator (De Oratore)*, trans. James M. May and Jakob Wisse, New York: Oxford University Press.

Colclough, David (2005) *Freedom of Speech in Early Stuart England*, Cambridge: Cambridge University Press.

Corbett, Edward P. J. (1990) *Classical Rhetoric for the Modern Student*, New York: Oxford University Press.

Crawford, Robert (ed.) (1998) *The Scottish Invention of English Literature*, Cambridge: Cambridge University Press.

de Man, Paul (1979) *Allegories of Reading: Figural Language in Rousseau, Nietzsche, Rilke, and Proust*, New Haven, CT: Yale University Press.

——(1982) 'The resistance to theory', *Yale French Studies* (63): 3–20.

——(1986) *Blindness and Insight: Essays in the Rhetoric of Contemporary Criticism*, ed. Wlad Godzich, London: Routledge.

Derrida, Jacques (2004) *Dissemination*, trans. Barbara Johnson, London: Continuum.

Dillon, John and Tania Gergel (trans.) (2003) *The Greek Sophists*, London: Penguin.

Dixon, Peter (1971) *Rhetoric*, London: Methuen.

Douglass, Frederick (1996), 'I hear the mournful wail of millions' [1852], in *The Penguin Book of Historic Speeches*, ed. Brian MacArthur, London: Penguin: 260–63.

Duncan, Ian (1998) 'Adam Smith, Samuel Johnson and the institution of English', in Robert Crawford (ed.), *The Scottish Invention of English Literature*, Cambridge: Cambridge University Press: 37–54.

Eagleton, Terry (1981) *Walter Benjamin or Towards a Revolutionary Criticism*, London: Verso.

——(1983) *Literary Theory: An Introduction*, Oxford: Basil Blackwell.

Edwards, Michael and Christopher Reid (eds) (2004) *Oratory in Action*, Manchester: Manchester University Press.

Erasmus, Desiderius (1978) *On the Method of Study*, trans. Brian MacGregor, in *Collected Works of Erasmus*, xxiv, ed. Craig R. Thompson, Toronto: University of Toronto Press.

Fish, Stanley (1989) 'Rhetoric', in *Doing What Comes Naturally: Change, Rhetoric, and the Practice of Theory in Literary and Legal Studies*, Durham, NC: Duke University Press.

Fontana, Benedetto, Cary J. Nederman and Gary Remer (eds) (2004) *Talking Democracy: Historical Perspectives on Rhetoric and Democracy*, University Park, PA: Pennsylvania State University Press.

Genette, Gérard (1982) *Figures of Literary Discourse*, trans. Alan Sheridan and intro. Marie-Rose Logan, Oxford: Basil Blackwell.

Gleason, Maud (1995) *Making Men: Sophists and Self-Presentation in Ancient Rome*, Princeton, NJ: Princeton University Press.

Gouge, William (1976) *Of Domesticall Duties*, Amsterdam: William J. Johnson, Theatrum Orbis Terrarum.

Gowing, Laura (1996) *Domestic Dangers: Women, Words, and Sex in Early Modern London*, Oxford: Clarendon Press.

Graff, Gerald (1987) *Professing English Literature: An Institutional History*, Chicago, IL: University of Chicago Press.

Gross, Alan (1990) *The Rhetoric of Science*, Cambridge, MA: Harvard University Press.

Halpern, Richard (1991) *The Poetics of Primitive Accumulation: English Renaissance Culture and the Genealogy of Capital*, Ithaca, NY: Cornell University Press.

Harris, Robert (2006) *Imperium*, London: Hutchinson.

Heard, Rachel (2006) 'Caught *in medias res*: Female Intercession, "Regulation" and "Exchange"' in Jennifer Richards and Alison Thorne (eds), *Rhetoric, Women and Politics in Early Modern England*, London: Routledge: 51–69.

Honohan, Iseult (2002) *Civic Republicanism*, London: Routledge.

Hoskins, John (1935) *Directions for Speech and Style*, ed. Hoyt H. Hudson, Princeton, NJ: Princeton University Press.

Howell, Samuel Wilbur (1971) *Eighteenth-Century Logic and Rhetoric*, Princeton, NJ: Princeton University Press.

Hutson, Lorna (1994) *The Usurer's Daughter: Male Friendship and Fictions of Women in Sixteenth Century England*, London: Routledge.

Ionesco, Eugene (1958) *The Bald Prima Donna: A Pseudo-Play in One Act*, trans. Donald Watson, London: Samuel French.

——(1964) *Notes and Counter-Notes*, trans. Donald Watson, London: John Calder.

Jakobson, Roman (1956) 'Two aspects of language and two types of aphasic disturbances', in Roman Jakobson and Morris Halle, *Fundamentals of Language*, The Hague: Mouton.

Jameson, Frederic R. (1982) 'The symbolic inference: or, Kenneth Burke and ideological analysis', in Hayden White and Margaret Brose (eds), *Representing Kenneth Burke: Selected Papers from the English Institute*, Baltimore, MD: The Johns Hopkins University Press: 68–91.

Jardine, Lisa and Anthony Grafton (1986) *From Humanism to the Humanities: Education and the Liberal Arts in Fifteenth- and Sixteenth-Century Europe*, London: Duckworth.

Jarratt, Susan C. (1991) *Rereading the Sophists: Classical Rhetoric Refigured*, Carbondale, IL: Southern Illinois Press.

Jasinski, James L. (2001) *Sourcebook on Rhetoric: Key Concepts in Contemporary Rhetorical Studies*, Thousand Oaks, CA: Sage.

Joyce, James (1980) *Ulysses*, London: The Bodley Head.

Kahn, Victoria (1985) *Rhetoric, Prudence, and Skepticism in the Renaissance*, Ithaca, NY: Cornell University Press.

——(1986) 'Humanism and the resistance to theory' in Patricia Parker and David Quint (eds), *Literary Theory/Renaissance Texts*, Baltimore, MD: Johns Hopkins Press: 373–96.

——(1994) *Machiavellian Rhetoric: From the Counter Reformation to Milton*, Princeton, NJ: Princeton University Press.

Kames, Lord (Henry Home) (1763) *Elements of Criticism*, 2 vols, 2nd edn, Edinburgh.

Kastely, James L. (1997) *Rethinking the Rhetorical Tradition: From Plato to Postmodernism*, New Haven, CT: Yale University Press.

Kennedy, George (1963) *The Art of Persuasion in Greece*, London: Routledge.

——(1972) *The Art of Rhetoric in the Roman World 300 B.C. – A.D. 300*, Princeton, NJ: Princeton University Press.

——(1980) *Classical Rhetoric and its Christian and Secular Tradition from Ancient to Modern Times*, London: Croom Helm.

——(1994) *A New History of Classical Rhetoric*, Princeton, NJ: Princeton University Press.

Kerford, G.B. (1981) *The Sophistic Movement*, Cambridge: Cambridge University Press.

Kinney, Arthur (1983) 'Rhetoric and fiction in Elizabethan England' in James J. Murphy (ed.), *Renaissance Eloquence: Studies in the Theory and Practice of Renaissance Rhetoric*, Berkeley, CA: University of California Press: 385–93.

Kirkpatrick, Andy (2005) 'China's first systematic account of rhetoric: an introduction to Chen Kui's *Wen Ze*', *Rhetorica* (23): 103–52.

Kofman, Sarah (1993) *Nietzsche and Metaphor*, trans. Duncan Large, London: Athlone Press.

Kohrs Campbell, Karlyn (1973) 'The rhetoric of women's liberation: an oxymoron', *Quarterly Journal of Speech* (59): 74–86.

Kyd, Thomas (1986) *The Spanish Tragedy*, ed. Philip Edwards, Manchester: Manchester University Press.

Lanham, Richard A. (1991) *A Handlist of Rhetorical Terms*, Berkeley, CA: University of California Press.

Leff, M. (1983) 'Topical invention and metaphorical interaction', *Southern Communication Journal* (48): 214–29.

——(1996) 'Commonplaces and argumentation in Cicero and Quintilian', *Argumentation* (10): 445–52.

Lentricchia, Frank (1983) *Criticism and Social Change*, Chicago, IL: University of Chicago Press.

Lewalski, Barbara Kiefer (1985) *Paradise Lost and the Rhetoric of Literary Forms*, Princeton, NJ: Princeton University Press.

Longinus (1927) *Aristotle The Poetics, 'Longinus' On the Sublime, Demetrius On Style*, London: William Heinemann; New York: G. P. Putnam's Sons.

Luckyj, Christina (2002) *'A moving Rhetoricke': Gender and Silence in Early Modern England*, Manchester: Manchester University Press.

Lyotard, Jean-François (1993a) 'The Sublime and the Avant-Garde' in Thomas Docherty (ed.), *Postmodernism: A Reader*, New York: Harvester Wheatsheaf.

——(1993b) *The Libidinal Economy*, trans. Iain Hamilton Grant, London: Continuum.

Lyotard, Jean-François and Jean-Loup Thébaud (1985) *Just Gaming*, trans. Wlad Godzich, Manchester: Manchester University Press.

Mack, Peter (2002) *Elizabethan Rhetoric: Theory and Practice*, Cambridge: Cambridge University Press.

——(2005) 'Rhetoric, ethics and reading in the Renaissance', *Renaissance Studies* (19.1): 1–21.

McKenna, Stephen J. (2006) *Adam Smith: The Rhetoric of Propriety*, Albany, NY: State University of New York Press.

Mailloux, Steven (ed.) (1995) *Rhetoric, Sophistry, Pragmatism*, Cambridge: Cambridge University Press.

Meyer, Michel (1994) *Rhetoric, Language, and Reason*, University Park, PA: Pennsylvania State University Press.

Miller, Thomas P. (1997) *The Formation of College English: Rhetoric and Belles Lettres in the British Cultural Provinces*, Pittsburgh, PA: University of Pittsburgh Press.

Milton, John (1998) *Paradise Lost*, ed. Alastair Fowler, London: Longman.

Monfasani, John (1976) *George of Trebizond: A Biography and A Study of his Rhetoric and Logic*, Leiden: E.J. Brill.

Montaigne, Michel de (1993) *The Complete Essays*, ed. M. A. Screech, London: Penguin.

Murphy, James J. (1974) *Rhetoric in the Middle Ages: A History of Rhetorical Theory from Saint Augustine to the Renaissance*, Berkeley, CA: University of California Press.

——(1983) *Renaissance Eloquence: Studies in the Theory and Practice of Renaissance Rhetoric*, Berkeley, CA: University of California Press.

Myrick, Kenneth (1935) *Sir Philip Sidney as a Literary Craftsman*, Cambridge, MA: Harvard University Press.

Neel, Jasper (1995) 'The degradation of rhetoric: or, dressing like a gentleman, speaking like a scholar', in Steven Mailloux (ed.), *Rhetoric, Sophistry, Pragmatism*, Cambridge: Cambridge University Press: 61–81.

Nietzsche, Friedrich (1979) *Philosophy and Truth: Selections from Nietzsche's Notebooks of the Early 1870's*, ed. and trans. Daniel Breazeale, Amherst, MA: Humanity Books.

——(1983) 'Nietzsche's Lecture Notes on Rhetoric: A Translation', trans. Carole Blair, *Philosophy and Rhetoric* (16): 94–129.

Norris, Christopher (1988) *Paul de Man: Deconstruction and the Critique of Aesthetic Ideology*, London: Routledge.

Olson, Gary A. (1990) 'Jacques Derrida on Rhetoric and Composition: a conversation', *Journal of Advanced Composition* (10), www.jac.gsu.edu/jac/10/Articles/ 1.htm, accessed 23 December 2005.

Palmer, David J. (1965) *The Rise of English Studies: An Account of the Study of English Language and Literature from Its Origins to the Making of the Oxford English School*, Oxford: Oxford University Press.

Parker, Patricia (1987) *Literary Fat Ladies: Rhetoric, Gender, Property*, London: Methuen.

——(1996) 'Virile style', in Louise Fradenburg and Carla Fraccero with Kathy Lavezzo (eds), *Premodern Sexualities*, London: Routledge: 199–222.

Peacham, Henry (1577, 1593) *The garden of eloquence*, London.

Plato (1964a) *Gorgias*, trans. W. D. Woodhead, in *The Collected Dialogues of Plato, including the Letters*, eds Edith Hamilton and Huntington Cairns, New York: Pantheon Books.

——(1964b) *Phaedrus*, trans. R. Hackforth, in *The Collected Dialogues of Plato, including the Letters*, eds Edith Hamilton and Huntington Cairns, New York: Pantheon Books.

Pocock, J. G. A. (1984) 'Verbalizing a political act: towards a politics of speech', in Michael J. Shapiro (ed.), *Language and Politics*, Oxford: Blackwell: 25–43.

Pope, Alexander (1966) *Poetical Works*, ed. Herbert Davies, Oxford: Oxford University Press.

——(1987) *Selected Prose of Alexander Pope*, ed. Paul Hammond, Cambridge: Cambridge University Press.

Potkay, Adam (1994) *The Fate of Eloquence in the Age of Hume*, Ithaca, NY: Cornell University Press.

Puttenham, George (1936) *The Arte of English Poesie*, eds Gladys Doidge Willcock and Alice Walker, Cambridge: Cambridge University Press.

Quintilian (2001) *Institutio Oratoria*, trans. Donald A. Russell, Cambridge, MA: Harvard University Press.

Rainolds, John (1940) *Oratio in laudem artis poeticae*, eds William Ringler and Walter Allen, Jr, Princeton, NJ: Princeton University Press.

Rebhorn, Wayne A. (1995) *The Emperor of Men's Minds: Literature and the Renaissance Discourse of Rhetoric*, Ithaca, NY: Cornell University Press.

Rhodes, Neil (2004) *Shakespeare and the Origins of English*, Oxford: Oxford University Press.

Richards, I. A. (1936) *The Philosophy of Rhetoric*, New York: Oxford University Press.

Richards, Jennifer and Alison Thorne (eds) (2006) *Rhetoric, Women and Politics in Early Modern England*, London: Routledge.

Robinson, Mary (2003) *'A Letter to the Women of England' and 'The Natural Daughter'*, ed. Sharon M. Setzer, Peterborough, Ontario: Broadview Literary Press.

Rousseau, Jean-Jacques (2001) 'Essay on the Origin of Languages', ed. and trans. Victor Gourevitch, *The Discourses and Other Early Political Writings*, Cambridge: Cambridge University Press: 247–99.

Saussure, Ferdinand de (1966) *Course in General Linguistics*, eds Charles Bally and Albert Sechehaye with Albert Reidlinger and trans. Wade Baskin, New York: McGraw-Hill.

Schiappa, Edward (1995) 'Isocrates' *philosophia* and contemporary pragmatism', in Steven Mailloux (ed.), *Rhetoric, Sophistry, Pragmatism*, Cambridge: Cambridge University Press: 33–60.

——(1999) *The Beginnings of Rhetorical Theory in Classical Greece*, New Haven, CT: Yale University Press.

Schrift, Alan D. (1990) *Nietzsche and the Question of Interpretation: Between Hermeneutics and Deconstruction*, Houndsmills: Macmillan.

Shakespeare, William (2005) *The Complete Works (Second Edition)*, eds Stanley Wells, Gary Taylor, John Jowett and William Montgomery, Oxford: Clarendon Press.

Shaughnessy, Mina (1977) *Errors and Expectations: A Guide for the Teacher of Basic Writing*, New York: Oxford University Press.

Shelley, Mary (2003) *Frankenstein, or The Modern Prometheus*, ed. Maurice Hindle, London: Penguin.

Sherry, Vincent (2004) *James Joyce: 'Ulysses'*, Cambridge: Cambridge University Press.

Sidney, Philip (1985) *The Countess of Pembroke's Arcadia (The Old Arcadia)*, ed. Katherine Duncan-Jones, Oxford: Oxford University Press.

——(1989) *Sir Philip Sidney*, ed. Katherine Duncan Jones, Oxford: Oxford University Press.

Sim, Stuart (1992) *Beyond Aesthetics: Confrontations with Poststructuralism and Postmodernism*, New York: Harvester Wheatsheaf.

Simons, Herbert W. (2004) 'The rhetorical legacy of Kenneth Burke', in Walter Jost and Wendy Olmstead (eds), *A Companion to Rhetoric*, Oxford: Blackwell: 152–68.

Simpson, Michael (2004) 'The Morning (Post) after: the vertiginous career of rhetoric in Coleridge's "Fears in Solitude"', in Michael Edwards and Christopher Reid (eds), *Oratory in Action*, Manchester: Manchester University Press: 99–116.

Skinner, Quentin (1996) *Reason and Rhetoric in the Philosophy of Hobbes*, Cambridge: Cambridge University Press.

Smith, Adam (1985) *Lectures on Rhetoric and Belles Lettres*, ed. J. C. Bryce, Indianapolis, IN: Liberty Fund.

——(1998) *An Inquiry into the Nature and Causes of the Wealth of Nations: A Selected Edition*, ed. Kathryn Sutherland, Oxford: Oxford University Press.

Sonnino, Lee A. (1968) *A Handbook of Sixteenth-Century Rhetoric*, London: Routledge and Kegan Paul.

Sprat, Thomas (1959) *History of the Royal Society* [1667], St Louis, MO: Washington University Studies; London: Routledge.

Steadman, John M. (1968) *Milton's Epic Characters: Image and Idol*, Chapel Hill, NC: University of North Carolina Press.

Struever, Nancy C. (1970) *The Language of History in the Renaissance: Rhetoric and Historical Consciousness in Florentine Humanism*, Princeton, NJ: Princeton University Press.

Tacitus (1914), *Dialogus, Agricola, Germania*, trans. William Peterson, London: William Heinemann; New York: Macmillan.

Vickers, Brian (1970) *Classical Rhetoric in English Poetry*, London: Macmillan.

——(1971) 'Shakespeare's use of rhetoric', in Kenneth Muir and S. Schoenbaum (eds), *A New Companion to Shakespeare Studies*, Cambridge: Cambridge University Press: 83–98.

——(1988) *In Defence of Rhetoric*, Oxford: Clarendon Press.

Wardy, Robert (1996) *The Birth of Rhetoric*, London: Routledge.

Watson, Foster (1912) *Vives and the Renascence Education of Women*, London: Edward Arnold.

Wess, Robert (1996) *Kenneth Burke: Rhetoric, Subjectivity, Postmodernism*, Cambridge: Cambridge University Press.

Wilson, Thomas (1982) *Arte of Rhetorique* [1553], ed. Thomas J. Derrick, New York, London: Garland Publishing.

Wisse, Jacob (1989) *Ethos and Pathos: From Aristotle to Cicero*, Amsterdam: Adolf M. Hakkert Publisher.

——(1992) 'Review of Brian Vickers, *In Defence of Rhetoric*', *Mnemosyne* (65): 537–44. Oxford: Clarendon Press, 1988 (repr. with corrections and additions 1989).

Wordsworth, William (1970) *The Prelude, Or Growth of a Poet's Mind (Text of 1805)*, ed. Ernest de Selincourt, corrected Stephen Gill, Oxford: Oxford University Press.

——(1979) *The Ruined Cottage and The Pedlar*, ed. James Butler, Ithaca, NY: Cornell University Press.

——(1992) *Lyrical Ballads*, ed. Michael Mason, London: Longman.

Yates, Frances (1984) *The Art of Memory*, London: Arc Paperbacks.

Yeats, W. B. (1959) 'Per Amica Silentia Lunae' [1917], in *Mythologies*, London: Macmillan.

——(1990) *The Poems*, ed. Daniel Albright, London: J. M. Dent and Sons.

Young, Iris Marion (1990) *Justice and the Politics of Difference*, Princeton, NJ: Princeton University Press.

Zerba, Michelle (2004) 'The frauds of humanism: Cicero, Machiavelli and the rhetoric of imposture', *Rhetorica* (22): 215–40.

Index